REACH OUT and TEACH

Meeting the Training Needs
of Parents of Visually
and Multiply Handicapped
Young Children

by Kay Alicyn Ferrell
National Consultant in Early Childhood,
American Foundation for the Blind

PARENT HANDBOOK

with contributions by

Sherrill Butterfield,
Boston College

Zofja Jastrzembska,
American Foundation for the Blind

Kristen Rapsher
New Jersey Commission for the Blind
and Visually Impaired

Consulting Editor: Judith A. Eisler
Photos: Janet Charles
Illustrations: Cynthia Stoddard
Design: John B. Waldvogel
Art Director: Stephen Fay

AMERICAN FOUNDATION FOR THE BLIND
NEW YORK

REACH OUT and TEACH

PARENT HANDBOOK text, photos and illustrations
copyright ©1985
2nd printing 1986   3rd printing 1992
by American Foundation for the Blind,
15 West 16th St., New York, NY 10011

Library of Congress Cataloging in Publication Data

```
Ferrell, Kay Alicyn, 1948-
   Reach out and teach.

   Includes bibliographies.
   1. Blind--Education.  2. Visually handicapped
children--Family relationships.  3. Child development.
4. Perceptual-motor learning.  5. Children, Blind--
Family relationships.  I. Title.
HV1626.F47  1985       649'.1511      85-6227
ISBN 0-89128-127-4  (pbk.)
```

REACH OUT AND TEACH
PARENT HANDBOOK ISBN 0-89128-127-4
REACHBOOK ISBN 0-89128-128-2

Printed in the United States of America

These materials were developed in part with Federal funds from the United States Department of Education, Special Education Programs, under Grant #G008103230 ("Meeting the Training Needs of Parents of Visually Handicapped/Multihandicapped Young Children"). However, the contents of this publication do not necessarily reflect the views or policies of the Department of Education, and no official endorsement by the Department of Education should be inferred.

DEDICATION
to the Parents, Children,
Clients and Staff of

Bureau of Educational Services for the Blind
Workshop Building No. 11
Newington, Connecticut

Dallas Services for Visually Impaired Children
Dallas, Texas

Granby Group Home
Granby, Connecticut

The Lighthouse
New York Association for the Blind
New York, New York

New Jersey Commission for the Blind
Newark, New Jersey

Orchard Hill School
South Windsor, Connecticut

Perkins School for the Blind
Infant and Toddler Program
Watertown, Massachusetts

Woodrow Wilson School
Elizabeth, New Jersey

Contents

Project Staff
for
Meeting the Training Needs of Parents of
Visually Handicapped/Multihandicapped Young Children

Susan Jay Spungin, Ed.D.
Project Director

Kay Alicyn Ferrell, Ph.D.
Materials Development Coordinator

Sherrill Butterfield, Ph.D.
Product Content Specialist

Richard E. Gibboney
Susan Islam
Media Specialists

Zofja Jastrzembska
Workshop Coordinator

Susan M. Kershman, Ph.D.
Evaluation Consultant

Kristen Rapsher, M.Ed.
Correspondent Teacher

Delma Ward
Wilbert Suber
Pam Smalls
Project Secretaries

Additional thanks to:

Nancy Akeson and Lois Harrell,
Variety Club Blind Babies Foundation,
San Francisco, California

Jay Boyle,
New Jersey Commission for the Blind,
Newark, New Jersey

Catherine Brooks,
American Foundation for the Blind,
New York

Mary Lynne Dolembo,
Children's Special Education Center,
Kansas City, Missouri

Harriet P. Foiles,
Delta Gamma Foundation for Visually
Impaired Children, St. Louis, Missouri

Lawrence Gardner,
Columbia University Teachers College
New York

Margaret L. King,
American Foundation for the Blind,
New York

Mary Anne Lang, The Lighthouse,
New York Association for the Blind

Robert Long, Ed.D.,
Connecticut Board of Education and
Services for the Blind,
Wethersfield. Connecticut

Ruth Migliorelli, Parent,
Pelham Manor, New York

Yonnine Mingus,
American Foundation for the Blind,
New York

Sheri Moore,
American Printing House for the Blind,
Louisville, Kentucky

Consuelo Mosquera, Parent,
New York, New York

Mary Ellen Mulholland,
American Foundation for the Blind,
New York

Linda Norris,
Massachusetts Commission for the Blind,
Boston, Massachusetts

Louise Reynolds,
Tennessee Services for the Blind,
Nashville, Tennessee

Rigden Family, Plano, Texas

Robin Roller,
Houston Lighthouse for the Blind,
Houston, Texas

Glen Slonneger,
Virginia Department for the Visually
Handicapped, Richmond, Virginia

Maureen Vinton, Parent,
Eastchester, New York

A Note to Parents

Reach Out and Teach was written for parents, and about parents —and with the help of 500 parents across the country, who worked with the American Foundation for the Blind to develop and test the HANDBOOK and REACHBOOK over a three-year period. Funded by the United States Department of Education, it is designed to help meet the training needs of parents of young visually and multiply handicapped children. During the first year of the project, the American Foundation for the Blind asked parents what they wanted and needed to know in order to help them through their children's infant and preschool years. Some of the parents were still going through this period with their children; others were parents of older children looking back at their preschool experiences. Over one-third of the parents had children who had one or more handicapping conditions in addition to blindness or visual impairment. Some of the children attended a residential school for the visually handicapped; the vast majority of the parents saw their children every day, regardless of the type of school their children attended.

During the first year, the American Foundation for the Blind also asked teachers, teacher-trainers, and blind adults what *they* thought parents of visually handicapped infants and preschoolers needed to know. While it is useful for parents to consider professional viewpoints in making educational decisions, *Reach Out and Teach* is based ultimately on what parents felt was important; parents' opinions — from what they most needed training in (identifying educational opportunities) to what they least needed training in (providing a balanced and nutritious diet) — were the deciding factors for whether or not a topic was included in the HANDBOOK.

Once the books were written, other parents were asked to read them, use them with their children, and then tell the Foundation how *Reach Out and Teach* could be improved. Some parents did this on their own, at home, while others attended one of six workshops held in Houston, Texas; Boston, Massachusetts; St. Louis, Missouri; Sacramento, California; Nashville, Tennesee; and Charlottesville, Virginia. Still another group of parents worked along with a teacher who had attended a workshop. The books were then revised according to their suggestions, and the result is the *Reach Out and Teach* you have today. What you read in these books is there because other parents of visually and multiply handicapped children *wanted* it there, and *not* because a professional decided it *should* be there.

Reach Out and Teach represents a continuing commitment by the American Foundation for the Blind to blind and visually impaired infants and preschoolers, their parents, and their families. In a very real sense, these books contain *your* ideas, *your* suggestions, *your* hopes, and *your* fears. They also reflect *our* belief in you as parents, and in the ability of all blind, visually impaired, and multiply handicapped children to grow and learn to their greatest potential.

Susan J. Spungin, Project Director

American Foundation for the Blind
New York, January, 1985

Introduction

From the very moment of birth, parents are placed in the unique position of helping their children learn about the world. Many different activities are part of what we call parenting — nurturing, loving, disciplining playing, and teaching.

As parents, you teach your children as the opportunity arises, not according to any plan. By having toys or pots and pans on hand, and by allowing your children to play with them, you have set up situations where they can learn about how things work and how things go together. By giving them toys, you provide both the *means* and the *opportunity* necessary to help learning take place. By playing with your children yourself, you give them a *reason* to practice new learning. This is how children learn concepts, or general rules about how their world works — "If I drop this, it will fall" or "If I open this door, I will find the milk." These concepts are important for future learning, and each one fits on top of the last one, much like bricks do when building a house.

Usually children learn these concepts without their parents doing anything more than just being parents. But when you have a visually or multiply handicapped child, you may need to create more learning opportunities more often. These materials were designed to help you do just that.

About These Materials

If you are not handicapped yourself, it is difficult to imagine what it is like for your child and how he will be able to grow and learn like other children. If your child is multiply handicapped, it probably seems even more unlikely that he can become an independent, functioning adult. But it can, and often has, happened.

Reach Out and Teach was written to give parents the information they need (and have asked for) to raise their visually or multiply handicapped children. But, particularly in chapters "Taking Off," "Picking Up," "Thinking It Through," and "Coming Across," the information on skill development and learning is no different than what you would find in any book on infant and preschool child development. The information contained in these chapters is information that *every* child needs to learn in order to grow and develop, regardless of how visually or multiply handicapped he is. True, there is also information on how parents can modify a skill so that a child who cannot see can learn it a little easier, or a child with cerebral palsy can learn to do it in a different way — but the basic skill and way of teaching it are the same for *all* children. There are differences, certainly, but those differences are more in terms of:

How things are learned
When they are learned
How fast they are learned

All children have their own style of learning, and they all learn at their own pace. Many children also do some things very well and take longer to learn others. The point is that every child is an individual. And your visually or multiply handicapped child is, too.

Sure, it's overwhelming. It may not even seem possible. But it is. These first few years are one of the few times in a child's life when the types and amounts of experience can really make a difference in his development, no matter how visually or multiply handicapped he is. You never know what will make a difference for your child, whether he is 1 week old or 4 years old; but you will *certainly* never know if you don't try.

How to Use These Materials

Reach Out and Teach consists of four parts: (1) a PARENT HANDBOOK containing information on early child development with activities and ideas you can use at home to help your child grow; (2) a REACHBOOK, or workbook, with sections to help you keep track of your child's growth and development; (3) a set of slide presentations, which are intended to give a quick introduction to the information in the PARENT HANDBOOK; and (4) a TEACHER'S MANUAL to help teachers adapt the materials for their own work.

The PARENT HANDBOOK and REACHBOOK are for your use, with or without the help of a teacher or counselor; they have been written so that you can use them by yourself.

The PARENT HANDBOOK and REACHBOOK refer back and forth to one another. They were written in such a way that you can read the HANDBOOK and then practice what you read by doing exercises in the REACHBOOK. Each time you finish reading a section in the HANDBOOK, a page reference, noted in an arrow, will direct you to relevant material in the REACHBOOK that will help you to see how you or your child is doing on that particular topic. As you finish a REACHBOOK section, another arrow will direct you back to the HANDBOOK to continue reading. Every time you read a new section, you will have a chance to apply what you have read *to your own child* or *to your own situation* before going on to a new section.

You can start now, with the PARENT HANDBOOK. Finish reading this introduction. At the end, there is a an arrow that tells you to turn to page 5 in your REACHBOOK. The first several pages in the REACHBOOK are similar to a baby book — records of height, weight, immunizations, doctor's reports, and so forth. If you are a parent of an infant, you can start right now to keep track of this information. If you are a parent of an older child, you may not want or be able to write in the information about your child's earlier years, but you can start keep track from today on.

When you finish page 18 in the REACHBOOK, you will find another arrow that tells you to turn back to page 7 in the HANDBOOK. Turn to this page and continue working through the chapter.

You can do as much or as little of *Reach Out and Teach* as you want. Some people like to skip around to find a topic that is important to them at that moment, and others like to start at the front and read straight through to the end. It is really your choice.

Because children grow and develop and change, the first time you assess your child you might find either that (1) she has learned some, but not all skills in that section; or (2) she has learned all the skills in that section. If #2 is the case — great; you can go on to another section. But if your child has learned only some of the skills, you will want to come back to each assessment from time to time and check on what your child has learned. This is called "reassessment" and is explained more fully on pages 18–19 of the HANDBOOK. The summary charts provided throughout the REACHBOOK will help you reassess because they help you see at a glance what your child is doing, and whether or not you've started to work on a particular skill yet.

Whenever you reassess and go back to an assessment page of your REACHBOOK, try to use a pen or pencil in a different color and always write the new date in at the top of the page. Based on your new assessment, update the summary chart in the REACHBOOK. Continue to do this as your child grows.

Start now to keep records in your REACHBOOK.

Turn to page 5 in the REACHBOOK ➔

GETTING STARTED:

Learning About Learning

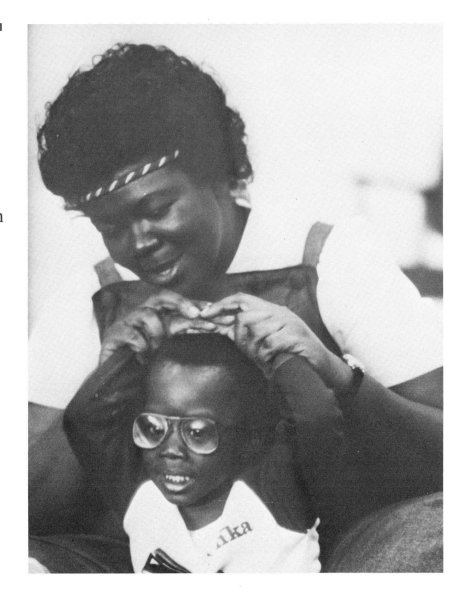

GETTING STARTED:
Learning About Learning

Reading Your Child's Signals

Reading the messages, or signals, that children send can be a special problem with visually or multiply handicapped children. They do not always react to other children and adults the same way that sighted, nonhandicapped children do. For example, a baby with good vision looks intently at people, especially when being held. Adults, then, look back and smile, talk to, and tickle the baby in response. Children with visual impairments, however, often do not look at their parents, simply because they cannot see them. But this can make parents feel as if their child is ignoring or rejecting them. Parents feel bad, so they don't talk and play with their baby, when in fact talking is just the thing to help the baby focus on and pay attention to her parents.

Certainly a visually or multiply handicapped child's signals are hard to read. When a child is lying quietly in the crib, it's easy to think, "She likes it best when she's left alone," or "She's happy to lie in her crib," or "Such a good baby!" If a baby cries or stiffens when picked up, it's easy to think she would rather *not* be picked up. Look at it from the baby's point of view: If you did not see well enough to learn about your world through your eyes, then you would *have* to use your ears; and if you moved around and made a lot of noise, you *could not* use your ears. It makes sense, then, to lie perfectly still and listen! And it makes even more sense to be afraid, when suddenly you're picked up and moved around, and you don't even know who's doing it, or why, and to react by crying or stiffening your body.

The world of the young visually or multiply handicapped child is confusing at best, and can be frightening. Information comes to the child in pieces, and sometimes one piece of information does not fit with another piece. But that does not mean the world will always be so confusing. By understanding what it's like to have a visual impairment, you can help your child put the pieces together.

Talk to your child before you pick her up. Tell her what you are going to do, and then tell her again as you are doing it.

Give your child a few seconds to adjust to being picked up before you start walking. Take time for a little extra squeeze.

Look for your child to respond. She may breathe a little faster, hold her head a certain way, or open and close her hand. All children develop their own way of responding — you just have to find it!

If your child has a hearing impairment, talk to the side where hearing is best. If her right ear is best, for example, position her so that her right side is closest to you.

Wear the same perfume every day so your baby learns that when she smells that perfume, you are close by.

Let your baby touch your beard or mustache every time you hold her so that she knows it is you even if you don't speak.

Carry your baby with you as you shop or wash dishes so she enjoys and gets used to movement.

When you hold or carry your hearing impaired child, hold her so that her back is against your chest. This helps her to feel the vibrations of your voice as you are talking. Because you also want your child to interact with you and learn to focus on your face, vary this position so that sometimes her side is against your chest, and sometimes she faces you with her hands on your chest.

Watch your child and see how she reacts to loud noises.

Imagine what it would be like if *you* were visually handicapped — how would you put your world together?

Visually and multiply handicapped children need to be picked up, tickled, played with, and taught by their parents just as much, if not *more*, than nonhandicapped childen. But when they don't talk yet, it is up to you, their parents, to anticipate their learning needs, just like you do their needs for food, sleep, and clean pants. And this you already do better than anyone else. Remember though, when you touch your child, it is important to give some warning. Before picking your child up, talk about what you are going to do. If you let your child know you're near, she will not be startled by your touch and will know what to expect.

Turn to page 19 in the REACHBOOK

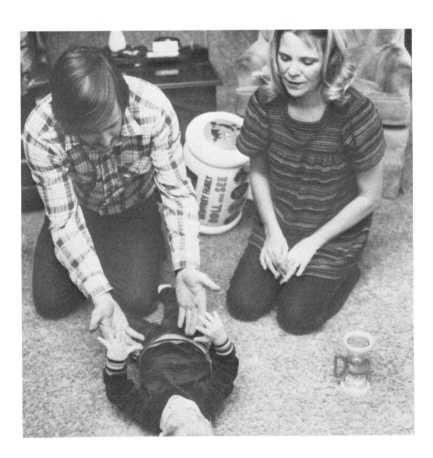

Who is Really Doing the Teaching?

If you already have access to an early childhood teacher or a teacher of the visually handicapped, you may be saying to yourself, "How is my parenting different from the teacher's teaching? They sound pretty much the same." There are some very important differences between the way a teacher teaches and the way a parent teaches. A teacher teaches children using lesson plans, special equipment, and usually a curriculum guide of some sort, during specific hours of the day for a given number of days a year. Parents, on the other hand, usually do not write lesson plans, read a curriculum, buy special equipment, or limit the amount of time they spend with their children. But parents *do* have a commitment to their children that connects them throughout their lives. A teacher may have more experience with visually or multiply handicapped children than you do, but that is exactly how they can help: by giving you teaching ideas, by sharing ideas about your child's future educational and job opportunities, and by observing your child in a different setting. (Children often act differently at school than they do at home.) You and the teacher work together as partners for your child's growth and development.

Parents still teach, but in a much broader sense than teachers do. As a parent, you are a nurturer and caregiver for all your children. As a natural teacher, you help all your children make discoveries about the world outside the classroom. And you act as an advocate for your children, insisting that they receive appropriate services from the educational system. You also:

Know your children better than anyone else does. You know how to approach them, and you have a better idea of what they are ready to learn.

Spend more time with your children than a teacher does. You live with your children over a period of many years, not just a school year, and you are able to take advantage of many more natural opportunities — things that happen throughout the day, in the normal course of family living — to teach them.

Give your children toys and provide common, everyday materials to help your children learn in natural situations that can be applied to other situations outside the home.

Provide your children with the opportunity to practice what they have learned, and a chance to experience the world under your guidance.

Act as a role model. By starting early, you teach your children good habits that will last a lifetime.

Keep your children involved in the family so that the family learns how to interact with a handicapped person, and your children learn how to act with others.

Every moment you spend with your children is a teaching moment. It might be playing, or talking, or running errands, or just *being* — but you are teaching your child just the same.

Turn to page 20 in the REACHBOOK

Using Natural Interaction Times

When children are visually or multiply handicapped they have other ways of understanding and learning about the world:

Exploring with their hands
Listening
Using their sense of smell and taste
Moving their body parts in space and time
Using their remaining vision

By touching and talking to children you can teach them a great deal about themselves, the family, and the world around them. One of the best ways to do this is to take advantage of natural interaction times — when parents, babies, and even older children do a lot of touching and talking. Dressing, bathing, feeding, and diaper changing are all natural interaction times. During these times you can:

Use a wide range of voice tones, inflections, and volumes.

Imitate the sounds your child is making, or say words that sound like those sounds (your child's "ba-ba" could be "bottle").

Be specific when talking to your child so he knows what you're talking about. You give your child much more information when you say, "Good boy, you waved bye-bye," than when you say, "Good boy, you did it." (Did what?)

"Boy, you're dirty! How did you get so dirty?"

"Let me check that diaper. Are you wet? You're not wet, you're drenched!"

Give lots of description and connect what's going on now to what happened before and/or to what will happen later. For example:

"Umm-m-m! Smell that apple pie baking in the oven! It sure smells good! We had a lot of fun picking the apples from the trees and cutting them into pieces at home. Tonight, we'll eat our apple pie with ice cream on top — yum-yum!"

Talk to the baby as you change diapers, touching different body parts and commenting specifically on what you're doing. For example:

"What's the matter? Do you want to be changed? Well, come on. Let's go change your diaper. We'll get this baby some dry pants.

"Up you go. Let's unsnap your pants and get your diaper unpinned. Want to help me? Here, pull your pants so they come unsnapped. Good! You unsnapped your pants!

"Let's get that dirty diaper off. Such a wet diaper! Can you feel how wet it is? It smells dirty, too, doesn't it?

"Oh, you don't like that cold washcloth. Well, I'll get you a warm one. There, that's better.

"How about some powder? Here, smell it. Doesn't this powder feel good when I rub it on you? C'mon, help me rub it on.

"Now you smell so good! I'm going to kiss that little belly, and those little hands and feet. Here I go! (Kiss, Kiss, Kiss)

"Hold still now, so I don't stick you with this pin when I put it in your diaper.

"There you are now, all clean and dry. You smell so good!"

In that one short interchange, you have planted the seeds for your child to learn many different concepts: clean/dirty, wet/dry, pinned / unpinned, warm/cold. By using scented powder, you let your child know that smell is an important part of the world, too. You gave many opportunities for him to babble and imitate what you were saying. And you taught him about his body parts when you kissed, tickled, and talked about his belly, hands, and feet.

Your baby wants and needs to be included in family interactions. Mealtimes are great times to talk about sounds, smells, and people:

"Well here we go again. Time for dinner! Daddy is on your left, and your sister is on your right. Mommy is across from you."

"Mmmm! Doesn't that smell good! What is it? You're right, it's spinach. Oh, and smell this lemon! The lemon smells sweet but it tastes sour. Here, you try."

"What did you do in school today?"

"There's the telephone. Will you answer it, please, daddy? Oh, the telephone is for me? Okay. Be right back."

"Are you banging your spoon on the table?"

"Ooops! Spilled the milk. Let's clean it up."

"Boy, that celery is noisy when you chew it."

"Uh-oh, the cake is burning! I can smell it!"

Talking, Touching, and Playing

Another area that is extremely important to your visually or multiply handicapped child is exploring objects with hands. Your child will benefit from playing with and just being exposed to a variety of objects with different textures. Try sandpaper, a soft doll, a piece of carpet, a sponge, and other objects with rough, smooth, prickly, or fuzzy tectures. You can build these "touch-and-feel" concepts into other play and interaction times, such as letting your child:

Feel the washcloth before you wet it in the bath water, and then again after it's wet.

Feel different clothes as you talk about how they feel — soft, fuzzy, scratchy, nubby, silky.

Feel different food textures: cookies can be hard or soft; pudding is soft and sticky; jello is liquid when it is first made and then becomes soft and jiggly.

Often, when children have some residual vision, they will hold objects close to their eyes. While this may look funny, it is a good practice to encourage. Other ways you can help your child use his vision during your everyday routines include:

Talk about the things around you that you may take for granted. For example, your child may only see a dark blur where you see the front door. By pointing out the door to your child and letting him touch it, you give meaning to that dark blur, and understanding to your child.

Bring toys and other objects close to your child, if possible, or take your child close to the objects. But experiment. Depending on your child's eye condition, bringing things too close may actually block out whatever vision he has. Take the cue from your child:

How close does he get on his own?

At what distance does he seem to pay attention?

When do his eyes fixate and appear to focus?

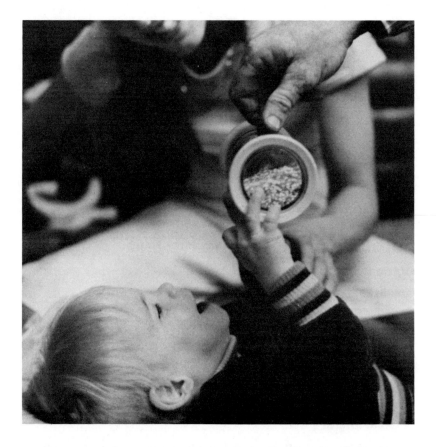

Give your child a chance to see. Try not to hurry all the time (only when you need to!). Just as you have learned to give your baby time to adjust when you pick him up, so too, you need to give him time to adjust visually. It may take him longer to focus, or to adjust to lighting changes, or to make his eyes move at the same time in the same direction. Give him a chance to respond.

Chapter 2 will give you more help on these and other questions about your child's vision.

In summary, visually and multiply handicapped children learn by touching, listening, smelling, tasting, moving, and looking. You can help your child by talking, touching, and playing with him during natural interaction times and by giving him toys that vary in texture, weight, smell, sound, and color. The more sensory experiences you can provide, both one at a time and simultaneously, during your everyday routines and special family occasions, the better.

Your creative, on-the-spot teaching will go a long way towards helping your child grow and learn.

Turn to page 23 in the REACHBOOK ➤

Excuses and Expectations

Parents of visually and multiply handicapped children often wonder whether their children will learn and grow up like sighted children do. Parents often ask, "Will my child learn to walk at the same time as sighted children?" or "Will my child learn to talk around the same time sighted children do?" or "Will my child be able to go to kindergarten?"

These are questions about developmental *milestones*. A milestone is a specific behavior that children are expected to do at a certain age. But the time for reaching a developmental milestone is often different for visually or multiply handicapped children and they may reach milestones later than sighted children do. One of the reasons for this is that it is difficult for children with a visual impairment to imitate and learn actions that they are unable to see. But it *is* possible to teach visually and multiply handicapped children what they cannot pick up through imitation, and these books are designed to help you do just that.

Sometimes visually and multiply handicapped children are slower to reach developmental milestones simply because no one expects them to do certain things. It's easy to think that a child cannot use a spoon because she's blind. It is quite another matter to say, "Okay, she can't watch us eating; how can we show her how to feed herself with a spoon?" The first assumption is an excuse; the second is an expectation. With excuses, children may never learn. With expectations, there's a chance.

Turn to page 26 in the REACHBOOK ➤

How Teachers Teach

Most adults never went to school before they were 5 or 6 years old, so it is hard to imagine how babies and young children can be taught. It is even harder to imagine if the baby is visually or multiply handicapped. As a parent, you will be teaching your child in situations that normally occur at home and in situations that you create to help your child learn. To do this, it helps to know something about how teachers teach.

Basically, teaching is a process which has four steps:

1. Assessment
2. Planning
3. Teaching
4. Reassessment

1. Assessment

One of the basic principles in teaching is that anything new must build upon what is already known. For instance, if children do not know how to walk, they can't be taught to run; and if they do not know how to count, they can't be taught to add. For this reason, the very first step in the teaching process is to find out what the child knows, and how well he knows it. This is called assessment.

To do that, you need good observation skills — an ability to watch your child and, over time, to decide whether or not he has learned a particular skill. In all of the chapters that follow, you will be asked to observe your child and make some decisions about what he can and cannot do. The information you collect in the REACHBOOK will help you (and your child's teacher, if one is available) *assess* what your child is currently doing and to make a plan of what to teach next.

Turn to page 28 in the REACHBOOK

2. Planning

Once an assessment has been made, you will have a good idea of how much your child is able to do. A plan can then be made to teach those skills your child is ready to learn. This teaching plan is similar to what a classroom teacher uses in class, except it is for just one child — yours — and is specifically geared to your child's needs.

The REACHBOOK will help you find which skills your child has learned and which skills she needs to work on. The plan that you make, either alone or with a teacher's help, will guide you in teaching your child what is needed in order to reach the next developmental milestone.

In order to work, plans must be specific. They should describe the goal the child is working toward, and they should include simple, specific activities to be done with the child to help her reach that goal. For example, you may have found during your assessment that your child already knows how to hold a spoon, but she does not know yet how to scoop up food with a spoon and get it into her mouth. The plan will list "feeds self with spoon" as the goal, and then suggest ways to work on teaching this to her in small steps. Breaking down goals into small steps is called *task analysis*.

The easiest way to do a task analysis is to think about how you would go about doing an activity yourself: think about what you are doing as you are doing it. You should look at the skill you want to teach and decide ahead of time which steps are critical and should be taught. For example, it is not really important when brushing your teeth to wet the brush before you put on the toothpaste. That is an individual difference and an individual choice. What *is* important is that somehow toothpaste gets on the toothbrush, the toothbrush gets to the mouth, and the teeth get brushed.

Turn to page 29 in the REACHBOOK

Once you know your child's strengths (what she does well) and weaknesses (what she needs help doing), it is possible to make plans that will help her progress smoothly. If you know what your child is working toward, it is easier to use everyday activities to teach her, and you might be able to avoid the tenseness that arises in "contrived" learning situations.

3. Teaching

When you teach you will be working on the activities contained in the plan. Sometimes you will want to write down the way your child reacts to being taught. By using the observation skills you developed during assessment, you can observe your child as you teach and record the progress made. You want to do this because a very important part of teaching is *feedback* — letting your child know how well he's done. For visually and multiply handicapped children this is especially important because they cannot watch their own movements and tell how well they have done, or what exactly they have done, unless they get some very specific feedback on their performance. Teachers often call this "reinforcement." What you are really doing is helping your child to develop good feelings about himself. Remember to say:

"Good! You put your hand all the way around the peg."

"Marylou, you rolled over!"

"Almost got it — try saying 'sister' again."

"I'm proud of you."

"You did a nice job writing your letters. Next time, try not to smudge the papers with your arm."

"Good work! You sorted all the big and little pegs."

Teachers do not expect children to do things perfectly the first time. But feedback lets a child know where improvement is needed. More importantly, the child knows that *you* still think he can do it.

Turn to page 31 in the REACHBOOK

4. Reassessment

A child is reassessed during and after teaching to find out whether or not the teaching is successful, or whether it needs to be changed. If a child makes some progress and meets the goal, a new goal — the next step — is added to the plan.

Sometimes, the child does not learn what you or the teacher are trying to teach. If this happens, then you need to decide if the child understands what is being asked of her, and whether or not you need to come up with some alternative teaching strategies, or new ways to help the child reach the goal. Look again at your task analysis to find out if maybe you've missed a step somewhere and are asking your child to make too big a jump from one step to another. Sometimes, too, it helps to write down how the child behaved, or how well the child did. That way, you can go back and try to find whether or not the teaching worked, and if not — why not. If your teaching worked, move on to another step; if not, try a new approach to the same goal.

When you look at teaching as a process, you can begin to see that it follows a cycle:

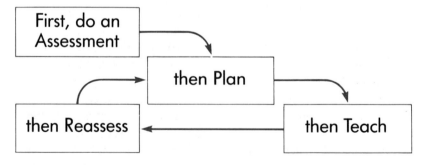

First, do an *assessment* to find out what your child can already do;

Then, make a *plan* to teach your child the next step;

Then, *teach*; and

Finally, continually *reassess* as you teach to find if your child has learned what you have tried to teach:

If the child did learn it, then move on to the next step.

If the child did not learn it, then make a new *plan* (with new activities) and try again;

Teach with the new plan; and

Then, *assess* how effective the *new* plan was in teaching the child.

Turn to page 32 in the REACHBOOK

Finding Help

National Parent Groups

One source of help you might want to look into is other parents of visually or multiply handicapped children. Parent support groups are made up of people like you who have found that it often helps to talk to someone else with the same problem. These groups either hold regularly scheduled meetings or just meet informally to share suggestions on parenting and educational issues. Parents of older visually and multiply handicapped children can give you helpful hints and tell you what it was like when their children were young. And all parents can share techniques that have worked in teaching their children. Your teacher or early childhood program director can help you find a parent group, or you can write to:

American Council of the Blind — Parents
c/o American Council of the Blind, Inc.
1155 15th Street, N.W., Suite 720
Washington, DC 20005
(202) 467-5081

The American Council of the Blind—Parents (ACBP) is a special interest group of the American Council of the Blind, an organization of blind and visually handicapped adults. Many members of ACBP are blind parents whose children may or may not be visually impaired, but the group does not restrict membership to blind persons. ACBP publishes a periodic newsletter and sponsors a national two-day parents meeting annually during the first week in July. Because officers are elected every two years, it is best to contact the national office of the American Council of the Blind, which will send your request for information to the appropriate officer.

National Association for Parents of the Visually Impaired, Inc.
2180 Linway Drive
Beloit, WI 53511-2720
(608) 362-4945
(800) 562-6265

The National Association for Parents of the Visually Impaired (also known as NAPVI) is an organization for parents of children who are blind, visually impaired, or multiply handicapped. Non-voting membership is available to other interested persons. It shares supportive ideas and information with other parents and families through an information bank and a quarterly newsletter, *Awareness*. NAPVI also publishes several books, including *Take Charge! A Guide to Resources for Parents of the Visually Impaired, Your Child's InFORMation JOURNAL,* and *How To Pack 'Em In: A Guide to Planning Workshops.* These and other NAPVI publications will help keep you up to date on developments in the education of visually handicapped children. NAPVI has several affiliate parent groups around the country and sponsors local and regional parent meetings each year.

Parents of Blind Children Division
National Federation of the Blind
1800 Johnson Street
Baltimore, MD 21230
(301) 659-9314

The Parents of Blind Children Division is composed of parents whose children are blind and visually impaired. It is a division of the National Federation of the Blind (NFB), a national membership organization of blind persons with affiliates in every state. The Division for Parents publishes a bimonthly magazine, *Future Reflections*; other publications and nonprint media are available through NFB. The Division sponsors state and regional parent meetings and a day-long national conference for parents during the first week in July.

Turn to page 34 in the REACHBOOK

You might find other parent organizations in your hometown by contacting your local school district or organizations that deal specifically with multiply handicapped children, such as United Cerebral Palsy, Easter Seal Society, and the Association for Retarded Citizens.

Community Resources

You may also want to find out what resources exist in your community for both you and your child. These resources depend on where you live — farm, city, small town, in the mountains — and are quite varied. For some of you this step will not be difficult; for others, it will seem like you are defeated before you even begin. But, you now begin your life as an assertive person. You will find yourself always on the alert, always asking questions until you get the answers you need and want. To find some of these answers:

Ask doctors and nurses

Ask friends

Ask clergy

Ask the school nurse

Ask the education department in your city

Look in the Yellow Pages for agencies that service not only visually impaired youngsters, but any handicapped child

Contact the American Foundation for the Blind for referrals of sources of help near you

Contact the three national parent groups listed in the last section

Contact a university or college nearby

Contact the Visiting Nurses Association

Contact a well-baby clinic

Contact your public health nurse

Ask the welcome wagon volunteers

Contact any source that you feel may direct you in obtaining help for you and your visually impaired youngster. You cannot begin too early to plan for the future.

Turn to page 35 in the REACHBOOK

Once you have found what is available to you, you need to make some decisions — based on your ability to cope and your willingness to direct your child's abilities — about how much, if at all, you want any kind of organized system to help you. Many organizations offer a range of services from home teaching to homemaker services and, as parents, you know best what services are needed by your particular family at this particular time. If you do call any of the agencies you found in the phone book, remember that they are there to help you — nobody's doing you a favor.

Expect all people you deal with to be:
Understanding
Empathetic
Professional
Courteous
Considerate
Flexible
Dependable
On time for appointments

At the same time, they should be able to expect you to be:
Friendly
Courteous
Flexible
Interested
Dependable
On time for appointments

It's a two-way street. You need each other.

Turn to page 42 in the REACHBOOK

Preschool Programs

During the infant and preschool years you will probably want to enroll your child in an infant stimulation or preschool program if one is available. Infant stimulation, early childhood education, early intervention, child development, preschool — all are names used to refer to a group of services available to handicapped children under 6 years of age and their families.

The availability of these programs varies from state to state. Only twelve states in 1984 — call your state department of education to find out if yours is one — have laws which require local schools to provide programs for handicapped children under 5 or 6 years of age.

Turn to page 43 in the REACHBOOK

If your state does have mandatory special education services for infants and preschoolers, all you need to do is contact the superintendent of your school district. But even if your state does not require educational services for preschool children, many local schools have early childhood programs because they are aware of the benefits to child and school alike. (About two-thirds of the children who graduate from preschool special education programs enter regular elementary classrooms and only need occasional help; many schools have decided the money spent on preschool programs actually saves money later.) Your local superintendent will know if your district has a program and can tell you whom to call.

Turn to page 44 in the REACHBOOK

But if your school district does not have an early education program, you are not necessarily out of luck. Education for the visually handicapped has a long history, and preschool programs for blind children began in the 1930s, long before the rest of the country recognized how important it was to work with children before school age. So there may be an agency, sorority, or volunteer organization in your area that has set up a program. Perhaps you already found it when you did the last exercise in your REACHBOOK. If you haven't found an early childhood program specifically geared toward children who are visually impaired, you might find one for all types of handicapped children at United Cerebral Palsy, Easter Seal Society, or the Association for Retarded Citizens. Use the information you wrote down in your REACHBOOK. Check out all possiblities.

Types of Preschool Programs

All preschool programs use one or more of the following ways of working with families:

1. **Home-based services,** where teachers, counselors, or consultants come to your home on a regular basis. All activities take place in your home and you have exclusive time with that teacher or other professional while they are there. Home visits usually last about an hour and can occur as frequently as four times a week or as infrequently as once a month, depending upon the size of the staff, the number of families served, and how far the staff must travel to reach all the families.

2. **Center-based services,** where you and your child must travel to a central location. All teachers, consultants, and counselors are located at the center and work with children individually and in small groups. Depending on how old your child is, you may be able to drop your child off for a class and return later when class is over, or you may be asked to help out in the classroom, or to join a parent discussion group.

3. **Home- and center-based services,** where some activities occur in your home and sometimes you must go to the center. Regardless of which model a preschool program uses, look for the following "good practices" in the program you work with.

Good Practices

1. **A certified teacher** of the visually handicapped and an orientation and mobility specialist, if not directly on staff as teachers, are at least involved in assessment, planning, and consultation. No other teacher is trained to understand how visual handicaps affect development, or how the child can learn to compensate for the visual impairment.

2. **An occupational or physical therapist** should be available to answer questions about your child's motor development and to work directly with your child if your doctor prescribes it. If a therapist is not available, the program knows where you can find one.

3. **You are involved** in the choice of which program your child receives and what goals your child works on.

4. **The program asks your permission** to assess your child, to obtain copies of medical records, and to take pictures of your child, and you are given a copy of any permission forms you sign.

5. **Any record on your child** contains a sheet of paper which tells you who has looked at your child's file and who has received copies

of any papers found in the file. Your child's file is confidential, and no one should be able to see it without a good reason.

6. **You are given copies** of your child's assessment report and individualized educational plan.

7. **You are kept up to date** on how your child is doing, including receiving ideas for activities you can work on yourself.

8. **You have a chance to meet** with other parents, either in a formal meeting or informally, over coffee or soft drinks.

9. **The curriculum** (what your child is taught) covers motor development, visual development, self-help skills, language and communication, social and emotional development, mental or intellectual or cognitive development, orientation and mobility, and sensory development (touch, smell, hearing, and taste).

10. **A variety of support services** (extra but necessary services that add to the quality and completeness of the program) are available. Some examples are social workers, speech therapists, low vision examinations, toy libraries, pediatricians, transportation, ophthalmologists, and psychologists.

The program you find may not use all of these good practices now, but you can work together with the program's staff to see that they are in place for the future. Every program learns from the people who are part of it, so share your ideas and feelings freely. All visually and multiply handicapped children will benefit as a result.

The pages which follow and the pages in your REACHBOOK will help you assess, plan, and teach your visually or multiply handicapped child, with or without the help of a preschool program or a teacher of the visually handicapped. They have been designed specifically to help you REACH OUT AND TEACH!

Turn to page 45 in the REACHBOOK

Notes on Additional Reading

Some people might like to have additional reading material to help get started. Here are a few suggestions. For complete information on these publications, see the Bibliography in the back of this HANDBOOK.

There are two booklets that are simple, easy to read, and fun: *Get a Wiggle On,* by S. Raynor and R. Drouillard, and *Move It,* by R. Drouillard and S. Raynor. You may enjoy them yourself, but they would also be ideal to give to an older child, relative, or friend to help them understand your baby's needs and how you try to meet them. If your child has multiple impairments, especially cerebral palsy, there is a similar booklet, *I Wanna Do It Myself,* by C. Gimbel and K. Shane. And less playful, but equally brief, for parents of young children with hearing loss as well as visual impairment: *A Handbook for Parents of Deaf-Blind Children* by J. Esche and C. Griffin; and *Infant Stimulation: A Pamphlet for Parents of Multihandicapped Children,* by S. Hoffman.

The following books are more extensive, with suggestions related to the child's level of development. They contain activities that will help children to develop in various ways and advice on handling situations that may present problems for the parents. *Show Me How: A Manual for Parents of Preschool Visually Impaired and Blind Children,* by M. Brennan; *Handbook for Parents of Preschool Blind Children,* by I. Davidson, et al.; *Workbook for Parents & Teachers—Teaching the Visually Impaired Preschool Child 2-5 Years Old,* by Galante; *Preschool Learning Activities for the Visually Impaired: A Guide for Parents,* Illinois State Board of Education; *Hints for Parents of Preschool Visually Handicapped Children,* by V. Murray; and *Get Ready, Get Set, Go!,* by J. Schuch. *Parenting Preschoolers: Suggestions for Raising Young Blind and Visually Impaired Children,* by K. Ferrell, deals briefly with many of the topics of *Reach Out and Teach* and might provide an overview for yourself and others. All of these deal mainly with children who are only blind or visually impaired. *A Comprehensive Program for Multi-handicapped Children: An Illustrated Approach,* by S. Jerard et al., is along the same lines, and gives very concrete directions for training severely multiply handicapped children. It is rather long and deals separately with various areas of development, so it will be discussed again in future chapters.

The Visually Impaired Child: Growth, Learning, Development— Infancy to School Age, by C. Halliday, deals with child development in general and how it is affected by loss of vision. It provides advice to parents in more general terms than the five books just listed, but it goes far deeper into the reasons for it. There is also a four-page article that takes a similar approach, "Developmental Needs in Blind Infants," by R. Dubose. Although the author uses technical terms, it is clearly written.

Play is a very important part of any young child's life. *Games and Toys for Blind Children of Preschool Age,* by Pielasch, Ed., et al., relates toys and activities to the child's development and learning. A small commercial catalog, *Some Children Are More Special Than Others. . . A Guide to Mattel Toys for Parents of the Visually Handicapped Child* from Mattel, Inc., also relates toys to areas of development. *Touch Toys and How to Make Them,* by R. Barquist and E. Timburg, gives directions for making various toys for blind and visually handicapped preschoolers. *Homemade Toys for Mother and Child,* by M. Miller, also gives directions and, in addition, relates the activities to development. However, it is not specifically for blind and visually handicapped children; many of the games assume the child can see. Selection and adaptation are needed. The same applies to *How to Fill Your Toy Shelves Without Emptying Your Pocketbook: 70 Inexpensive Things To Do Or Make,* by Southwest Education Dev. Lab., Austin, and *Toy Workshops for Parents: Bridging a Gap. Baby Buggy Paper No. 201,* P. L. Hutinger, et al.

The following longer books will be referred to more than once in this HANDBOOK, each time noting the chapters most relevant to the subjects under consideration. *Our Blind Children,* by B. Lowenfeld, Chapters 5 and 13, and *Can't Your Child See?,* by E. P. Scott, J. E. Jan, and R. D. Freeman, Chapters 3, 4, 7, and Chapter 6 (which refers specifically to the multiply handicapped) deal with the parent's role in the development of the young blind child. As a whole, *Can't Your Child See?* concentrates more on the early years than does *Our Blind Children. Understanding the Deaf-Blind Child,* by P. Freeman, Chapters 1 through 5, cover the same topics in relation to the child who also has severe hearing loss.

There are three more books that give advice and information in particular areas of child development rather than on parenting in general, so they, too, will be referred to in more detail in other parts of this HANDBOOK. They are: *Raising the Young Blind Child: A Guide for Parents and Educators,* by S. Kastein, I. Spaulding, and B. Scharf, which deals with blind children; *Beginning with the Handicapped,* by V. Hart, which is concerned with very severely multiply handicapped children whose impairments may include blindness or visual loss; and *Handling the Young Cerebral Palsied Child at Home,* by N. R. Finnie, which deals only with cerebral palsy.

Another book that touches on nearly every subject dealt with in this HANDBOOK is *The Road to Freedom: A Parent's Guide to Prepare the Blind Child to Travel Independently* by R. Webster. Because it is concerned with a single extremely important achievement — understanding and mastering the environment — it will be referred to repeatedly. The book deals with the child whose only serious handicap is blindness, but much of it is applicable to other children as well.

A different kind of book that you may enjoy is *Elizabeth,* by S. Ulrich. Written by a mother about her blind daughter, it is as much a personal experience for the reader as it is for the author.

Finally, a periodical that could be helpful: *VIP Newsletter* of the International Institute for Visually Impaired, 0–7, Inc. contains suggestions, questions and answers, and news items for, and often by, parents of young blind and visually impaired children.

TALKING IT OVER:

You, Your Family and the World

Vision
Attitudes toward blindness
Family interactions
Behavior
Parent rights
Questions for your eye specialist
How your child feels about himself

TALKING IT OVER:

You, Your Family and the World

In many of the chapters of *Reach Out and Teach* the emphasis is on your child — what he needs to learn, how you can help him learn it, and how his visual impairment and other handicaps affect his learning. This chapter, "Talking it Over," is a little different. There is more to life than learning, and there is more to parenting than teaching. How you and your child feel about yourselves, how you and your child deal with other people's feelings and with their sometimes thoughtless comments, and how you can best get through these growing times together are also important. "Talking it Over" will try to help you with some of these issues.

Dealing With Your Child's Handicap

As a parent who may just be learning about your child's eye condition or other handicap, it is important to understand that no one's experience is exactly like yours. Other parents may share some parts of what you are going through, but no two people bring the same history to the situation. *Your* background, *your* experiences, and *your* feelings are your own, and no one else's. No one can tell you how you feel, second-guess what you think, or explain what you are going through.

It doesn't really matter how you were told or when you first heard that your child was blind, visually handicapped, or multiply handicapped; your reaction did not depend on who told you, how you were told, where you were told, or even who was there when you first learned. But you will probably never forget the effect it had on you.

The way people respond to a handicapping condition depends a lot on how much contact they have had with handicapped children and adults. If the only blind adult you've ever seen was begging on a city street, you might feel pity or disgust for him and even for all blind persons. If your club gives a holiday party for crippled children in the hospital every year, you might have a different idea of what being handicapped means. If your response to the big telethons on television is to give money (or not to), you probably have another idea of the word "handicapped." Then again, if you grew up in a small town where the only handicapped persons were elderly, you might associate "handicapped" with being old. Or, particularly when you think of blindness, you might think of celebrities like Ray Charles, Stevie Wonder, or Jose Feliciano — all famous and successful singers. Before you even know that your child is blind or visually handicapped, you already have a concept of what "blind" means.

But that doesn't mean anything anymore — now it is your child that is visually or multiply handicapped. Everything you ever saw, thought, or heard about blindness no longer counts. What *does* count is where you go from here.

Turn to page 55 in the REACHBOOK

Understanding Your Child's Vision

If you are like most adults in this country, you wear glasses. Those glasses either (1) put things that are far away in focus, (2) put things that are close up in focus, or (3) do both, but to different degrees. But you also have a child who is visually handicapped — or you wouldn't be reading this book. What does blindness or visual impairment actually mean in terms of what your child can see?

First, a definition of terms: For most educational uses, *blindness* means a total loss of vision — no awareness of light or where it is coming from. *Low vision* means a range of visual abilities, from being capable of seeing newspaper print to having only light perception (awareness of light), and everything in between. Low vision persons are also sometimes referred to as *partially seeing*.

Legal blindness is included in the definition of low vision, but refers only to visual abilities with a measured acuity of 20/200 or less in the *best* eye, with correction (that is, with glasses on). For your purposes, legal blindness is nothing more than a classification system used by the government to limit the number of visually handicapped persons who are eligible for special services. While this is important for you in terms of benefits (such as Supplemental Security Income, infant programs, braille books, etc.), it does not tell you much about what your child *is able* to see since many legally blind persons are able to read regular size print with the help of low vision aids. (See the "Looking Ahead" chapter for more information on low vision aids.)

Visual acuity can best be described as how sharply the eyes focus. It is usually meaured using a Snellen chart, a long chart with black letters placed 20 feet away from the person being examined. Each line of identically-sized letters corresponds to the size of an object that can be seen clearly by the "normal" eye at various distances of 20 feet and beyond. A person with "normal" acuity would therefore be able to read the smallest size of letters when the chart is 20 feet from her eyes, and her acuity would be described as "20/20" — or, "She sees at 20 feet what the normal eye sees at 20 feet." All acuity measures are thus discussed in terms of the "normal" eye. Legal blindness, 20/200, means that the legally blind individual must be 20 feet or closer to something that the person with normal vision can see at a distance of 200 feet.

Obviously, unless you are trying to qualify for services, acuity is not very useful when dealing with infants and preschoolers since (1) most of their activities occur within 10 feet of their bodies, and (2) they won't be able to read the Snellen chart until they can identify letters. Fortunately, there are alternatives to the Snellen test that your eye specialist can use with young children:

Lighthouse Low Vision Cards: Designed for near-point (close-up) instead of distance measurement, these cards use figures of a house, apple, and umbrella, instead of letters.

National Society for the Prevention of Blindness "E" Test: Designed primarily for preschoolers, the child only needs to identify the direction in which the "E's" legs are pointing. If the child cannot yet identify right, left, up, down in words, she can point or use another "E" card to match the direction.

Stycar Vision Test: Designed for lower functioning children, this test utilizes balls of various sizes which are rolled past the child. The smallest size observed by the child indicates the best measure of acuity.

Forced Choice Visual Preference Test: With this relatively new technique widely used by perceptual psychologists, the child is shown a series of black-lined cards. The lines are carefully measured to correspond to the Snellen chart distance acuities. The child's attention to the lined card is interpreted to mean that the child is able to see it at that acuity. When the child no longer pays attention, it is because the lines are no longer discernible to her — she sees the card as solid gray because the lines quite literally "melt" into one another.

Any one of these tests will help give your eye specialist an acuity measure that can be used to assist you in obtaining services. Although some specialists may not be familiar with or have the equipment to perform all these tests, they might be able to refer you to a university or medical center that can. If not, don't worry; explain to the eye specialist that your child needs to qualify for services. In many cases, doctors have completed an eye report form by stating "unable to test at this time," which is usually accepted by agencies until the child is older.

Unfortunately, the "unable to test" comment is used by some eye specialists when they are not experienced with very young or severely handicapped children. When you are trying to find out what your child can see, however, *do not accept* "unable to test" from your eye specialist. You deserve more than that — you *need* more than that if you are going to help your child learn.

Turn to page 57 in the REACHBOOK

Questions You Should Ask Your Eye Specialist

There are many, many different eye conditions. Some involve structural damage to or malformation of the eye (such as cataracts or optic nerve hypoplasia); some are part of an overall syndrome (such as Down's Syndrome or Usher's Syndrome). Some are hereditary characteristics passed on from generation to generation (such as albinism), while others are caused by an infection during pregnancy (such as rubella or cytomegalo virus), or by an accident at birth (such as brain damage caused by a lack of oxygen).

This chapter will not describe every possible eye condition; there are other books that provide such information. (See Notes on Additional Reading at the end of this chapter.) What the "Talking it Over" chapter *will* do is describe the manifestations, or consequences, of visual impairment, any one of which may be shared by several different medical diagnoses. This chapter also suggests questions for you to ask the eye specialist so you will have specific answers about your child's particular visual problem.

Question 1: **What caused my child's visual problem?**

Your first question will probably be about cause, because you want to know why this happened to you, and why it happened with this particular child. Possible causes might be:

> **Infection:** caused by a virus that is transmitted to the developing fetus while still in the mother's womb. Rubella (German measles) and cytomegalo virus are common. In some cases, the infection occurs during birth (such as herpes or other venereal diseases) or after birth (such as encephalitis).

Chromosomal: caused by a change in the child's genes, or the dominance of one gene over another. Some chromosomal changes are unpredictable, such as Down's Syndrome (now often referred to as Down Syndrome) or Trisomy 21, while others are predictable because of family history. Chromosomal changes may also result from chemical and environmental causes.

Perinatal: caused by an event occurring at or around the time of birth, such as prematurity, anoxia (lack of oxygen), or a forceps delivery.

Chemical interactions: caused by exposure of the developing fetus to drugs (tranquilizers, nicotine), alcohol, or some unknown substance.

Environmental: caused by something in the surroundings, such as exposure to Agent Orange in Vietnam, or proximity to a pesticide. Environmental causes are not likely to be pinpointed immediately and are difficult to prove. They usually involve a lot of study and investigation before a cause-and-effect relationship can be drawn.

Question 2: **Is this eye condition hereditary?**
This question may have already been answered when you asked Question 1. If not, be sure you get an answer. If the eye condition is hereditary, you will want to talk with a genetic counselor to find out:

The chances that any of your future children could have the same thing;

The chances that this child's children will have the same eye condition; and

The chances that any of your other children will be carriers (that is, they don't have the eye condition themselves, but they could pass it along to their own children).

Question 3: **Will my child's eye condition change?**
Some eye conditions are stable, and you can expect that your child's medical needs will not change as she gets older. Other eye conditions will deteriorate, or get worse, as your child gets older. Your eye specialist should be able to tell you:

If the eye condition is stable;

If the eye condition will improve;

If the eye condition alone will get worse; or

If your child's general health will get worse along with the eye condition.

You will also want to know *when* this improvement or deterioration will take place, and if it might be helpful for you to talk to a different medical specialist (such as a neurologist, physical therapist, or orthopedist).

Question 4: **Where is the problem located?**

The problem with your child's vision can usually be traced to a specific part of the visual system. The visual system includes the brain as well as the eye, and when both are functioning correctly they allow an individual not only to see, but to interpret what is being seen. If only part is damaged or not working correctly, vision will be impaired.

The way the eye works can be greatly simplified by tracing the path taken by a visual image:

1. **Light rays first enter** the eye through the *cornea*, the clear outer covering of the eye, then

2. **Pass through the *pupil*,** the opening in the middle of the *iris* (the colored part of the eye)

3. **To the *lens*,** which changes shape, bends the light rays to the proper angle, and directs them through the *vitreous humor*, a clear substance that helps the eye to hold its shape,

4. **To the *retina*,** the lining of the eye, which is composed of millions of photoelectric cells. The most sensitive part of the retina is the *macula*, and in the center of the macula is a tiny pit known as the *fovea*. The fovea is the point of sharpest vision. Light rays are then transported through the retina

5. **To the *optic nerve*,** and conducted to the *visual cortex* in the back of the brain. The brain then interprets the light rays to form a visual image — what we see.

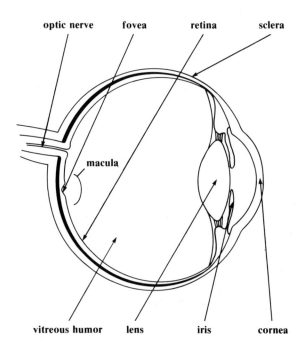

optic nerve   fovea   retina   sclera

macula

vitreous humor   lens   iris   cornea

The point at which the eye is damaged or impaired explains something about what your child is able to see:

If the problem occurs between the front of the eye (the cornea) and the lens, vision might be blurred or hazy all over.

If it occurs between the lens and the retina (in the vitreous), vision might be blurred or blocked completely in some or all areas of the visual field. (Visual field refers to what you can see in front of you, from left to right, up and down, without moving your eyes.)

If the problem is with the retina, several possibilities exist: vision could be blurred or blocked out completely in the center of the visual field; blurred or blocked out in the peripheral, or side, parts of the visual field; a combination of these two; blurred or blocked out in spots.

If the problem is with the optic nerve, vision might be blurred, weakened, or blocked completely.

If the optic nerve is well formed and the problem occurs somewhere between the retina and the visual cortex of the brain, the visual image formed on the retina may not be transmitted to the part of the brain that interprets the visual image; or it may be transmitted in parts; or it may be transmitted in whole or in part only some of the time.

If the problem is in the visual cortex of the brain, the ability to interpret the visual image is affected. It may be lost completely, mixed up, or only functioning in parts.

Question 5: **Do my child's pupils react to light?**

Light enters the eye by passing through an opening called the pupil. The size of the opening changes according to the amount of light that is coming in. You may have noticed that when you are outside in bright sunlight your pupils (or those of someone with you) are very small — almost like pinpoints. When you are in a room where there is not much light, however, your pupils are very large, and you can barely see the iris, or colored part of your eye. Your pupils adjust automatically to make sure that *enough,* but not *too* much, light reaches the retina.

Sometimes, however, the pupils do not react the way they should. Either because of the particular eye condition, or because of some medication your child is taking, her pupils may not *dilate* (get bigger) or *constrict* (get smaller) the way they should. This could make a difference not only in *what* your child is able to see, but *when* she is able to see. For example:

If your child's pupils do not dilate very much, it means that her ability to see, even in very bright light, will be limited. There may simply not be enough light passing through the pupil to form an image on the retina, or the image that is formed may be very weak.

If your child's pupils always seem to be dilated, it means that her ability to see in bright lighting situations may be affected. Her eyes are not able to limit the amount of light coming through and so her vision is "washed out" in bright light. She will probably do better in dim lighting, or on a cloudy day outside, because there is less light present to pass through the pupils.

If your child's pupils seem to be dilating and constricting all the time, it means that your child has very little control over the amount of light entering her eyes — and so do you. It will be hard to find the right lighting situation because it will keep changing as your child's pupils change. This condition is called *hippus*.

You can experience something of what it is like when your pupils do not constrict by setting up a situation in which you are looking at something across the room, but must look past a bright lightbulb (a bare lightbulb hanging from the ceiling or a lamp with the shade removed). Place yourself so that the lightbulb is between you and whatever it is you are looking at, and try to focus on the object beyond the lightbulb. You will probably find that everything in your field of vision is washed out; you might be able to see the object, but you can't see it clearly or in detail. If your pupils did not constrict or get smaller, your whole world would be like this unless the light around you was controlled.

If your child has this problem, take care that she does not spend a lot of time facing windows with sunlight streaming through, or facing lamps that are directly in front of her. She will do better if the light is *behind* her. With the light in back of her, you can keep it out of her eyes, yet still use the light to shine on her toys or food, or just around the room.

Try not to position yourself in front of a window when you are talking to or playing with your child. Sunlight will literally pour in around you and all your child will see is a dark figure. She will not be able to tell if you are smiling, frowning, or grimacing, and any hand gestures you make will be lost.

Glare is a particular problem when the pupils do not constrict. Look for glare from tabletops, desks, mirrors, and even toys, and move them or your child around to get rid of the brightness shining directly into her eyes.

Get down on your child's level. From where you are standing or sitting, the lighting often seems to be fine and there does not appear to be any glare. But from your child's viewpoint, just the opposite could be true. If you notice that your child is not paying attention or has her eyes closed, she might actually be trying to keep the light out of her eyes.

Be particularly aware of contrast if your child's pupils have difficulty reacting to light. High-contrast colors (such as yellow and black; black and white) are good for getting your child's attention. On the other hand, a pale pink shirt laying on a white sheet may be very difficult for your child to see.

As you can tell from the suggestions given above, the value in asking your eye specialist about how your child's pupils react to light is in finding out what you can do to make it easier for her to see. Just because the pupils react, however, does not necessarily mean that your child has vision; it means only that the pupils are working. Because a pupillary response is what is known as a low-level brainstem response, it is almost like breathing — it happens automatically, without the individual having to think about it. So, *use* the answer to this question to help you plan your child's living and learning environment, but do not stop asking questions yet; there is more you need to know.

Question 6: **What is my child's tracking like?**
This question will probably surprise your eye specialist. Tracking refers to the way the eyes follow moving objects, and not everyone uses the word. How a child tracks tells you something about what he is able to see and how he is able to coordinate both visual and motor activities.

Tracking can be checked out either with a penlight; a toy, bottle, or other object; or with the face of a live person. The eye specialist is looking for:

How *smoothly* the eyes follow a moving object;

Whether the eyes move *together;*

How *far* they move; and

In what *direction* they move.

If your child is able to fixate on a moving object and follow it with his eyes, his visual and motor systems are working together. You also know that he is able to fixate, or focus, on objects and that he is able to pay attention for at least a few seconds.

Tracking that appears "bumpy" — where the eyes appear to focus on the moving object but seem to get left behind as the object moves, and then catch up again — could mean only that the visual and motor systems are not quite working together yet. On the other hand, if the eyes always seem to "lose" the moving object in a particular place (such as when the object is on the right side, or when it is in front of the nose), it could mean that the visual field has some areas or spots where vision is not as good as others. If the eyes are not able to cross the midline — that is, if the eyes follow an object until it reaches the center of the body, but cannot move past that point — the child might be in a stage of his motor development where his reflexes are not allowing independent body movement. (See Chapter 3, "Taking Off," and the section on reflexes.)

Both eyes usually move together, in a coordinated fashion. Sometimes, however, one eye seems to wander off or drag behind the other eye as it follows a moving object. This could mean a child has difficulty in coordinating motor actions, but it could also indicate poorer vision in the eye that falls behind. Your eye specialist will want to look into this possibility further as your child grows.

Like every other aspect of your child's growth, tracking skills become more sophisticated as he gets older. Developmental research and observation suggest that children learn to track horizontally, from right to left or left to right, first; then vertically, or up and down; then on a slant, say from top right to bottom left; and then, in a circle. As your child learns to do these skills, the eye specialist will continue to look for how smoothly he tracks and whether or not he can focus on the object or light regardless of where it is located in his visual field.

Multiply handicapped children, particularly those with cerebral palsy or brain damage, will usually have difficulties in tracking, primarily because movement in general is more difficult to control. But these children can learn to follow moving objects if they are given an opportunity to practice. Because their response time might be slower, however, both you and the eye specialist should be sure to move objects slowly, and back up if necessary, to help the child maintain his focus.

Question 7: **What is my child's central vision like?**

Central vision is the eye's best focusing point. It refers to a particular portion of the retina where rays of light are the most sharply focused. Some eye conditions, such as macular degeneration, affect central vision severely; other eye conditions, such as retinitis pigmentosa, affect central vision only in the final stages. You want to ask the eye specialist about your child's central vision, however, because the answer will indicate something about how sharply your child sees, whether or not she is missing what is going on or what you are trying to teach her, and whether or not she can see colors.

Central vision occurs at the *macula*, that part of the retina where rays of light are best able to focus. In that area, the retina is made up largely of cones, cells that are responsible for transmitting color as well as sharpness. If your child has a problem with central vision you can also expect that colors will be difficult for her to learn, and that her visual images will always be slightly out of focus — at least in terms of what *you* are used to.

Another reason to ask your eye specialist about your child's central vision, however, is to find out if your child might be missing out on some of the activities going on around her. If, for example, you always hold her bottle directly in front of her face, she may not see it clearly. If you held it slightly *off-center*, however, it is possible that she could see it more clearly and in more detail. With younger children and children whose movement is limited because of some other handicapping condition, it is particularly important that you move the task to a position where they have a better chance of responding. As they grow older, children themselves learn to scan and move their eyes so that they can find the best possible focus.

Question 8: **What is my child's field of vision like?**

Just as important as central vision is the entire field of vision. If there are no problems with the visual field, an individual would be able to look straight ahead and still see objects held at approximately the level and position of his two temples. In some eye conditions, an individual has a restricted field — that is, he cannot see quite that far out to the sides. Other eye conditions may result in areas, or spots, in the field where vision is reduced or missing altogether.

The visual field also includes the area in front of the individual extending up and down. And the same problems can occur. If a child's lower visual field is not functioning, you would expect him to run into low objects (e.g., chairs, water fountains, wastepaper baskets), and perhaps to have difficulty with stairs, curbs, and even on playgrounds. If the upper field were affected, the child might have difficulty recognizing faces (unless the adults came down to face him at his level), or might not see bedposts, corners of tables, or an open cabinet door.

Again, your reason for asking the eye specialist about your child's visual field is to find out what *adaptations you* need to make at home until your child learns to scan, move his head, and generally make his own adaptations.

Question 9: **What is my child's best viewing distance?**

The answer to this question will depend on your child's age as well as her particular eye condition. Children's ability to *accommodate*, or focus at different distances, improves as they get older. In part, this focusing ability involves development and maturation — rays of light are focused on the retina as they pass through the lens of the eye (see page 38). When an infant is first born, the lens is much like the baby's muscles — relatively soft and unable to move. With development and *use*, however, the lens becomes more flexible (again, like the muscles), and the lens will be able to change shape when necessary. It is the change in shape which causes an object to be focused on the retina, and it is the distance of that object from the lens which brings about the change in shape.

If there is no visual impairment, this ability to focus at different distances is practiced and perfected over time until a child can see an object close to the body as well as when it is ten feet from the body. Depending on the eye condition, however, accommodation could be severely limited. Your eye specialist should examine your child's response to objects at many different distances in order to determine the best viewing distance for her. Just remember that how your child responds will depend on how she feels, whether or not she likes the eye specialist, whether or not she likes whatever it is the specialist is using to get her attention, *as well as* the distance.

Accommodation may change from day to day, and from situation to situation.

Why even bother asking the eye specialist, then? Because, first, you do not want to rely on a distance visual acuity that the eye specialist obtained from use of the Snellen chart. You want to know more about how your child functions in the space closest to her body. Second, determining the best viewing distance at least gives you a point of comparison. You can start working with puzzles, books, writing skills, or even eating skills at this distance, and then gradually get closer or farther away as you encourage your child to look.

And third, your child's viewing distance will tell you more about the type and size of toys you should buy. If your child's best viewing distance is two inches from the nose, it will not make a lot of sense to practice accommodation with a soccer ball — it is too big. If your child's best viewing distance is ten inches, however, a soccer ball might be just the right size to get and maintain her attention. Many people assume that children with a visual impairment automatically need everything larger, but bigger is not necessarily better. If you're not careful, you can use something that is so large that it is literally "out of sight."

Question 10: **How does this eye condition affect my child's mobility?**

This may be another one of those questions that you are better able to answer than your eye specialist, if only because you have had more of a chance to observe your child's movement. If your child is not yet moving, however, or if your child's mobility is limited because of another handicap, you should ask your eye specialist what to expect. Eye conditions which might affect your child's mobility include:

Field restrictions, where small or large areas of the visual field could be blocked out completely, or severely limited in their ability to receive light.

Tunnel vision, an extreme field restriction that is almost like looking through a straw. Vision is limited to a small amount of central vision. Objects are best seen at a distance, while the world closest to the body is usually missed.

Glaucoma, or abnormally high pressure within the eye, may, or perhaps should, limit a child's choice of activities because of loss of peripheral (side) vision. Contact sports, for example, may be ruled out because a hard blow to the head could result in detachment of the retina and total loss of sight.

Poor central vision, which requires a child to scan the environment constantly to find the clearest image. The child's mobility may be slow, deliberate, and cautious until self-confidence is gained.

Difficulty in adjusting to changing lighting conditions, such that a child might be temporarily confused or unsure of himself.

Use of only one eye, such that depth perception (ability to recognize an object's size and position in space) is affected. A child may have problems with steps, curbs, platforms, stages, and other fall-offs.

High refractive error, such that clear vision is limited to an area very close to the body (myopia), or to an area some distance from the body (hyperopia). Again, the child's movement will be cautious and slow.

Question 11: **Are my child's eyes sensitive to light?**
This question may have been answered already when you asked Question 5. If you are not sure, ask again. You may in fact have noticed that your child blinks or closes her eyes tightly whenever you go outside into bright sunlight, or when bright lights are directed into her eyes. With some eye conditions, such as glaucoma, the bright light can actually cause pain, and you will want to be sure that if this is the case your child can be protected.

Sunglasses are made even for small children these days, and your eye specialist might be able to provide you with specially made sunglasses that screen out most of the bright light.

For babies or children who have difficulty supporting sunglasses on their tiny noses, a sunbonnet or other hat with a brim may help screen out the light.

Regardless of whether or not your child is so sensitive to light that it is painful, you should expect that she will have difficulty moving from indoors, where it is relatively dark, to outside, where the sunlight may be very bright. If someone suddenly turns on a ceiling light in a dark room where you've been sleeping, you know what it is like — you are disoriented, you can't open your eyes, and when you do get your eyes open, the room seems overly bright. A child who is sensitive to light will experience this every time she moves from one type of lighting situation to another.

Give your child a chance to adjust. Try not to move quite as fast as you normally would, and when you notice that your child is having difficulty, stop and talk to her. Explain what is going on and reassure her.

Question 12: **Does my child have light perception?**
Light perception is the awareness of light. To get an idea of what light perception means, close your eyes, turn towards a bright lamp, and pass your hand back and forth between your face and the lamp. What you experience is similar to what a blind individual with light perception experiences.

If your child has light perception, it means that he will be able to tell when the lights are on, whether the day is sunny or clouded over and, when he gets older, in what direction he is moving. As he grows you can help him put meaning to light and dark by pointing out when the lights are on (and letting him turn them out), talking about the weather, pointing out where the sun is, and generally just making him aware. You are not ignoring his blindness by doing this, but helping him to use whatever light perception he has to his best advantage.

Question 13: **Does my child have light projection?**
Light projection is an ability to know where light is coming from. Whereas light *perception* refers only to an awareness of light, light *projection* means that the light can be *localized*.

Your eye specialist, however, may not be able to tell you whether your child has light projection or not. Particularly when your child is young, you are better qualified to answer this question because your child's ability to tell where light is coming from will be demonstrated in her daily life, and not necessarily performed on cue in the eye specialist's office.

Still, you want to be aware of your child's ability to localize light, and you want to encourage it whenever possible. It can be a great help to your child in terms of her mobility: For example, if you live in the city, walking along a city block and knowing when the buildings stop — because a new stream of light is now coming from the right — can you give a little extra warning and prepare you for the curb and street ahead.

Question 14: **Will glasses or contact lenses help?**

Many eye conditions are corrected by prescription eyeglasses or contact lenses, but many others cannot be corrected. Be sure to ask your eye specialist because improvements are being made daily.

Eye conditions that involve a field loss or brain damage are generally not helped by eyeglasses or contact lenses.

Question 15: **Will low vision aids help?**

Ask your eye specialist about low vision aids for your child, regardless of your child's age at the time of your appointment. (Before talking to the eye specialist, read about low vision aids in Chapter 7, "Looking Ahead.") The eye specialist will at least know that you are aware that low vision aids exist and that they might be useful to your child at a later time, even if they are not useful now.

Whether or not low vision aids are useful is related to your child's stage of learning. Depending on the eye condition, low vision aids can be very helpful to children who are learning academic skills (reading and writing readiness) and those who are becoming more independent in their mobility (walking to school or to a neighbor's house, for example). But be cautious of using low vision aids for their own sake: Bigger is still not always better, and the adjustment to the aid might slow your child down in either his learning or his mobility.

Some professionals are beginning to question the use of low vision aids with young visually handicapped children. They feel that the aids, particularly magnifiers, actually make reading more difficult for a child because they enlarge the size of the print too much and cause fatigue. This will probably be debated for many years, and you will need to make *your own* decisions about their usefulness, based on the needs of your child.

Reread these 15 questions for your eye specialist before you take your child to his next appointment. You can take your REACHBOOK with you, and use the questions as they are listed there.

Questions for your Eye Specialist

1. What caused my child's visual problem?
2. Is this eye condition hereditary?
3. Will my child's eye condition change?
4. Where is the problem located?
5. Do my child's pupils react to light?
6. What is my child's tracking like?
7. What is my child's central vision like?
8. What is my child's field of vision like?
9. What is my child's best viewing distance?
10. How does this eye condition affect my child's mobility?
11. Are my child's eyes sensitive to light?
12. Does my child have light perception?
13. Does my child have light projection?
14. Will glasses or contact lenses help?
15. Will low vision aids help?

Turn to page 58 in the REACHBOOK

Questions Your Eye Specialist Should Ask You

As the people who spend the most time with their child, parents can provide the eye specialist with valuable information about how the visually or multiply handicapped child is *using* her vision. There is a big difference between what your child is *physically capable* of seeing, based on the eye specialist's examination, and what she *does* see. The *physical* ability to see depends on the structure and general health of the eye. But *what* you actually see depends on how you *use* what you have, and this depends on your learning experiences and on how well you adapt to or compensate for your visual impairment.

The *use* of vision is as much a part of development as every other skill area discussed in *Reach Out and Teach*. And it will be subject to the same basic principle — the more chances your child has to use what vision she has, the more she will be able to do with it.

When talking with your eye specialist, however, you want to say more than, "I *think* she can see." If the eye specialist's physical examination of your child indicates to him that there is little chance for your child to be seeing very much, or if the eye specialist feels that your child is so brain damaged that vision is highly unlikely, he will not pay much attention to what you *think*. But, if you can give specific examples of how your child seems to be using her vision, the eye specialist will have to pay attention.

The eye specialist should be interested in your answers to the following questions:

Question 1: **Have you noticed your child holding his head in an unusual way?**
The way your child holds his head could mean that he is compensating for a loss in some part of his visual field. For example, if he tilts his head backward and seems to be looking through the lower part of his eyes, it could mean that he does not see very well in the upper part of his visual field. Or, if he holds his head to one side, it could mean either a side-vision or central-vision loss. Watch your child and try to figure out if he always holds his head in a certain position, or if he does so only in certain situations, such as in rooms with an overhead light or when he is outside. Keep a record of these times in your REACHBOOK and be prepared to tell your eye specialist about them. Be careful, however, that the head position you observe is not because your child is unable to balance his head, or because he has some other handicapping condition.

Question 2: **How does your child act when she is around bright lights or sunlight?**

Many times the first indication you have that your child has light perception is when you go outside and she closes her eyes tightly or squints. This at least tells you that she is aware of lights. And it might indicate that she has an eye condition that makes her particularly sensitive to light. Again, keep a record of the times when light appears to bother her and tell your eye specialist about it.

Question 3: **Does your child reach for toys and other objects?**

Reaching behaviors can tell you a great deal about *how far* your child can see, *where* he can see, and *how much detail* he can see. Observe your child for such behaviors as:

Reaching for objects only when they are on one side of his body, or only when they are directly in front of him. This could mean that he has difficulty seeing in certain parts of his visual field.

Reaching for objects that are close to his body.

Not noticing a favorite toy when it is out of his reach or more than a certain number of feet away.

Stopping as he walks through the kitchen, stooping down, and picking a raisin up off the floor.

Frequently reaching for an object and missing — either his aim is off, or he reaches beyond the object, or he does not quite reach far enough.

Only reaching for objects that he hears, touches, or smells first.

Question 4: **Does your child hold objects close to one or both of her eyes?**

Bringing books, toys, and other objects up close to the face is *good*. It tells you, first, that your child is not able to see things at a distance and, second, that she is motivated to use her vision and has learned what she has to do in order to see better. She may also move her own body close to objects, such as sitting very close to the television or pressing her nose against the hall mirror. Your child cannot hurt or strain her eyes by doing this, and you should try to encourage her to do it whenever necessary. If your child does this, however, try to determine if she uses both eyes or if she seems to prefer one eye over the other. If she seems to prefer one eye, it could mean that vision in the other eye is weak, or that she gets a double image when she uses both eyes because they do not focus together. Your eye specialist will want to know about this because he may be able to correct this condition if it is caught early enough.

You may have observed other actions by your child that make you think that she is using some of her vision, and you should share these observations with the eye specialist, too. Remember that you are there to learn as much as possible about your child's vision —

no question is too obvious or too silly or too time-consuming. Either you, the insurance company, or the government is paying for the eye specialist's time. You not only *deserve* to find out as much as possible, the eye specialist *owes* it to you.

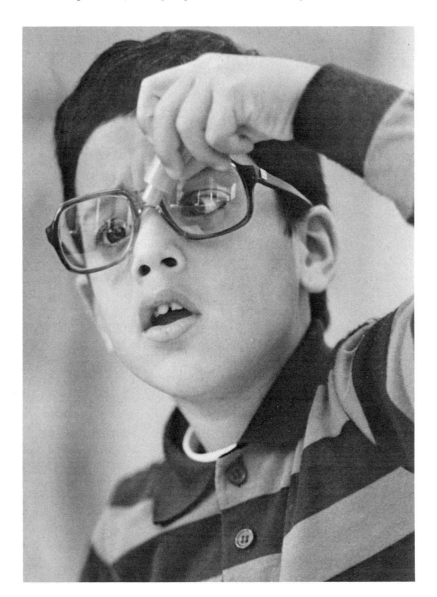

Turn to page 61 in the REACHBOOK

Your Child's Self-Concept

Everybody has a self-concept. How people think and feel about themselves affects everything they do and say. When you feel good about yourself, you can be proud of your successes; on the other hand, if you don't feel good about yourself, you might not even realize that you were successful. How you feel about yourself may make a difference in the way you:

Walk	Win or lose some games
Say hello	Work
Talk to strangers	Wear your hair
Eat	Act at a party, and even
Dress	Sleep

Your self-concept might even make the difference between:

Working and not working
Studying and not studying
Learning and not learning
Growing and not growing
Being independent, and always being dependent on someone else

Self-concept is a funny thing: As adults, it is tied in with everything that has ever happened to us, from early infancy. Some people have even suggested that your self-concept begins to form before you are born — as you hear your mother talk about her pregnancy and how she feels. While self-concept before birth is a bit difficult to understand, it is easier to see how your own feelings about yourself developed in infancy — as your parents cuddled you and responded to your crying; as you learned to move about your world; and as you discovered what you could do for yourself. Your self-concept, your idea of who you are and who you want to be, is the sum total of your hopes, dreams, limitations, doubts, failures, successes, should-haves, should-have-nots, concerns, and ideals. Sometimes, you feel better about yourself than at other times, but usually, almost always, you know *who* you are.

It may surprise you to learn that developing a good self-concept is not always easy for visually and multiply handicapped persons to do. But if you become dependent on other people for certain parts of your everyday life, it is difficult to take pride in what you can do on your own. Another reason why developing a positive self-concept is hard for visually handicapped persons is because, quite simply, they cannot see very well. This does not mean that they can't have a good self-concept, but it does mean that they may need a little extra help to get there.

Giving a "little extra help" is nothing new to you at this point. You are probably becoming accustomed to the role of "translator" — looking for events and things that might slip past your child if you did not take the time to point them out or explain them. Self-concept, however, seems different. But it isn't really; like all the other areas discussed in *Reach Out and Teach*, self-concept develops gradually, and in a specific order. Two first steps in developing a good self-concept are found in the "Thinking it Through" chapter of these materials. They are body awareness (knowing the body) and self-awareness (knowing that you are an individual). "Thinking it Through" will give you specific suggestions for working on these first steps with your child. But keep in mind that you are really helping your child to develop a personality.

Turn to page 63 in the REACHBOOK

Shaping Your Child's Personality

Body-awareness and self-awareness are just the beginning. The entire home atmosphere is important for your child's self-concept because it leads to his becoming his own little person, with his own quirks, likes and dislikes, limitations, and talents.

Many of the things you say and do as your visually or multiply handicapped child is growing up will have a direct influence on his personality. You may remember events from your childhood which made an impression on you and helped make you the person you are today. If your mother was always away from home working, you may have decided that you would only work in a job that would allow you to spend time with your family; if your father was always after you to "clean your plate — there are children in China who are starving," you may have decided that you would never say that to your children; if a neighbor always made you feel welcome, you may have decided that you would always try to do the same for the kids in your neighborhood; if your brother was the kind of person who always made the best of a situation and who didn't let bad luck get him down, you may have decided that you, too, could be that way.

There are many ways that you can help your child grow and develop in a healthy way, ways that will make the most of his good points and minimize what he cannot do because of his visual impairment. A clergyman who has worked with blind adults put it this way:

> This means that you, even more than the rest of us, need to come to a mature understanding of yourself — because your adjustment to life and to the blindness of your child is so important to *his* adjustment. More than any other person, you are involved in the total growth and the future of the child; if you fail to become sufficiently involved, he will lose the support he needs in growing; if you become too involved, you will choke his growth and stunt it. . . .

> Don't be discouraged. Your child can grow to live a life of total adjustment to his total environment, loving God and his fellow men (both blind and sighted). His chances for doing this will be greatly enhanced if you, his parents, are both able to give to him a deep, mature, nonpossessive love — a love for him *as he is,* while making every attempt to aid him to grow to something stronger and completely independent, save for his dependence on God.
>
> —Thomas J. Carroll (1961)

Turn to page 64 in the REACHBOOK

Remember, though, that you are people, too, with *your own* quirks, likes and dislikes, limitations, and talents. No parent can be perfect, and no parent can do the "right" thing all the time. There are things that your parents did that you promised yourself you would never do when you had a family. And, while you may have succeeded in doing some things differently than your parents did, you can be fairly sure that your children are promising themselves that *they* will not do some things that you do now. It's an endless cycle: All parents try to do their best, but there is always another way.

Take heart from Father Carroll's words: Don't be discouraged. And as your visually or multiply handicapped child grows, keep these thoughts in your mind:

Give your child choices, from a simple choice of juice or milk, to the more complicated choices of which clothes to wear, which book to read, and even which therapy (arm exercises or leg exercises) to do first.

Tell your child when he does something good.

Tell your child when he does something wrong, but do so in a way that lets him know that you still love him. Some people have suggested that before you correct your child for a mistake, you should start off by commenting on something good, such as:

> "This picture you drew is really lovely. Next time, though, please try to keep all your crayon marks on the paper. You can help me clean the table."

Other professionals suggest that when you yell and scream at your children, you should be sure to focus on what they *did* instead of on them. Notice the difference between these two ways of saying the same thing:

> "Just who do you think you are, Johnny? You can't talk to me like that! You're nothing but a rude, smart-mouthed brat!"

> "That is no way to talk to me or any other adult, Johnny. It makes me angry. It's rude, impolite, and sounds like you don't like me very much."

Both of those comments accomplish the same thing; they discipline Johnny, show him who is the boss, and even make him feel guilty. But the first example attacks Johnny as a person, while the second example acknowledges your feelings and tells Johnny what he did was wrong.

While discipline is important, particularly in a situation like the one above, it is also important to recognize that your child has feelings, too. In the example above, obviously something made Johnny upset. What you may want to do is talk to Johnny about his feelings and *why* he said what he said, and then give him another way of expressing himself:

> "Okay, Johnny, I understand that you really wanted to go outside and play in the sandbox. But you still cannot talk to an adult that way. If you're that angry, go to your room and cry, or go tell your mother about it, or ask me why I said no. Maybe we can talk it out."

Try not to think that every one of your child's achievements, no matter how big it seems to you, is so remarkable. What you are really saying is that your child is so visually impaired or so multiply handicapped that you never thought he would be able to do the things that other children do all the time. This message — that your expectations for your child are lower — will be communicated to your child if you continue to be amazed, and may affect this own expectations and even his motivation.

Sure, this is difficult. If you are not handicapped yourself, it is natural that you would try to imagine how you would learn some skills without using your vision or when your brain damage makes even the slightest movement hurt. But you must try to put aside those feelings and focus on what your child can do given his particular handicap and his desire to learn.

Separate out those limitations caused by his visual or multiple handicap from those limitations caused by his particular personality. It is all too easy to blame everything on your child's blindness: he can't lift his head because he doesn't see anything; he has to eat with his fingers because he can't see what is on the spoon; he doesn't sleep at night because he doesn't know the difference between night and day; he couldn't see that little girl, so she has no reason to get mad at him for stepping on her. All of these are excuses. Your child *can* learn to do all of these things — lifting his head, eating with utensils, sleeping at night, and minding his own body to show consideration for others. *Why* he has not learned them has more to do with *your* expectations for how he behaves.

Do not sell your child short. There are very competent blind, visually impaired, and paraplegic wheel-chair bound adults who have learned how to behave in public and how to think of others. They have not used their handicaps as an excuse. If you do, you are setting up your child for a future where he can always find the easy way out.

Your child does not need special consideration in every area of his life. Decide which areas are really affected by his visual or multiple impairment, such as:

Walking to school	Using ditto sheets
Reading	Playing soccer
Knowing what a bird is	Making friends

and devise ways to help him over the hurdles. But at the same time, give him the same duties and responsibilities that every child has sometime during the growing years, such as:

Setting the table	Delivering newspapers
Doing dishes	Taking out the trash
Making his own bed	Watering the plants
Brushing his teeth	Taking a bath
Feeding the dog	

Even children who have no control over their bladders can learn to catheterize themselves and thus take care of their toileting needs. A child is expected at some point to take responsibility within the family whether it be going to the bathroom by himself or sweeping the floor. The handicap only makes a difference in *how* those responsibilities are carried out.

When you were in school, was there ever a time when your class was allowed to take a test with books open. What do you think your reaction would have been had you found out later that your class was the only one allowed to use open books? At first you might feel lucky, as if you had gotten away with something. But, thinking about it, maybe the teacher was unintentionally saying that *your* class was not as smart as the others and needed some extra help. How would that make you feel?

Continue to use words like "see," "look," "blind," and so forth in your everyday conversation. These words are commonly used by almost everyone, and your child will hear them eventually, anyway. Besides, if you make a big deal out of it (by whispering those words, or saying "Oops, excuse me" when you use them), your child will wonder what is going on. He will soon learn that there is something special about those words.

Remember, if your child was born blind or visually handicapped, he doesn't know what good vision is. He will not realize that he is any different from anyone else unless he is made to feel that way. And, while you can be fairly certain that he will learn about his differentness when he attends school with other children, the attitudes and self-confidence he gains at home during the infant and preschool years can make that time when he becomes aware less traumatic.

It is normal to have mixed feelings about your children — *all* your children, blind or not, handicapped or not. Every parent does. But if you feel guilty about them and show it, the message to your child is: "You're different. I can't treat you the way I treat other kids."

Your child needs time to himself, sometimes alone and sometimes with other children and adults. It helps him to become self-reliant and independent.

Turn to page 65 in the REACHBOOK

Fear vs. Freedom

Remember the first night you stayed out until midnight and your parents were waiting up for you when you got home? You may have felt that they didn't trust you, or that they still thought of you as a little kid. Whether or not your parents showed it, they were honestly worried about you. Of course, they probably never told *you* that — they just yelled and told you never to do it again, at least not without calling home first.

The balance between fear and freedom is just as difficult for parents of preschool children to achieve. When your child is visually or multiply handicapped, it can be even more of a struggle. Like the parent who follows his child to the local store to make sure he gets there without getting lost, you as the parent of a handicapped child have to learn to give your child her independence without going crazy yourself.

If you think it's hard on you, your child's struggle between dependence and self-sufficiency is just as difficult for her. You are both learning, on a trial and error basis, what she is capable of, and when. It takes patience, energy, understanding, and love, but you *both* can reach that balance point if you are both willing to take the risk.

Dealing With Your Child's Behavior

Children are little people and, because they are, there will be times when they are annoying, exasperating, frustrating, or just plain naughty. Your visually or multiply handicapped child will not be any different. She will test you frequently to see how far she can go or how much she can get away with. Your response to these situations will determine who is in control in your household.

Throughout *Reach Out and Teach* you will find suggestions for developing your child's behavior and attitude in a positive way. There may come a time, however, when nothing seems to work. You have tried being reasonable; you have tried talking it out with your child; you have taken away one of her privileges; you may even have punished her in some other way. But now you don't know what to do.

Guidelines

In this situation, just like in any teaching situation, you need to remember three guidelines:

1. Don't Let Frustration Get the Best of You

Stop, step back, relax, and take a deep breath. Think about what is happening, and remember that your child is getting just as frustrated as you are. Once you have calmed down a bit, go back and try again.

2. Remember Who is in Charge

You are the adult. And *you* are in control of the situation and can make the changes that will result in your child's changing her behavior.

3. Be Consistent

If you expect your child to eat all her dinner one night and the next night tell her she doesn't have to because she is taking too long to eat, she will not only be confused, she will learn that she can work around you.

Cause-Action-Consequence

One way you can follow all three guidelines is to analyze the situation. Professionals who specialize in behavior management analyze behaviors according to a "cause-action-consequence" model. Under this model, every behavior is caused by some other behavior, either something the child does herself, or something done by someone near the child. And every behavior or action the child does has a consequence, or results in some other behavior.

As an example of "cause-action-consequence," look at something as simple as a baby's reaching for her bottle. The *cause* in this situation would be the adult's holding up the bottle so that the baby can see it. The *action* is the baby's reaching for and getting hold of the bottle. The *consequence* is the baby's drinking from the bottle and satisfying her hunger. In this case, everything went well: The baby *learned* that she could do something — reach for her bottle — that would make her happy. But at any point in this event, a breakdown could have occurred.

If, for example, the adult had not shown the baby the bottle, but had just put it in her hands, the baby's *action* would only be holding and drinking from the bottle. The *consequence* would have been the same, but the baby would not have been required to reach, and she would not have *learned* that her actions could produce such a happy result.

If, for example, the baby had not reached for the bottle, or if she had reached but not been successful, the *consequence* would have been frustration and crying.

Then again, if the baby's crying resulted in the adult's giving the bottle to the baby, the *cause* would have been the crying; the *action* would have been the adult's giving the bottle; and the *consequence* would have been the satisfaction of not being hungry. But what the baby *learned* is now quite different — *crying* brought about the satisfaction, *not her reaching*. Next time, the baby will not even try to reach; all she really has to do is cry.

Changing Behavior

This same model, or method of analysis, can be used to *change* your child's behavior. If there is something he does that you want to change, use your REACHBOOK to keep track of when he does it, and what happens after he does it. After you have kept notes for a day or a week, look at your notes and see if you can pick out a pattern. You may be able to eliminate whatever is *causing* the behavior you don't like, or you might be able to change the *consequence* so that your child does not want to do what he was doing. The REACHBOOK will help you look at this in more detail and make decisions about what behaviors you want to change and why.

Turn to page 67 in the REACHBOOK

Why It Seems Harder When Your Child is Handicapped

If you have children older than your visually or multiply handicapped child, you may have thought to yourself, "Of course I should discipline my son. He can't get away with that kind of behavior!" But often, with a handicapped child, such an attitude is easier said than done.

The reasons why it seems harder have as much to do with you as they do with your child. Many people fear blindness; if they had a choice, blindness would be the last condition they would want for themselves. Most people experience life through their eyes — when they remember a sunset, a favorite grandparent, or a television show. To be without those eyes, that vision, seems impossible. If you have ever felt this way, then your child's visual impairment might seem devastating to you because it represents your own worst fears.

And then, of course, your mind wanders to the subject of whether or not you had anything to do with your child's blindness. Maybe you feared it too much....Maybe you are being punished for something you did that you knew was wrong....Maybe you are being tested. In some cases, you may feel sure that you were the direct cause of your child's handicapping condition, perhaps because your father also had it, or because you had a virus before the baby was born, or because you were too old to have children in the first place.

But your own feelings and attitudes are only part of the problem. With time, patience, and understanding, you can change your ideas about blind people, and you can stop blaming yourself for everything that happens to your child. Sometimes the hardest part, however, is dealing with other people.

Grandparents

Grandparents can be difficult. Grandchildren are a source of pride, something to brag about. If the grandchild is handicapped, however, grandparents are likely to have mixed reactions. Try not to judge your parents and in-laws too harshly: Remember that they are older than you are, and their attitudes about handicapped people were formed in the days when handicapped people were neither seen nor heard. While blind children have attended public school for years, other handicapped children were not seen routinely in public schools until 1978, when the Education for All Handicapped Children Act went into effect. If you think *you* had little exposure to handicapped people when you were growing up, you can be sure that your parents had even less. And if they *were* exposed, chances are that their views of handicapped persons were not very positive. Your visually or multiply handicapped child can have more of an effect on your parents than he does on you.

Grandparents have been known to react in several ways:

If your child's grandparents:
1. Avoid visiting your home, or avoid asking about the handicapped grandchild in letters or on long-distance telephone calls,

Then you should:
Be sure that you always mention the child.

Ask them to baby- or child-sit for you.

Try to get them to talk to you about their feelings so that you can have a better understanding of them.

Give them this book to read.

If your child's grandparents:
2. Tell you you're too hard on their poor little grandchild, or that you expect too much,

Then you should:
Reply that no one really knows what visually and multiply handicapped children can or cannot do.

Say that you want to be sure that your child has every possible opportunity to learn.

Remind them that they were sometimes hard on you, but that it helped you to learn.

Explain that you don't want your child growing up feeling any different from the other kids.

Give them this book to read.

If your child's grandparents:
3. Offer to take their grandchild for a weekend so you and your partner can have some time together,

Then you should:
Thank them!

If your child's grandparents:
4. Talk about the "poor child" and generally seem sad when around their grandchild,

Then you should:
Ask them to try to be more positive and happy because you're afraid your child will pick up the sound of their voices and think that he *should* be pitied.

Give them this book to read.

If your child's grandparents:
5. Continue to talk baby talk with him long past the time when he is a baby,

Then you should:
Explain that one of the ways visually handicapped children learn is through language, and that it's important for him to hear the kind of language he is expected to use himself.

Remind them that he is not a baby anymore.

Give them this book to read.

If your child's grandparents:
6. Offer to take him to therapy so that you can take that class you've always wanted to take,

Then you should:
Thank them!

Offer to return the favor sometime.

Tell them that if something comes up and they can't take him to therapy, you could skip class for a day.

If your child's grandparents:
7. Buy him baby toys (rattles, squeeze toys, etc.) even when he's 5 years old,

Then you should:
Tell them that being handicapped doesn't automatically mean that he isn't capable of doing some things on his age level.

Explain that handicapped or not, your child still has feelings, and he might think that his grandparents still see him as a baby.

Let them know it hurts *you* that they think he hasn't made any progress.

Give them this book to read.

If your child's grandparents:
8. Tell you that your child should be doing more at his age than he is doing now,

Then you should:
Tell them you have been working on it with his teachers, but that it is a little different for children who have visual impairments.

Tell them that every child grows and develops at his own pace, just as you did.

Point out the areas where your child is way ahead of the other kids, such as language.

Explain that hospitalizations and illnesses can make a child go two steps backward before he can get moving forward again.

Say that you've been working really hard on his walking right now, and that the other areas will catch up.

Ask them if they have any suggestions that might help.

Give them this book to read.

Friends and Neighbors

Neighbors and friends also pose problems. They may avoid talking about your child's eye condition or his obvious motor problem, or they may talk too much about it. In the first case, they might actually be waiting for you to talk about it first, thinking that perhaps you are not ready to talk about it. If they talk about the handicap too much, you may feel that they are trying to be too casual about a very serious matter. It is no easier for them than it is for you. Everyone is second-guessing everyone else, trying to do the right thing. It is important to remember that these people are your friends, they care about you, and they may turn out to be your best baby-sitters!

Strangers

But face it — the hardest part is not people you know, but the people you don't. The people who "tsk-tsk" over your child when they see him in the grocery cart; those who shake their head when your obviously handicapped child cries at the checkout counter for the chocolate bar that you've already told him he can't have; the ones who come up to you on the street and tell you that you don't belong, that you are lowering the property values. Almost every family has horror stories like these to tell, even families without handicapped children. In the early 1970s, when baby backpacks and slings were just becoming popular, a little white-haired lady approached one mom and told her that her daughter's neck would break if the mom continued to carry her baby around on her back. Dealing with strangers who think they know what is best for you and your family is not easy; you will probably have to ignore them, just like you will later tell your child to ignore people who call him names. It's part of life.

But the self-consciousness, the feeling that people are always looking at you, is not part of life. Somehow you can never quite get used to the feeling that you are being stared at, or that the folks whispering over there in the corner are really talking about you or your child. People who are overweight report some of the same feelings, and so do politicians and even actors. But just because *you* think you stand out does not mean that you do. With one exception: Have you ever seen a child screaming his head off while his parent is holding his hand, yanking him along the street? *That* is noticeable. And there will be times when that will happen between you and your handicapped child, and every passerby will think you're horrible and you yourself will feel terribly guilty.

But just remember: You're not the first person to be in that situation — and you won't be the last.

Turn to page 74 in the REACHBOOK

Family Interactions

So far, this chapter has concentrated pretty much on you and your handicapped child. But if you have a spouse (or partner) and other children, their concerns and ideas are important, too.

Attention

Attention is one of the biggest problems in families, particularly in today's hurried world, where one or both parents may be working and where television, church, and school activities require varying amounts of time from each member of the family. When a handicapped child comes into the family, this seems to complicate matters even further, especially in the beginning, with visits to doctors, hospitalizations, infant stimulation programs, and physical and occupational therapy.

If this was all that was involved, it might be manageable. But in real life, each one of these leads to a long list of other errands and responsibilities so that you seldom "just" go to the doctor's office (you have to stop at the bank to get money, and then later at the drug store to pick up a prescription), or "just" attend the infant program (you have to meet with the other parents while you're there for "therapy" and then you have to meet about next month's fund-raising activity). With all this going on — with all these demands on your time — someone is bound to feel left out.

Both adults and children will react to feeling left out in similar ways: Some will withdraw and appear depressed. Others may act out and get into fights or arguments. A child's school grades might fall; an adult might throw herself into work and spend long hours working overtime; a younger child might appear delayed in language or some other area of development. A couple's sex life might change. As hard as it is, you must try to schedule time for everyone. Here are some suggestions:

Plan to do some activities together — eating breakfast or dinner, housecleaning, or shopping, even if you know it will take longer.

Assign brothers and sisters a special responsibility with your handicapped child — reading a story to him, perhaps. It's nice to feel helpful and needed. But guard against giving your nonhandicapped children too much responsibility for the handicapped child, or they will learn to resent him.

Plan a special time of the day with the other children — reading books or doing homework, for example. One parent always planned a snack time after school for all her children to talk about the day's events at school and plan that night's homework.

Have a "quiet time" with your partner. It might only be 10 to 20 minutes, but make sure the kids know that is your time together and that the two of you are not to be disturbed unless it's an emergency. (Unless the kids are in bed, you can't do this until someone, a child or another adult, can take responsibility for the kids.)

Turn to page 76 in the REACHBOOK

Jealousy

Jealousy is another emotion seen frequently in families and sometimes more so in families with a handicapped child. Where there is a visually handicapped child, a lot of time is consumed by verbal explanation and physical help so that he can experience what other kids can see and experience with no special effort. There is no easy way to deal with jealousy, but understanding why it's occurring can help defuse potential confrontations.

Stress

You probably know by now that stress is also a frequent problem in families with handicapped children. There can be many sources of stress: anxiety about your child's medical condition; worries about paying medical bills; lack of time; arguments with your partner; or sources totally unrelated to your child's handicap — losing your job, seriously-ill family members, a leaky roof, no heat.

Again, there are no recipes for dealing with this family problem, either. If you at least recognize stress, you may be able to step back and take a few minutes daily to do something about it. If you find yourself getting snowed under and you don't think you can cope, *ask for help*. The medical and educational professionals who work with you family can probably refer you to a psychologist or other therapist. If you don't want your child's doctor or teacher to know

Signs of Stress

Tiredness or fatigue
Lack of interest
Boredom
No desire to go out
(shopping, movies, restaurants, etc.)
Never inviting friends over
Lack of sexual intimacy

that you're not doing too well, you can look in the yellow pages of your telephone book under "Mental Health," or check the listings for your local and county governments. Almost every town or county has some type of free or sliding-scale (the smaller your income, the less you pay) mental health and counseling service for its citizens. In any case, find someone to talk to, even if it's a neighbor or relative.

Embarrassment

At some point in the life of your family, someone is likely to be embarrassed by your child's blindness or other handicap. Your other children may refuse to play with him, or resent your interference if you try to force the handicapped child on your children's nonhandicapped friends. They may stop inviting their own friends over after school. This is normal. Pressures are very high on school children to conform, to be one of the gang, to be just like anyone else. A handicapped brother or sister makes you stand out a little bit in the crowd. Other suggestions in this chapter of *Reach Out and Teach* will help you help your other children. Luckily, the example you set — by attitude and action — will be the controlling factor in the long run. The embarrassment phase will eventually fade away.

Respite Care

When you need a lengthy period of time off, no matter what the reason, check with mental health/mental retardation agencies about a program called respite care. This is a service for families in which a trained and qualified adult comes to your home to care for your visually or multiply handicapped child while you are away for a weekend (or a week), or arrangements are made for your child to live in a residential facility for longer periods (usually up to a month). It is not a permanent arrangement, but it can give you that needed break.

Those same agencies might have a list of experienced baby- and child-sitters, too. If your child has severe complicated medical problems, you might want to check with a program called "Home-makers." Physical therapy and nursing schools frequently keep a list of students who need part-time work, and if a college or university is nearby, the department of special education may do the same thing. (If you hire a special education student, you will be contributing more to their education and to the making of a future teacher than money. It will probably be one of the best training experiences they will have.)

Turn to page 79 in the REACHBOOK

Your Rights As Parents

Many professionals talk about parents going through something called "the grieving process" when they learn of their child's handicap. According to this theory, parents first go through a stage of shock. This is followed by a sense of sorrow or grief, where parents are thought to mourn for the loss of the "perfect" child that most parents hope for and expect. Then comes denial, where parents deny that their child is really handicapped, or perhaps seek out other doctors to get second, third, and fourth opinions. Anger and resentment come next, and then, finally, comes acceptance.

These stages — shock, grief, denial, anger, and acceptance — are often used by the professionals who interact with you and your family to describe your feelings and sometimes your actions. The grieving process is only a theory, but it is widely believed, perhaps because it helps the *professionals* deal with your feelings. (It is easier to see similarities among people than it is, sometimes, to see the individuals.) You may, in fact, have all these feelings. But you also have certain rights:

1. The right to feel angry

Nothing in life prepares anyone for being handicapped, and when it is your child who is handicapped, it seems all the more unfair. You did not ask for this, and there is very little you can do to change it. Your sense of control over your own life and the life of your child is at risk. Be angry, but use your anger to get the best services you can for your child.

2. The right to seek another opinion

Everyone is told today that it makes good sense to seek a second opinion before having surgery, or before investing money, or before buying a used car. It should not be any different for you and your handicapped child, whether you are looking for medical care or an educational program. If you hear of a new treatment that might help you child, why shouldn't you look into it? Times change, and so do people; 25 years ago, parents of children with Down Syndrome (a condition that may involve a range of physical

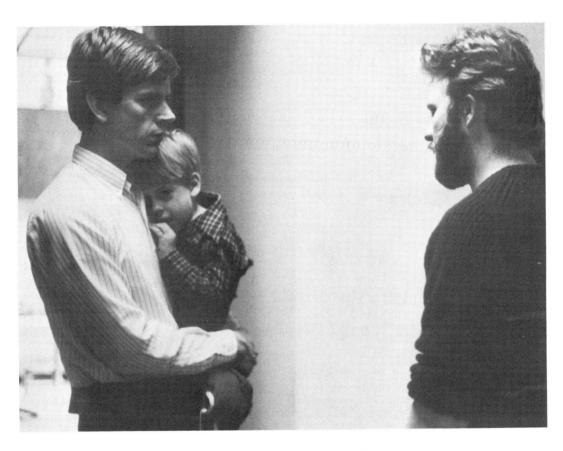

and/or mental problems) were advised to place their children in institutions. Today, studies have shown that the average intelligence of many children with Down Syndrome, when tested after pre-school training, is in the normal range.

3. The right to privacy

Many parents have talked about the effects a handicapped child in the family has on family members' privacy, not because the handicapped child does something, but because a handicapped child suddenly brings into the family circle a series of professionals who examine, give advice, and sometimes even judge the actions of individual family members. One parent said that the hardest part for her was "having to turn to experts — it was difficult to have to have someone tell me what to do with my child." Some aspects of your life are simply no one else's business. If you do not want to discuss something, or if you do not want your child's picture taken, it is your right to say "*No.*"

4. The right to keep trying

Parenting is not easy, but all parents try to do the best job they can. It sometimes becomes harder when well-meaning friends and professionals tell you that you have set goals that your child will never be able to reach, or that you must stand back and accept the fact your daughter is multiply handicapped and will never be able to walk. There is nothing wrong with you if you are not willing to give up. Your child has the greatest potential for learning now, in the preschool years, and no one knows what event or combination of events will make a difference for her. If the others turn out to be right — so what? You will have given your child the best chance she could have.

5. The right to stop trying

Well-meaning friends and professionals have also told parents that they do not work often enough or long enough with their handicapped children. "If you would just do this at home for 15 minutes a day on the weekends, it would make *such* a difference." The truth is that it could just as easily make no difference at all. *You* are the one who lives with your child; *you* are the one who is being asked to do one *more* thing; *you* are the one who is somehow expected to accomplish at home what trained teachers have not been able to do at school. If you just cannot do it tonight — okay. That is your decision.

6. The right to set limits

There are limits to what one person can do; you shouldn't expect yourself to think about your child all the time. And your child shouldn't expect to be the center of attention. You have limits, and your child has limits; learn to recognize both, and give yourself a chance to examine the situation before responding in anger or fatigue. You are not SUPER-PARENT.

7. The right to be a parent

Teachers who work with young handicapped children and their families are fond of giving parents activities to do at home. Even

Reach Out and Teach gives suggestions for home activities and talks about parenting as teaching. But you are mommy and daddy first. You cannot expect to be a teacher all the time, and even your child's teacher cannot teach all the time. (If you ask her teacher, he will probably admit that he is great at teaching other people's kids, but he can't do a thing with his own.) You and your child need time to fool around, giggle, tickle, tell stories, laugh, and just do nothing. Those times are just as much a part of your child's "education" as the time you spend following the activities in this or any other book.

8. The right to be unenthusiastic
No one expects you to be "turned on" all the time. Sometimes you feel sad, or you're worried about money, or your child, or you feel sick. If other people take that as a sign that you're "not adjusting" or that you're "not accepting your child's handicap," that is their problem. No one is excited about work every day; it can be tedious one day and new and interesting the next. The same is true of parenting: There will be days when your child thrills you with joy and days when parenting will seem like the most boring job on earth. You have a right to be "up" sometimes and "down" others.

9. The right to be annoyed with your child
There are days when you like your child and days when you don't, but that does not mean that you don't *love* her. Visually handicapped children are just as capable of being ornery as other children, and they should be disciplined. You may feel extremely guilty about doing it, but your preschooler will greet you the next morning as though nothing had ever happened.

10. The right to time off

You need time to yourself, time with your spouse or partner and other adult family members, and just plain time without kids.

Many parents describe the first time they went to the grocery store alone after their child was born as a tremendous feeling of freedom, even though they were doing a chore, and even though they didn't talk to anyone but the checkout clerk. There are many parts to your life, and each deserves as much attention and nurturing as does your visually or multiply handicapped child.

11. The right to be the expert-in-charge

You know your child better than anyone else: You spend the most time with her, you have lived with her longer than anyone else, you know what works and what doesn't. Teachers come and go, but *you* are the expert with the experience and first-hand knowledge about your child. And, as the expert, you have the right to be in charge of your child's educational, social, and medical decisions — at least until she is able to make them herself. Professionals do not live with the consequences of their decisions, so while you might want their opinions, remember that they are *only* opinions and not facts. They cannot tell you you're wrong, that you will regret it, that you're selfish, or that you're not looking far enough ahead. Nor can they make you feel guilty or pressure you into a decision. Parents are the single most important resource that children have.

12. The right to dignity

These rights of parents really boil down to the right to be respected and treated as an equal. You expect to be neither pitied nor admired, but you *do* expect to be listened to and supported in a nonjudgmental way. You expect to be treated as though your child were not handicapped. *And* you expect the truth — from the doctors, teachers, social workers, and therapists, who are there to help you; from your friends and neighbors, who owe you a chance to be someone other than "parent-of-a-handicapped-child"; and from your family members, who love you. You *deserve* to know why the doctor is looking into your child's ear; if she doesn't volunteer the reason, *ask* her. You *deserve* the courtesy of having professionals who visit you at your home arrive promptly for appointments. If a teacher is repeatedly late and does not have a satisfactory excuse, call the program supervisor and *ask* why. You *deserve* to be talked to as an adult; if you feel a teacher or therapist is talking down to you, *tell* him so. Sometimes, when you are the parent of a handicapped child, you have to risk being aggressive and, sometimes, even rude in order to obtain the dignity that is your right and your due.

None of these 12 rights apply *just* to parents of handicapped children; *all* parents share certain common experiences, whether they have one child or 10, and whether one child or all 10 children are handicapped. You cannot forget that you are an adult with your own needs, desires, hopes, and dreams. Enjoy your individuality — and enjoy your child.

Your Rights as Parents

1. The right to feel angry
2. The right to seek another opinion
3. The right to privacy
4. The right to keep trying
5. The right to stop trying
6. The right to set limits
7. The right to be a parent
8. The right to be unenthusiastic
9. The right to be annoyed with your child
10. The right to time off
11. The right to be the expert-in-charge
12. The right to dignity

What Every Child Needs for Good Mental Health

Love

Every child needs to feel:
that his parents love, want, and enjoy him;
that he matters very much to someone;
that there are people near him who care what happens to him.

Acceptance

Every child needs to believe:
that her parents like her for herself, just the way she is;
that they like her all the time, and not only when she acts according to their ideas of the way a child should act.

Security

Every child needs to know:
that his home is a good safe place he can feel sure about;
that his parents will always be on hand, especially in times of crisis when he needs them most;
that he belongs to a family or group;
that there is a place where he fits.

Protection

Every child needs to feel:
that her parents will keep her safe from harm;
that they will help her when she must face strange, unknown, and frightening situations.

Independence

Every child needs to know:
that his parents want him to grow up; and
that they encourage him to try new things.

Faith

Every child needs to have:
a set of moral standards to live by;
a belief in human values — kindness, courage, honesty, generosity, and justice.

Guidance

Every child needs to have:
friendly help in learning how to behave toward persons and things;
grown-ups around her who show her by example how to get along with others.

Control

Every child needs to know:
that there are limits to what he is permitted to do; and that his parents will hold him to these limits;
that though it is all right to feel jealous or angry, he will not be allowed to hurt himself or others when he has these feelings.

Children whose basic needs are satisfied have a better chance to grow up in good mental health and to become mentally healthy adults — people who are good parents, good mates, good workers, good neighbors, and good citizens.

Notes on Additional Reading

Of all the books for parents of blind children, *Can't Your Child See?*, by Scott, Jan, and Freeman, gives the greatest consideration to parents as persons, and to the child as a participating member of a functioning group of relatives and friends. Three chapters are particularly relevant to some of the problems discussed in "Talking it Over." Chapter 1 deals with the first diagnosis of visual impairment and all that follows from it; Chapter 2 is a brief discussion of eye conditions; and Chapter 5, "Living with a Visually Handicapped Child," is just that. If your child has additional handicaps, Chapter 6 would also be helpful.

Raising the Young Blind Child: A Guide for Parents and Educators, by Kastein, Spaulding, and Scharf, deals with the child rather than the parent. Chapter 4 and parts of Chapter 10 are about social and emotional development. Chapter 17 deals with the child's awareness of blindness.

Lowenfeld's *Our Blind Children* deals with the parent-child relationship in Chapters 1, 3, and 4. Chapter 2 gives some facts about blindness. There is a section on emotional growth in Chapter 5, and Chapter 6 addresses the attitudes of parents.

In *Handling the Young Cerebral Palsied Child at Home*, by Finnie, Chapter 2 deals with parents' problems, and in *Understanding the Deaf-Blind Child*, by Freeman, Chapter 10 discusses emotional development of the child.

From a different point of view, *Take Charge! A Guide to Resources for Parents of the Visually Impaired*, by Nousanen and Robinson, may be helpful to you in getting organized and finding information or services you may need.

National Parent Conference on Education of Children Requiring Extensive Special Education Programming proceedings (edited by Machalow) combine both approaches with regard to severely and/or multiply handicapped children. Part II and Part III (pages 61-65) deal with social and emotional factors in the context of interaction with service providers and support systems, and aim at helping the parent secure the best possible outcome for the child. *Selecting a Preschool: A Guide for Parents of Handicapped Children*, by Wintern, Turnbull, and Blacker, within the scope defined by its title, also combines information on services with a discussion of the social and emotional needs of both parents and children, and how these can be met most effectively.

The magazine *Exceptional Parent* has articles that deal with both the emotional and the practical aspects of dealing with disability, although usually not from the specific point of view of visual impairment.

If you have, or plan to have, other children, you may be interested in the *Newsletter* of the Sibling Information Network, which is concerned with the well-being of the brothers and sisters of handicapped children.

Finally, some very personal reports: *Elizabeth*, by Sharon Ulrich, is the story of the first five years of a blind child written by her mother. Conversely, "Growing Up Virtually Blind: A Self-Report," by E. Crowley, is an article by a woman blind from birth. And *Before and After Zachariah*, by E. Kupfer, is again written by a mother, in this case of a very severely handicapped child who could not be retained at home.

Refer to the Bibliography at the end of this HANDBOOK for additional information on any or all of these publications.

Chapter 3

TAKING OFF:

Motor Development

TAKING OFF:
Motor Development

Walking, running, bending, sitting, writing—many of us do these things everyday without thinking twice about *how* we do them, or how we *learned* to do them. You know you were not born doing all these things; but if you ask your parents, they will probably say that you just started to do them—that you just "learned them naturally."

Well, for a visually or multiply handicapped child, it is not always that easy. A lot of movements that we take for granted were learned because we could watch others doing them and then watch ourselves doing the same things. When you have good vision, it is easy to *imitate* what other people are doing. What's more, with good vision you can *practice* new movements and have an idea of how well you're doing or where you need to make changes. This is called *feedback*. Imitation, practice, and feedback are three very important steps in learning, and with good vision, they happen almost without thinking. If your vision is impaired, however, you need a little help.

LEARNING STEPS

FEEDBACK

PRACTICE

IMITATION

How to Help Your Visually or Multiply Handicapped Child Move

There is very little a visually handicapped child cannot learn, if she is given a chance. If your child has a motor impairment, there may be some very real limits to what she can do. But the important thing is to try.

How can you help your child learn to move? You can:
1. **Assess:** Find out what she does already and what she needs to learn next;
2. **Plan:** Find out what it feels like to do it yourself;
3. **Teach:** Show your child how she can do it herself; and
4. **Reassess:** Find out how well she has learned and where she needs to go next.

Because a visually handicapped child has trouble imitating movements she cannot see, it helps to put her through the movements so she gets the idea of how it feels to move the muscles and body parts in various ways. If you were learning to swim, you would not be able to see what other people were doing under water. You *could* just jump into the water and try to do what everyone else was doing, but it might be easier if someone who knew how to swim showed you first how to position your arms and then actually moved your arms through a few strokes to help you get the idea.

This is just what you can do with your visually handicapped child, only you may need to do it more often and for more movements. Sometimes, it helps to try it yourself before you put your child through the movements because that gives *you* a better idea of what you're asking *her* to do. Getting down on the floor and crawling like a baby may make you feel silly, but it sure makes you appreciate how much effort it takes to do it right!

Guidelines for Teaching Your Child

Before beginning to work with your child on motor skills, some guidelines should be established. Reread these guidelines from time to time and keep them in mind whenever you are teaching your child.

1. Don't Let Frustration Get the Best of You

The teaching of any skill, especially to your own child, can be frustrating. In Chapter 1, "Getting Started," feedback was talked about in terms of letting your child know when she is doing something right and what she can do better. Sometimes it may seem to you as if your child is always doing something wrong and you are not getting the kind of feedback *you* need to keep teaching. Or you may see that your child is learning small steps of a skill, but still cannot do the skill by herself. (For example, she can walk if you hold her hands, but will not even try to walk if you let go.) You think to yourself, "This is taking forever. Why am I even trying to teach her to walk?"

As a parent, you are involved on a very personal level with your child. Your expectations are very high, and when your child fails to learn something you feel as though you have failed as a teacher. Your child is also personally involved, and she begins to feel that she is failing you. Frustration levels build up, and pretty soon you find you don't want to work at all with your child because both of you just keep failing. You get angry, you may yell, and nobody makes any progress.

This feeling of frustration is perfectly normal for *all* parents. It is not peculiar to you and your visually or multiply handicapped child. These same feelings happen to *everyone* who tries to teach *anyone anything,* including teachers. The difference is that you are personally involved, while a teacher can more easily step back, analyze the situation, and come up with a new approach.

Think back to new situations in your life. Can you remember your father *trying* to teach you to drive, your mother *trying* to teach you to knit, your best friend *trying* to teach you a new game? What were your feelings in those situations? Did you always feel calm, happy, and peaceful? No. It is important to keep this in mind when you try to teach your child. It is also important to recognize *when* you are getting totally frustrated, and to step back, breathe deeply, wiggle your toes, stretch to the sky, or do anything that will give you a minute to calm down. A screaming match will not help. Sometimes if you relax, your child will relax, too, and you both can begin again. It is important that you finish your activity in some way, however, so that your child does not get the idea that all she has to do is put up a little protest and you will do all the work for her. The more this happens, the more difficult it is to stop this habit later.

Turn to page 81 in the REACHBOOK

2. Who's in Charge Here?

One of the important things that parents learn through experience is that they are the adults, and that adults make the rules of the house and are basically in charge. Your child does not rule the house. All parents make concessions to their lifestyles when children come into the family, but after the initial shock of how much time and care a child takes, adults adjust and develop some kind of schedule so that all family members survive day-to-day living. This sense of organization, scheduling, and who's in charge is necessary for the family to grow. It is important that this feeling of adults-in-control is given to all family members from the very beginning.

Remember — you're the boss!

3. Allowing Growth

There are two areas here to talk about: (a) providing the time to grow, and (b) letting go. First, you have been working very hard to help your child learn how to do something, such as walking. You have broken the skill down into the smallest steps, and your child can now do it from start to finish. The only problem is that it takes your child 15 minutes to walk across the room. You know what your days are like and most of the time you do not have 15 minutes just for walking, let alone for working on all the other tasks you want to do today. So, you help and do it for your child. It is easier and faster for you; he can do it by himself when there is time, and you can still practice on Saturday and Sunday, but not on Monday through Friday when you have two other children and no help.

The problem with stepping in and helping when you know your child can do it by himself is that your child soon learns that if he takes enough time doing something, you will probably step in and do it for him. Before you know it, your child is 8 years old, and he *still* wants to be carried.

Once a child knows all the steps and can participate in the skills, make him do it himself. He will become better and faster at it. He needs to grow and find out that he *can* do things by himself, and that you *expect* him to do things *by* himself and *for* himself.

This leads to the second aspect of allowing growth: Letting go. Sometimes you have ambivalent feelings about letting your child do things for himself. If he can take care of things by himself (such as dressing, or eating, or running to the store for a popsicle), you may think "Does he still need me? If I continue to do things for him, then of course he will need me." You want to protect your child from all of life's traps. You can make life easier for him by doing; after all, he can't see. But, let *him* try, let *him* fail, let *him* grow. And know that after each accomplishment you will still be needed to help conquer the next goal.

Use these guidelines as you teach your child:

1. Remember that frustration is normal, but don't let it get the best of you. Stop, relax, then try again.

2. Remember that you're the boss.

3. Remember that it may be easier and faster to do things for your child, but that you risk your child becoming a "done-to-er" instead of a "do-er."

Turn to page 82 in the REACHBOOK

Teaching Strategies

There are several strategies you can use that will make your teaching a little bit easier. You may not be able to use them all at once, or even on a daily basis, but each will help you work with your child in a natural manner and with as few problems as possible.

1. Use Common Sense

Teach new skills *when* they come up and *where* they come up. You want your child to learn motor skills for a purpose, not just for the sake of learning them. Try not to create special times just to work on motor skills, but instead work on motor skills when your child needs to use them. For example, work on reaching when you have a bottle or cookie that the child can reach for, and work on running when you're outside chasing after the dog.

2. Try it Yourself

Before you try to teach a motor skill to your child, think about how you yourself do it, or how you would like to be taught. Then do the skill yourself, slowly and deliberately, thinking about each step as you go. Decide which steps are important to learn and which are not really necessary.

3. Be Prepared

Make sure you have everything you need before you start. Most motor learning does not require any special equipment, but sometimes you will want to have a favorite toy available to encourage your child to lift her head or to reward her for trying to roll over. But if your child rolls over and you have to run into the next room to get her toy, she will have trouble connecting her action to your reward.

4. Be Spontaneous

It might appear that this strategy is inconsistent with number 3, being prepared, but actually the two are very much related. You have to be ready to jump on the "teachable moment" no matter when it occurs, which means you reinforce your child for her actions, or help her go one step further, when she's ready, not when you think it might be a good time. Spontaneity — following your child's lead regardless of the situation and helping her make connections between skills already learned and those that come next — is the mark of a good teacher.

5. Be Consistent

Use the *same* words and follow the *same* teaching steps. It can be very confusing for a visually handicapped child to hear that she's a good crawler one day, and then to hear that she's a good creeper the next day; or to skip a step on some days, but not on others.

6. Work from Behind

It is easier for your child to feel the movements you're showing her how to do, and it feels more natural to be moved from behind than to be pulled forward.

7. Give Less and Less Help

You may start out helping your child by placing your hands on hers and putting her through the movements. Gradually, though, you will want to move your hands to her wrists, then her elbows, and then perhaps her arms as she learns to do more and more on her own.

8. Let Your Child Help

Whether it's choosing clothes, setting the table, or picking up toys, give your child a chance to feel needed.

9. Give Enough Time

It often takes visually and multiply handicapped children longer to do tasks or perform motor skills. Give them enough time to finish.

Learning to Move

All children follow the same basic pattern in learning to move. They all:

- **Use large muscles before they use small muscles**
  They can turn over before they can write.

- **Control the upper part of their bodies before they can control the lower part of their bodies**
  They can lift up their heads before they can stand on their feet.

- **Move their arms, before they can move their fingers**
  They can push up on their hands and arms before they can hold their bottles.

- **Make big, uncoordinated movements before they can do small, coordinated movements**
  They can play patty-cake before they can pick up a raisin with two fingers.

Your visually or multiply handicapped child will follow the same pattern. The timing may be different, but it will be the same pattern just the same. Recognizing that these are the steps your child will go through will help you to set your expectations. Knowing that movement proceeds

from Large to Small
from Head to Toe
from Trunk to Arms and Legs
from Simple to Complex

you won't expect your child to run before walking, or to write before feeding himself. Growth and development is a very complex process in which each new thing learned is based on what has already been learned and leads to what will be learned next.

Turn to page 83 in the REACHBOOK

How Children Learn

When children learn they also go through certain stages. First, of course, they go through the imitation-and-practice stage in which they receive feedback on how they are doing. If they learn the skill they have *gained* some new knowledge or a new way of doing things.

Next, they have to be able to *maintain* what was learned. Remember how you would memorize words for a spelling test and then forget some of them when the teacher gave a review test the following week? Well, those you spelled correctly on the review test were *maintained*. Those you forgot were *not* maintained. In motor development, almost every skill must be maintained because each new movement depends on the last movement learned. For example, children cannot walk before they have learned to stand alone. And they must *maintain* the ability to stand or they will not be able to walk.

The last stage of learning is *applying* the newly learned skill to new and different situations. In your spelling list you have *applied* what you have learned if you can correctly write the word in a letter without having to look it up. In motor development children *apply* their ability to walk when they start walking outdoors, or when they start walking without their parents telling them what to do. *Applying* what you have learned to new and different situations is the highest stage of learning, and it means that your child is thinking on his own and no longer has to be taught all the different ways of using a new skill. Applying skills to new situations is what we are working toward in all of our activities because that is how our visually and multiply handicapped children will grow to be more independent.

Some children never learn to apply what they have learned in this way. The reasons are many: sometimes they have not been given a chance to do things on their own; sometimes no one has shown them that it is possible to do an old skill in a new place; and sometimes they simply are not able to learn to apply what they have learned. If they are not able to do this, they can still be taught to use the skills they do know in each new situation as it comes up.

Applying or using what has already been learned in new situations can be a problem for visually handicapped children because their poor vision does not allow them to see the possibilities of using old skills in new situations. This is where you, as parents come in — by reaching out, teaching, and encouraging children to learn, maintain, and transfer as much as possible. You *show* your children the possibilities until the day when *they* can see the possibilities themselves and take off on their own.

LEARNING STAGES

Turn to page 84 in the REACHBOOK

First Things First: Motor Prerequisites

There are five important areas of motor skills that must be developed before children can walk, run, and jump:

The child's *reflexes* must not interfere with his ability to move

Muscle tone must be neither too tight nor too loose

The child must be able to *balance* his body

The child must be able to *rotate* or *turn* body parts

The child must be able to *protect* or *catch* himself when he starts to fall or lose his balance

Each of these areas has several different parts to it. Let's look at them one by one.

Reflexes

Reflexes are automatic movements that children do not control themselves. They are an important part of learning to move because they give children their first experiences with bending and stretching their body parts. Reflexes are usually present at birth: If you stick a finger in a baby's mouth she will suck, and if you stroke her cheek she will turn and search for your finger with her mouth. Without these reflexes the baby would not be able to eat.

The same is true of motor reflexes: They are all necessary. They seem to disappear as the baby grows older, but actually they become part of her overall movement pattern. If you work with a teacher or physical therapist, you may find that each looks for and talks about many different reflexes; three that are particulalry important for early movement experiences are discussed here.

Asymmetrical Tonic Neck Reflex

The asymmetrical tonic neck reflex (ATNR) is the reflex that makes babies go into an "off-balance" position in which the arm and leg on one side of the body are bent, and the other arm and leg are straight. The baby's head is turned toward the arm that is straight. To see if your child still has the ATNR, lay him on his back, and turn his head to one side. If he has an ATNR, you will see the arm and leg straighten out (or extend) on the side toward which you turned his head, while the arm and leg on the other side will bend (or flex).

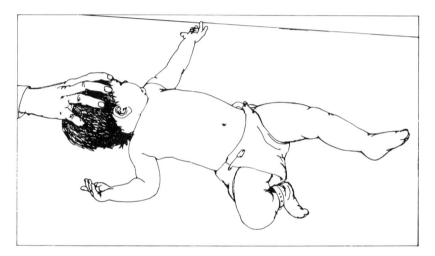

Some children will not show a perfect ATNR pattern when tested. In the illustration below, for example, only the leg on the side toward which the head is turned is straight, but both the leg and arm on the other side are flexed.

This still shows an ATNR pattern, even if it does not fit the typical example given above.

If your child does not have an ATNR, do not worry. The ATNR must fade away or, more exactly, become integrated and assimilated into the child's total motor pattern, thus seeming less pronounced, before a child can balance or turn body parts independently. Imagine what would happen if a baby had an ATNR and tried to sit alone: If he turned his head to the right to see or hear something, his right arm and leg would straighten, his left arm and leg would bend, and over he would go! Your child may not have an ATNR because it has already blended into his overall movement pattern.

If your child does have an ATNR, check with your doctor or physical therapist to find out if it is expected at this stage of his development. An ATNR that does not fade away as your child tries to learn new motor skills may mean that he should have a complete physical. It is best to check with a specialist to be sure.

Because reflexes are automatic, there is little you can do to change your child's ATNR. But you can discourage it a little bit by doing some of the following:

Place your child on his tummy and encourage him to push up on his hands. It's harder to go into an ATNR from that position.

Hold your child so that both arms are in front of him.

Play patty-cake and other games in which you clap your child's hands together. Sometimes it helps to hold your child with his back against your chest, and then move his arms forward at the elbow.

If your child is older and has what's known as an "obligatory ATNR" — that is, if every time he turns his head, his arms and legs go into the ATNR position — a physical therapist can suggest many different ways to position your child so that he will not be able to go into an ATNR.

Symmetrical Tonic Neck Reflex

The symmetrical tonic neck reflex (STNR) is the reflex that allows babies to turn one body part without turning another. You can tell if your baby has an STNR by laying her on her tummy over your knees. Be sure she is supported and cannot fall. If you raise her head, the arms will straighten and the legs will bend; if you push her head down, the legs will straighten and the arms will bend.

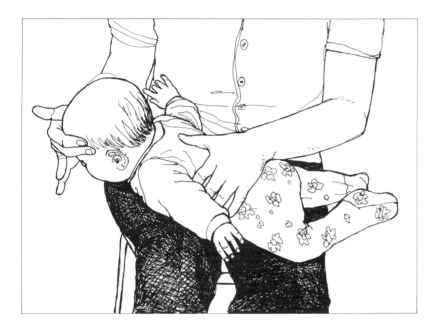

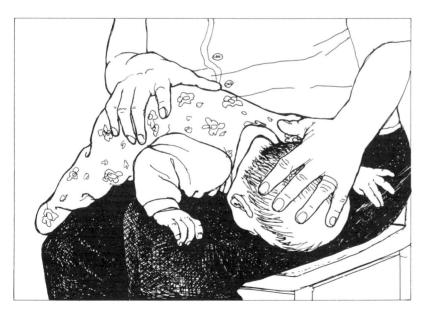

The STNR is the reflex that helps babies to push up on their arms when lying on their tummies. Later, it helps them to get into a crawling position. The STNR fades away or blends in when babies learn to crawl; if it didn't, they would not be able to move their arms and legs separately. Visually handicapped babies need to spend time on their tummies to practice using this balance reflex.

Some ways you can help this reflex are:

Again, give you child time lying on her tummy.

If your child has trouble lifting her head in this position, put your hand on her backside and push down a bit.

Gently rub the shoulder area, between the neck and the shoulder, moving from the neck out. This helps loosen up the shoulder area and helps the arms to move forward.

If your baby balances on her tummy with her arms and legs in the air, you can help her get out of this position by moving her arms forward from the shoulders (one of your hands on each shoulder), and giving her backside a little gentle push downward. While this "balancing act" looks cute and looks like it takes a lot of work, it actually uses the wrong muscles. Right now, you want your baby to bend her legs more and bring her hands forward and onto the floor to bear weight. If she spends too much time balancing on her tummy, the opposite muscles — those that would keep her from crawling — will develop faster, and you might notice that she's too tight in her legs and shoulder area.

Extension or Landau Reflex

The extension reflex will eventually help your child to stand. It causes the straightening, or extension, of the legs, back, and neck. Without this extension, the legs would not be able to bear weight and the body would not stand upright.

To see if your child has the Landau reflex, place him carefully on his tummy over one of your knees, or very carefully hold him in the air so that his arm and legs are *not* supported. His head should rise automatically and his legs should straighten. If you push down on his head, the legs will bend at the knees and the arms will bend at the elbow.

To help the Landau reflex along:

Continue the same exercises described above.

Give your child some "standing practice" by standing him on your lap (support him at the trunk or waist).

If your child does not seem able to bend his legs, check with a physical therapist. Too much extension can be as much of a problem as too little extension, and a physical therapist can show you ways to break up this extension and give your child some other movement experiences.

These three reflexes are important for your child's first movement experiences. However, each is needed only at a particular stage of development to help your child learn a new skill, and should subsequently blend in and become part of your child's overall motor pattern. In some multiply handicapped children these reflexes do not blend in. If you find your child is more than 9 to 12 months old and still has one or more of these reflexes, check with your doctor. If possible, you should also talk to a physical therapist to get some ideas about how to position your child so that these reflexes do not make it impossible, or more difficult, for him to learn in other ways.

Turn to page 85 in the REACHBOOK

Muscle Tone

Often young visually and multiply handicapped children are said to have poor muscle tone — they feel "loose," "soft," or "wobbly," and may have trouble lifting their heads or standing up. They just can't seem to take any weight on their hands or on their legs. Or the opposite may be true: The child is "tight" all the time and doesn't seem to cuddle up or bend. Doctors have special words for these two conditions: Muscle tone that is too soft, is referred to as *hypotonic*; that which is too tight, as *hypertonic*. At any point in time, the visually or multiply handicapped child may seem too tight or too loose: If the child is suddenly picked up, for example, she may stiffen up because you have surprised or frightened her. And just like other children who want to do things their way, they can react by going limp if you make them do something.

The point is that they should not be too soft or too tight *all the time*. Good tone — enough to support the child's weight but not so much that her walk is stiff or unnatural — is essential for good movement, especially for walking, running, and sports. And part of the way good tone is developed is by movement itself — all those things you do with a baby to teach her about her body and the world.

If you think your child has poor muscle tone, check with your doctor or physical therapist. Again, it is possible to position children so that poor tone does not interfere with learning.

How is your child's muscle tone? Check it out in your REACHBOOK.

Turn to page 88 in the REACHBOOK

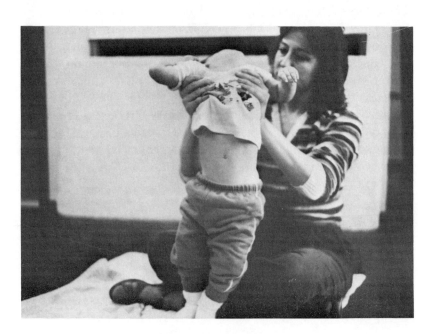

You can improve your child's muscle tone by:

Giving her the same movement experiences you've been doing so far. Partly, muscle tone is a response to movement—the more your child moves, the better feeling she will have for her own muscles.

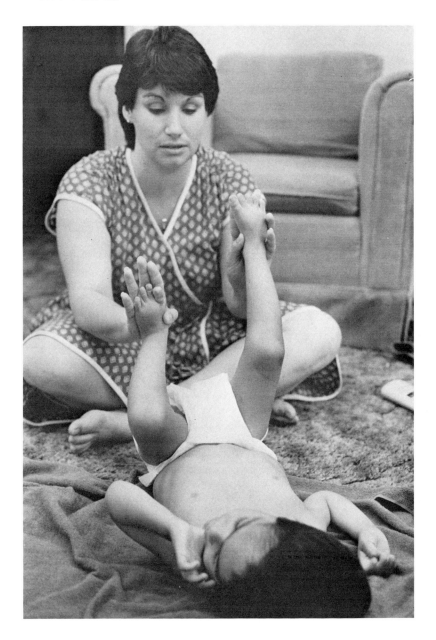

Doing exercises with your "soft" child: leg lifts, arm raises, arm crosses, leg crosses; moving arms and and legs together, opposite arms and legs together, and so forth. You may start out doing all the work, but as your child gets used to the movement, you will find that she will help you or start to do some of the exercises herself.

Massaging your child with lotions and soft cloths to stimulate the skin and help make her aware of her body parts.

Balance

Balance is a child's ability to hold body parts upright. This ability starts first with the head, then continues down the body with the shoulders, trunk, hips, and legs. In older children, balance is part of running, jumping, standing on one leg, bicycling, and ball throwing.

Because, as with all motor development, balance develops from head to toe, a child will not be able to sit until he has head and trunk balance, or to stand before he also has hip and leg balance.

At what stage is your child's balance? Go to your REACHBOOK and find out.

Turn to page 89 in the REACHBOOK

You can help your child improve his balance by:

Giving him chances to sit or stand alone.

Giving him some support and then letting go for a few seconds. See if he can catch himself before he loses his balance.

Carrying your baby with you in an infant carrier, knapsack, or sling as you do your daily chores. This gives the baby the feeling of balance and movement in space even if you're the one actually doing it.

Giving him lots of time laying on his tummy. Your child may act like he doesn't like this position. He probably won't — *until* he has learned to balance, and turn his head and lift it up off the floor.

Many people have said that visually handicapped babies do not like lying on their tummies because they cannot see. They still need to learn to balance their heads and bodies, however, and they still need to push up on their hands. (The next chapter will tell you more about why taking weight on the hands is important for learning to hold objects.) The key, then, is to *make* the position interesting:

Place a toy, mirror, or musical instrument in front of the baby to keep his attention.

Better yet, get down on the floor with him! Talk to him and encourage him to hold his head up. Put your hands over his, if necessary, so he can feel what it's like to push with his hands.

Use a penlight or flashlight to get his attention. As he lifts his head, move the light higher and higher. Cover the light with colored cellophane if you can; sometimes the white light is too bright for visually handicapped children and makes them uncomfortable. If your child doesn't seem to pay attention, try moving the light back and forth.

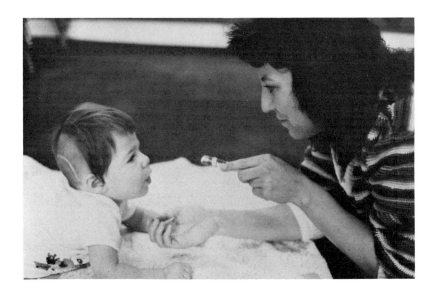

Sitting

When children first learn to sit they have trouble keeping their balance. It helps them to keep from falling over if they bend their arms and hold them at shoulder level, with their hands almost behind their shoulders. This is natural at first, and part of learning to balance. But, like most things, it should not go on forever. Work on bringing your baby's hands in front of her body by:

Sitting behind her and moving her hands forward with yours to play patty-cake or to play with other toys.

Encouraging her to reach out and find favorite toys that you've placed in front of her.

Stretching out your legs in a "V" and sitting your child between your legs. Gently push her to the right or left or forward, helping her to stretch out her arms to catch herself.

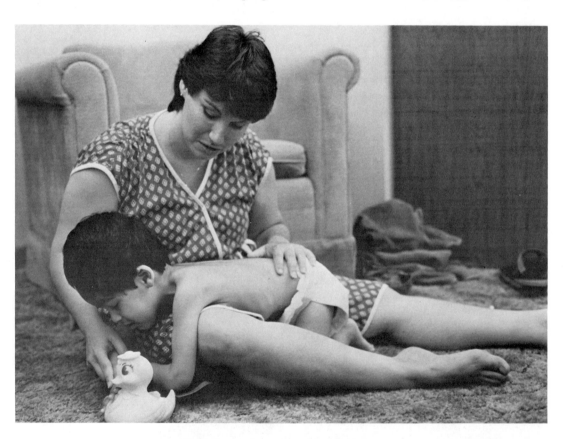

Continuing to place her on her tummy. Many times the shoulders are tight when the hands are held in this kind of an extreme position.

Pushing up on the hands while lying on the tummy gives babies feedback on what it feels like to extend the arms forward and helps to loosen up the shoulder area.

By doing these activities, you will be working (in this chapter and the next) on other important motor skills as well: on grasp, rotation, and protective reactions, at the same time as you are working on balance.

Sometimes children will try to get a larger base of support while sitting because it's easier to balance in this position. One of the ways they do this is by sitting in a "W" position in which the knees are bent and each foot is out on the side. This puts a lot of strain on the knees and on the thigh muscles. It is not a good position for learning to walk because the lower leg muscles are not used at all, while the upper leg muscles are used too much. If your child seems to need a wider base of support for sitting, show her how to sit "tailor" or "Indian" style; ring style (feet touching in front), or side sitting (the foot of one leg against the thigh of the other, with the foot of that leg out to the side).

Walking

Once your child has learned to walk, there are many activities you can do to increase her moving balance. Just like when first learning to sit, all babies begin walking by keeping their feet wide apart, and holding their hands and arms up high. But this, too, should disappear as they get older and gain more experience.

Some visually handicapped children continue to walk with their feet spread far apart, even though their hands come down to their sides. Try it yourself: With your feet wide apart, you feel "safer" because with a broader base of support it is not as easy to tip over. But *you* have learned to walk safely with your feet closer together, and so can visually handicapped children.

To help your child practice walking you can:

Give your child a chance to walk frequently. It builds up his self-confidence — and yours.

Be sure your child has an opportunity to walk on many different surfaces — rugs, bare floors, grass, sidewalks, gravel, tile, etc.

See that your child has a chance to walk on both even and uneven surfaces — steps, hills, sloping driveways, etc.

Make games out of balance activities. Trampolines are good for balance but so are old inner tubes. Rocking boards are easily made. See-saws provide a different kind of sensation but help balance just the same.

Safety

A word or two about making the environment safe for your visually handicapped child: When your child begins walking, it will be harder for your to keep up with her. While you want her to do things on her own, you also don't want her to get hurt, or to have a bad experience that might make her think twice about practicing newly learned skills again. Remember, when you cannot see very well, some of the predictability of your world is lost — you can't always expect the doors to be closed or the toys to be picked up off the floor, and while you're learning about your house, you can't even be sure where the steps are.

So, look in your home for "baby traps," and then find a way to make it safe for all your children:

Place a gate at the top of a flight of steps going down.

Tape down the edges of throw rugs or scatter rugs so the floor won't suddenly slip out from under a running or walking child.

Try to remember to keep room and closet doors closed, or place a heavy object against a door to prop it all the way open. If you've ever awakened in the middle of the night and stubbed your toe or banged your head on an open door, you know how much it hurts!

Sharp edges on tables can be a problem when your child is the same height as the table. First, add foam or tape to the edges to prevent accidents. Then, follow the suggestions in this chapter under "Orientation." Rubber-like corner guards can also be purchased.

Remind all your children, including your visually handicapped child, to put their toys away and not leave them on the floor where they can be tripped over.

Keep glass items, such as coffee tables and lamps in a protected place — for example, in a corner with chairs on either side. That way they will be less likely to get broken and to cut your child.

Kid-proof your cabinets: Keep poisonous cleaners in a cabinet out of your child's reach, or lock them up. Do the same for drugs and medications. Keyless locks that are easily opened by adults but difficult for children are available.

Use a bathmat or rubber stick-ons to keep your children from slipping in the tub.

Cover electrical outlets with an outlet shield so that plugs are not exposed. Outlet caps are also available for outlets that are not being used.

Other ideas on "child-proofing" your home are available from the Child Safety Institute. (See page 48 of your REACHBOOK for the address.)

Orientation

As your child becomes more and more active you will need to teach him more and more about "orientation" — a word used to describe blind people's ability to know where they are in space. Do you remember how, as a child, you would play tag? When you were "it," your friends blindfolded you, spun you around in circles, and then you tried to catch someone. Remember how dizzy and mixed up and *disoriented* you were? Well, it is important for blind children to learn early about their environment so that they can make sense out of the world and keep from getting confused. To help your child develop a good idea of the space around him, try these ideas:

Different rooms in your house have different odors, different floor coverings, and different sounds. As your child begins to walk around on his own, point these differences out to him:

"Feel the cold tile on your feet? You're in the kitchen."

"That's right, you found the rug to the living room."

"The ticking noise is from the big old clock in the hallway."

"The traffic is noisier when you're in the front of the house."

"Do you smell the cookies baking in the kitchen?"

Tape a piece of cloth that feels interesting on the door to your child's bedroom. Self-adhesive paper in brocade or other textures is also good. Use the same fabric or paper on your child's chair at the dinner table and on the kitchen drawer or cabinet that it's okay for him to play in.

If you move the furniture around, either ask your child to help you do it or be sure you tell him what you've done. When you're accustomed to finding things in a certain place, it can be very upsetting not to find them there. This doesn't mean that you should *not* rearrange furniture — it is actually good practice for your child to think about a new way of doing things — but it *does* mean you have to include your child in the process.

Begin teaching compass directions — north, south, east, west — early. Knowing that the sun always rises in the east and sets in the west may someday help your child to find his way home.

As you walk around the neighborhood with your child point out driveways, corners, mailboxes, trees, etc. These will become useful landmarks. For example, "If I walk out my front door, walk left, and count three driveways, I'll come to Mrs. Smith's house."

Teach your child to use sidewalks as clues. If you're supposed to be following the sidewalk and you're walking on grass or dirt instead, something's wrong.

Play follow-the-leader such that your child has to follow the sound of your voice as you walk around the room. Do this outside, too, as your voice will be more difficult to locate in a large space without echoes.

When walking with your older child, ask him to tell you where he's been and how to get back where he came from.

Set up travel games: "You got to the kitchen by walking through the hallway. Now can you go back to the hall *without* walking through the kitchen?"

Teach your child to trail walls, both to find his way and to give him a sense of control over where he is and where he's going. Trailing is done by lightly curving the fingers and holding the back of the hand against the wall but slightly ahead of the body. The wall is not used for support, but is almost like a grounding.

Jumping

Jumping is particularly hard for visually handicapped children to learn because they cannot watch anyone to see how it's done. It is hard to explain jumping in words. Yet jumping is a good activity for using up energy and at the same time giving the child the feeling of moving through space. Many of the activities already mentioned will help with this.

Try it yourself: Very slowly, go through all the movements you need to jump with two feet:

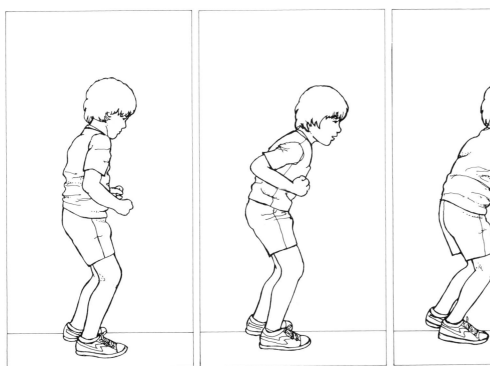

1. Bend knees, and swing arms back

2. Bend arms and move them forward

3. As arms go forward, push against floor with feet

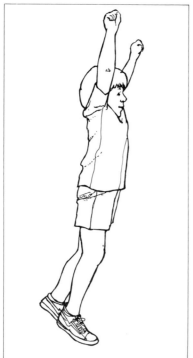

4. Bring feet up in the air, continuing to swing arms forward and up over the head

5. Land on feet, bending knees slightly to break the shock of landing

6. Straighten knees and stand up

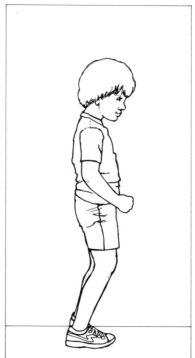

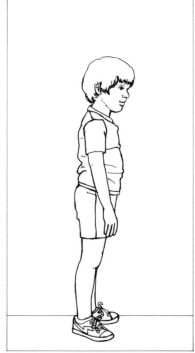

Now that you've done it yourself you know how it is done. But how do you explain all these steps to a young child? If your child does not learn to jump easily, as part of the other games and activities you do with her, you can move her through the process yourself:

1. **Show her** how to bend her knees.

2. **Show her** how to swing her arms forward and backward.

3. **Push on** her feet with your hands.

4. **Start on** the edge of the couch or bed with your child jumping into your arms so she gets the idea of movement through space and not jumping in one spot.

5. **If your child's** muscle tone is normal, use a stable chair to practice bouncing.

6. **Practice jumping** in place — bounce your child while you are holding her in your lap. But, again, be sure that her muscle tone is okay. If your child has problems with muscle tone, particularly if she is too tight, jumping in place is not a good idea. It actually increases her tone and will work against your efforts to make her muscle tone more normal.

Running

There is nothing quite like running and feeling the wind in your face. For young children, it is a release of energy, a source of power ("You can't catch me!"), and a developer of body sense (knowing where and how to move your body in space). As parents of visually handicapped children it might be scary to think of them running:

"She can't see where she's going."

"She'll run into something."

"She could fall down and break a leg!"

Any one of these *could* happen, of course. But since there are so many benefits to running, the best idea is to help your children to run safely. You can do that by:

Carrying your child as *you* run.

Running together, hand-in-hand.

Running together, each holding the end of a rope.

Asking another child to run with yours.

Making sure the area is free of obstacles.

Stringing some clothesline at the child's waist level to make a running track in the backyard. Place an auditory cue (bell, radio, beeper ball) at one end, and have your child run toward it holding on to the rope.

Telling your child only to run where she feels the sidewalk under her feet, and then only when she hears no traffic, or only in the park.

Moving Balance

Moving balance — all those activities that require children to move their bodies through space, such as running, jumping, skipping, and hopping — are very important for developing a child's good feelings about himself. As he learns to control his body, he also learns how he can control his world. *He* can do things; he doesn't have to wait to have things done *to* him.

Rotation

Being able to turn one body part without turning *all* body parts is an important part of motor development. Unfortunately, it is often overlooked because it is taken for granted.

Just like many of the motor skills already discussed, rotation of body parts is related to reflexes and balance. It also develops from head to toe: A child can turn her head before she can turn her hips. But before she can do either, the ATNR (asymmetrical tonic neck reflex) must no longer be obvious, and she must be able to turn her head anytime she wants to without the rest of her body parts bending or straightening.

How is your child's "turning ability?" Check it out in your REACHBOOK.

← **Turn to page 91 in the REACHBOOK**

Do not be upset if your child is not doing all the things in the REACHBOOK. Many of those twisting and turning motions depend on good vision — you turn around because something has caught your eye. This doesn't mean visually handicapped children cannot *learn* to do these skills, but it does mean that you have to show your child how to do them and create opportunities for practice.

Crawling

Why is rotation so important? Simply because it makes for easier movement. Without rotation your body would move very stiffly, like a board. Try this:

1. Lay on your back.
2. Now roll over without turning any body parts.

It can't be done, can it? Okay, try something else:

3. Crawl without moving your hips.

What did you do? In order to crawl without moving your hips you would have to slide your knees forward together, doing a kind of bunny hop, like this:

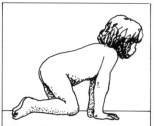 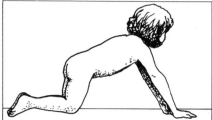 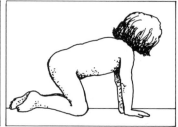

Many visually handicapped children do not crawl. They start walking without ever really going through a crawling period. As you have just learned yourself, however, crawling gives children the chance to practice hip rotation. Children who do not have hip rotation tend to have a "waddle walk" — they walk by shifting their weight from one foot to the other, usually with their feet spread apart for balance and their legs straight.

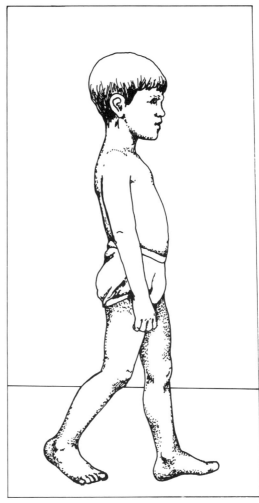

Far left: "waddle" walk

Near right: normal walk

You may have heard that blind children do not crawl because it is not interesting for them: They cannot see, so they don't make the effort to go after toys or other objects while lying on their tummies. Certainly every child is different; there are many nonhandicapped children who skip the crawling stage. But for blind children crawling is the time when they can really practice hip rotation. If your child is not walking yet, but can get on hands and knees, teach her to crawl:

1. **Try it yourself.** Get down on the floor and crawl very slowly. Feel the way your body moves.

2. **When your child** is on hands and knees, put your hand behind her feet and give a little push. This will give her the idea of moving forward.

3. **Show your child** how it feels to crawl by moving her arms and legs for her. Move the right hand forward first, then the left knee, then the left hand, then the right knee. As you get used to moving her arms and legs for her, you can move the left hand and right knee together.

4. **When your child** is on hands and knees, encourage her to reach out to you or to a toy with one hand. This makes her

shift all her weight to the other side and helps practice balance as well as rotation.

5. **Some blind children** crawl with their heads down on the floor. This looks funny but doesn't actually interfere with their crawling. If your child does this, try to get her to raise her head by using lights or by massaging the back of her neck. If it is not corrected, you may find that your child will *walk* with her head down, too.

In a a normal crawl, children move opposite arms and legs forward, instead of both arms or both legs at the same time.

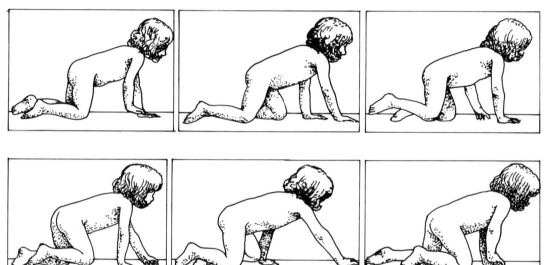

Practicing Hip Rotation

If your child is already walking, you can still practice hip rotation. The balance activities described earlier, such as the rocking board, are good for rotation, and so are these ideas:

Get a hoola hoop for your child and teach her how to use it. You may have to put your hands on her hips and move them for her so she gets the idea of the movement.

Place a ladder flat on the floor. Tell your child she can only step in one space (between two rungs) at a time, and she shouldn't touch the sides of the ladder or the rung with her feet. This keeps her feet forward and makes her turn her hips.

Teach your child how to ride a bicycle or big wheel. You can loosely tie her feet to the pedals and pull the bike by the handlebars to give her the idea of pedaling.

Go swimming. Kicking the legs is also hip rotation.

Walk up and down steps. Children usually crawl first, then walk up steps (two feet per step, two hands holding on), then crawl down backwards, then walk down (two feet per step, two hands holding on), then they learn to use just one hand. Every time she lifts or lowers a foot or knee to the next step her hips must rotate.

Take your child roller-skating. In order to keep from falling down, the feet must point forward and the leg movement must come from the hips.

The important thing to remember about rotation is that it allows for more natural movement and leads to greater mobility — the ability to get around the world on your own. What your child cannot pick up on her own, you can teach her.

Protection

The last area of motor development is protective reactions — the instinct to catch yourself when you feel you are falling. These, too, are related to balance and rotation.

How well can your child catch himself? Check it out in your REACHBOOK.

Turn to page 94 in the REACHBOOK

Forward Protection

Protection reactions toward the front of the body develop first. Until children are able to catch themselves when falling forward, they will not be able to sit alone without support. Many of the activities you are already doing will help to develop protective reactions, but you can also try these:

1. **Sit on the floor** with your legs spread in a "V" or with feet touching, and place your child sitting between your legs. He

can lean against your tummy for support. Put your hands on his, lean forward (so your baby also has to lean forward), and pull out his hands to touch the floor. Do this several times, rocking back and forth from sitting up to hands on the floor.

2. **In the same position**, place a ball between the baby's legs. Choose a ball large enough to fit the child's body — so that his hands fit comfortably on top of the ball while the ball is between his legs and on the floor. While your child is holding on to the ball, slowly roll it forward. This will give him the feeling of stretching out his arms while still giving him some support.

Many children first reach a "frog" position before they can sit alone. This is fine and gives lots of good feedback to the arms and body. It leads to forward protective reactions.

Side Protection
Side protection comes next. You can use the same activity as above, only push your child to the side. He should fall against your legs. As he and you become more sure of yourselves, try doing it without your legs as a guide.

Side protection must be developed before children will crawl. Catching themselves on the sides is one of their first experiences with shifitng weight and learning to balance.

Back Protection

Back protection comes before children are able to walk alone. Your child can practice catching herself when she falls backwards using the same kinds of activities you used to practice front and side protection — just change the direction.

Remember to do all these activities gently, without scaring your visually handicapped child. Always give feedback on what you are doing and how she is doing.

Overprotection

As visually handicapped children grow and develop they will naturally have their share of spills, scrapes and bruises. Let them. This is part of growing up and learning about their world and their own abilities. It is tempting as parents to try to protect your children from getting hurt. But you will not and cannot always be there for them. Because your child is visually handicapped it is even more tempting to do things for him — this is when you need to remember that your child will learn a lot about himself by the tone you set. If you think that blindness is something the two of you can work on together, then your child will have that "I can do it" attitude, too. But if you are worried a lot of the time, then it is going to be difficult to hide that worry from your child. One of the ways it comes out is by being overprotective. It will not be long before your child gets the idea that he is someone to *be protected*. He will do less and less on his own as he depends on you and others more. Sometimes it helps to talk to other parents about these feelings, and this is where parent organizations can help.

You might also want to read the section on your child's self-concept in the "Talking it Over" chapter. It will give you some more ideas on how to build your child's good feelings about himself while he struggles to do more on his own.

Mannerisms

Often visually handicapped children develop mannerisms — habits that are also sometimes called "blindisms" — right around the time when growing children usually become most active. These can take many forms, but the most common are rocking and eye-poking. There are many theories on the cause of these mannerisms. Some people say it is a way of releasing energy: The child is not getting enough activity, so the blindisms are a way of letting off steam. Some have suggested that they develop when children do not receive enough vestibular stimulation — movement such as being thrown up in the air or carried on the parent's back that develops the inner ear and the awareness of movement in space. Others say it is nothing more than a bad habit, like twirling your hair or tapping your pencil. The problem is that both rocking and eye-poking are really obvious. Visually handicapped children who do these things only draw attention to themselves and to their handicap. The children look different.

You may see your child rocking or eye-poking when she's sleepy or left alone. Part of the reason she does this may be because she has not yet learned how to occupy her time. Most young children have a short attention span and get bored easily; when this happens, they go off to find something to do. But visually handicapped children have to be *taught* to do this. You don't realize there are other things to do and play with if you don't see them.

You can help your child be a "self-starter" by doing the following:

Talk to your child from across the room. Let her know you are there even if she can't feel or smell you.

As soon as your child begins to rock or poke her eyes, go to her: "Now, let's see. What can we do now? Would you like a new toy to playing with? Try this."

Be frank about telling your child that rocking, eye-poking, or even playing with her hair does not look nice. Remember that she cannot see others doing it, so she has no idea of how it looks.

Try not to make a big deal out of the mannerism. Many children like the attention and continue to do it harder and faster when their parents yell at them.

You don't always have to be the one to redirect your child's activities. Sometimes a simple "Can you find something else to do?" will remind your child that there's a whole world of things to do out there.

So far, you have read about basic motor development and what children must learn in order to move freely and easily. Your REACHBOOK contains a chart that will help you keep track of your child's progress. Use the chart to find out what your child does now, what she needs to do next, and what you can do to help your child TAKE OFF on her own!

Turn to page 95 in the REACHBOOK

Notes on Additional Reading

Most of the books mentioned in the "Getting Started" chapter also deal with motor development. The following concentrate on motor development in particular.

In *Raising the Young Blind Child: A Guide for Parents and Educators,* by S. Kastein, I. Spaulding, and B. Scharf, Chapters 2, 8, and 13 deal with motor development in the blind infant, toddler, and young child, respectively.

If your child has additional handicaps, one or more of these may be helpful: *I Wanna Do It Myself,* by C. Gimbel and K. Shane, pages 21–33, and *Handling the Young Cerebral Palsied Child at Home,* by N. R. Finnie, Chapters 1, 3, 4, and 16 for cerebral palsy; *Beginning with the Handicapped,* by V. Hart, Chapter 3 for children who are severely multiply handicapped; and for those who are hearing impaired, *Understanding the Deaf-Blind Child,* by P. Freeman, Chapter 8. *A Comprehensive Program for Multi-handicapped Children: An Illustrated Approach,* by S. Jegard et al., addresses a variety of multiple impairments. Chapter 2 is on gross motor skills and Chapter 3 on fine motor skills. Finally, *A Practical Guide to the Training of Low Functioning Deaf-Blind,* by M. Watson and J. L. Nicholas is intended for both parents and professionals working together as a team with severely impaired deaf-blind children.

A toy catalog that relates toys and activities to development, *Toybrary: A Toy Lending Library for Parents and Children*, from the Nebraska Department of Education, may be helpful.

And a quarterly for teachers of visually impaired preschoolers, *National Newspatch,* from the Oregon School for the Blind has suggestions for both parents and professionals.

For more details on all of these publications, check the Bibliography at the end of this HANDBOOK.

Chapter 4

PICKING UP:

Using One's Hands to Learn About the World

Developing grasp
Learning to reach
Learning to let go
Wrist rotation
School readiness

PICKING UP:

Using One's Hands to Learn About the World

Chapter 3, "Taking Off," talked about suggestions and activities for helping your child learn to use his body to move around from one place to another. Most teachers refer to this as "gross motor development." In this chapter you will read about "fine motor development" — suggestions and activities for helping your child learn to use his hands. This includes playing with toys as well as getting information about objects, textures, people, sizes, letters and, eventually, learning to read and write.

The Motor Development Process

Fine motor development occurs in much the same way as gross motor development. All children:

- **Use large muscles before they use small muscles**
  They will bat and pat toys with an open hand before they will reach out and grasp a toy in mid-air.

- **Control the upper part of their bodies before they control the lower part of their bodies**
  They will lift their heads by pushing up on their hands before they will walk by themselves and push a popper toy at the same time.

- **Move their arms before they move their fingers**
  They will use their arms for balance in sitting before they will sit and manipulate toys in their hands.

- **Use big, uncoordinated movements before they use small, precise movements**
  They will swipe at and rake up a raisin before they will use their thumbs and forefingers to pick up that same raisin.

This *process* of motor development is always the same, regardless of how visually or multiply handicapped your child is. If you keep this process in mind, it will be easier to observe what your child is doing and to understand what he needs to do next. Remember:

The Motor Development Process
from Large to Small
from Head to Toe
from Trunk to Arms and Legs
from Simple to Complex

Turn to page 97 in the REACHBOOK

Four Important Fine Motor Skills

There are four important skills that every child must learn before she can go on to higher and more complicated tasks:

1. She must learn to *grasp* objects
2. She must learn to *reach* out to objects
3. She must be able to *release* objects deliberately
4. She must be able to *turn* her *wrist* in various directions

All other fine motor activities are built upon these four skills. When your child learns these, she will be well on her way to using her hands to get information about her world and to take care of herself because grasp, reach, release, and wrist rotation are very much a part of braille writing, handwriting, dressing, and eating.

The First Important Skill: Grasp

Grasp is the ability to hold on to objects and use them for specific purposes. Almost all babies have a reflexive grasp for the first few weeks after birth: If you place your finger in a baby's palm, his hand will automatically close, and the fingers curl around your finger and hold on tightly. This is called a reflexive grasp because the baby has no control over it and is barely aware that anything is even in his hand.

But just as motor reflexes are important because they give children their first experiences with movement, the grasp reflex is important because it gives babies their first experiences with using their hands. Gradually, as they continue to react reflexively to something being placed in their hand they become aware of what is there and begin to do "finger exercises": They will put their hands together and play with their fingers, straightening them out, curling them up, pulling on them; and they will somehow manage to get their fingers into their mouth, where they will suck and chew on them. This "mouthing" of their fingers often helps babies to comfort and soothe themselves in times of stress.

Not by coincidence, babies are also doing some significant balance activities at the same time this reflexive grasp is becomng more and more voluntary and under their control: They are pushing up on their hands as they lay on their tummies. At first, their hands are still fisted as they push, and only their heads come up. Then they will push more on the forearms and hands, and they start to lift their head and trunk. As they practice more, the elbows gradually straighten out and the hands open up, and soon babies can lift their entire head, shoulders, and trunk off the floor. All of the baby's weight at that point is supported by the hands.

This connection between weight-bearing and learning to use the hands is important. Blind and visually handicapped babies are often said to dislike lying on their tummies, either because they have no reason to lift their heads (they can't see anything), or because they have difficulty breathing, or whatever. But just as the "Taking Off" chapter pointed out the importance of the tummy or (prone) position for developing balance and rotation, so is the prone position important for developing grasp and manipulation. To see why, try it yourself:

Lie down on the floor in a prone position with your elbows bent and arms close to your sides. Keeping your hands fisted, push with your hands and forearms against the floor and lift the upper part of your body. What do you feel?

1. You notice that your hands are uncomfortable in a fisted position; and
2. You feel the tenseness throughout your arms and shoulders.

This weight-bearing on your hands gives *feedback* to the entire upper part of your body. You feel it in your joints and fingers. And if you had to spend a lot of time in that position, you would *open* your hands, *straighten* out your arms, and *raise* your head and trunk higher and higher. And, as you did so, you would learn *where* your arms were and *what* your hands could do. And pretty soon, you would be able to *shift your weight* to one side and support it with just one hand, as the other hand reached out and grabbed for a favorite toy.

That is the basic connection between weight-bearing and use of the hands: Weight bearing gives the kind of feedback that *first*, makes the baby aware of his arms and hands, and *second*, shows him how he can use them. The increased use of the hands for weight-bearing and weight-shifting activities occurs at the same time as grasp is becoming more deliberate and more precise. Visually handicapped children who do not receive this weight-bearing experience in the prone position (on the tummy) will have as much difficulty learning to use their hands as they will learning to move about independently.

If your child is multiply handicapped, and particularly if he has a motor impairment, you are probably wondering what all this means for his ability to use and learn from his hands. For various reasons, weight-bearing may be impossible, but learning to use the hands *is still* possible. You should talk to a physical or occupational therapist about it. While physical and occupational therapists understand the connection between weight-bearing and hand use, they may not be aware of how visually handicapped children depend on their hands for both *primary* information (that is, information they can't obtain in any other way), and to *verify* the information that is obtained through their other senses. (For example, to be sure that that sweet smell is really a banana that can be eaten, they will need to break off a piece and touch it.) Explain this to the people who work with your child, and ask for techniques and exercises that you can do with him to help make him aware of his hands and of what he can do with them.

Turn to page 99 in the REACHBOOK

Some activities you can do to help the child become aware of his hands and arms include:

Massage the arms and hands: Rub them with lotion or powder, moving from the shoulders down the arms, into the palm, and to the tips of the fingers. Use different textures as well: a washcloth, a blanket, corduroy, velvet, nylon, socks, brushes.

Work on the hands alone, moving from wrist to finger tips, and try other textures, such as a nylon scrub sponge.

Stretch out the arms and hands as you do for some of the balance activities described in Chapter 3, and push his palms against the floor. This will give his hands and arms some feedback.

Multiply handicapped children may show a preference for one side of their body, or one side of the body may be weaker than the other. You will want to work on that weak side, however, so it can develop as much as possible. One way to do this is to restrict or hold back the stronger hand so that your child has to use the other.

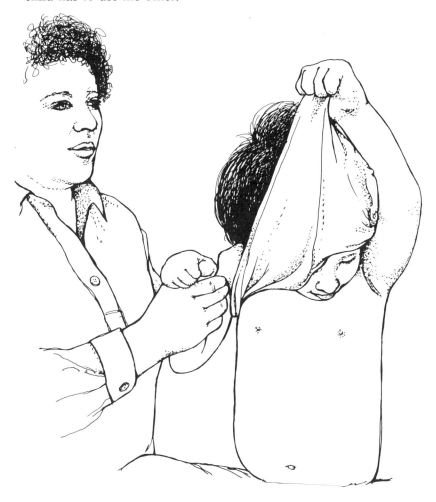

Another way to help the multiply handicapped child with developing the weaker side is to place a brightly colored sock on the preferred hand. Sew yarn pom-pom balls on the end of the sock if you want. Your child will use the weaker hand to play with the pom-poms and sock. Try to get him to pull the sock off.

Talk about what you're doing as you do it. These activities are excellent times for communication between parent and child —taking turns, describing feelings, naming body parts.

The teaching strategies you learned in Chapter 3 are useful in all activities. Remember especially the strategy of using common sense. These awareness exercises are not limited to 30–minute periods once a day. Nor should they be taken out of context—that is, worked on as an end in themselves, or done in isolation. The *natural* time to do them is while dressing and undressing. (Did you ever wonder why you get your child bathed and dressed to attend preschool, only to have the teacher or therapist remove his clothes for "sensory awareness" or "relaxation" time?)

Becoming aware of his hands and arms is only one part of your child's fine motor development. The awareness and feedback are necessary only because they prepare the way for his hands to become better able to obtain and use information. (Chapter 6, "Thinking it Through," contains more information on body awareness and its relation to self-awareness.) The ways in which objects are held become increasingly sophisticated, and then the other three important fine motor skills are developed: reach, release, and wrist rotation.

Types of Grasps

The *reflexive grasp,* discussed earlier, begins to fade away as a baby takes more and more weight on his hands, and is replaced by a series of different holding methods which, over time, involve more thumb participation. The next type of grasps, in the order of development, are:

A *raking grasp*, whereby the fingers—not the thumb—do all of the holding, and the palm is not even used. The strength of the grasp is felt in the fingers farthest away from the thumb.

A *palmer grasp*, whereby the fingers squeeze against the palm instead of against themselves, as they did in the raking grasp, and still the thumb is not involved. Some people also call this a *squeeze grasp*.

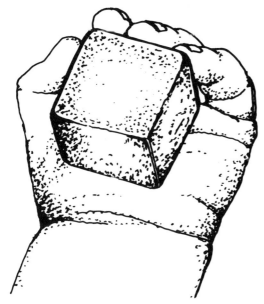

A *whole-hand grasp*, whereby the palm and fingers do the actual holding, but the thumb at last has become involved. The strength of the grasp is still between the palm and the fingers, particularly those fingers closest to the thumb), and the thumb exerts very little pressure on the object being held.

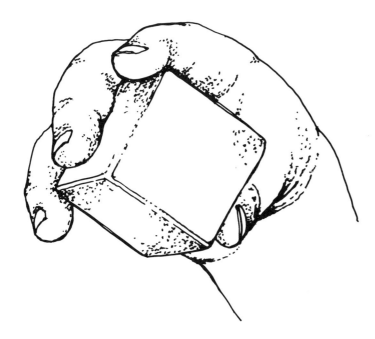

A *scissors grasp*, whereby the thumb is moved sideways toward the fingers. Objects of smaller and smaller size can be held between the thumb and index finger, but the tips of the fingers are not involved.

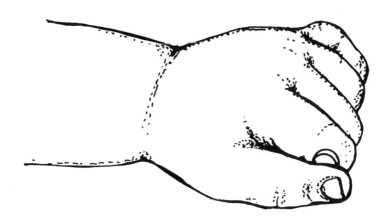

A *forefinger grasp*, whereby the thumb moves toward the underside (or palm side) of the forefinger, but the tips of the forefinger and the thumb are not directly opposed, or touching each other. With practice and experience, the thumb tip comes closer to the tip of the index finger.

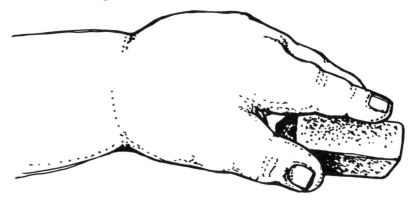

A *pincer grasp*, whereby the tip of the thumb and index finger are directly opposed, and the object is held between these two finger tips. Even this grasp does not become the high-level grasp that sup-

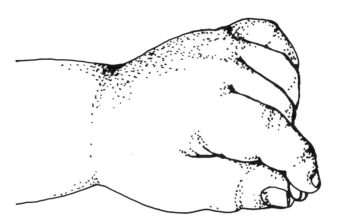

posedly makes humans different from animals overnight: At first the pincer occurs when the wrist is supported on a table or some other surface, and it is only later that the pincer occurs literally in mid-air, from above, without support to the wrist.

Notice that not only did the thumb and index finger gradually come together, but the strength of the grasp moved across the palm, from the little (or pinky) finger to the thumb. When this process is completed, your child will have a *mature* grasp, whereby the fingers do most of the work and the palm is used very little (and then only for support).

The development of grasp is not an end in itself, however. What you are leading to is not only the child's ability to obtain information, but his ability to *give* information to others—through handwriting, braille reading, and even art. A child's ability to do this is affected by his grasp as much as by his mental growth. To see why, try it yourself:

> **Use a palmar grasp** to hold a pen or pencil. That's right, place the pen across your palm and close your fingers around it. Now turn your wrist so the point of the pen touches the paper. Write your name.

Pretty sloppy, wasn't it? Many people are only able to print in this position, and then not very well. If you are trying to coordinate thinking, writing, and watching what you're doing, an inefficient grasp is not going to help you any.

Your child will also need to learn the correct way to hold a crayon or pencil. When your child is ready, start showing her how:

1. *Hold* the barrel of the pen between her thumb and index finger;
2. *Rest* the pen on the middle finger; and
3. *Support* the entire hand on the pinky or little finger.

Don't think that because your child is blind, you don't need to show her how to hold a pencil. Your child will still need to know how to write her name. But more importantly, this same hand position is used to hold a stylus for writing braille with a slate.

It is difficult to sit down with your child and *teach* grasp because grasp depends so much on what is occurring in other areas of development. But by observing the type of grasp your child shows now, you can choose the toys and activities that will help her move along to the next step.

If you still see a predominantly reflexive grasp, for example:

Give your child lots of opportunities to lay on her tummy and thereby push up on her hands.

Place various objects in her hand: a foam hair curler, a rattle, a peg from a pegboard, etc. Choose items which are about the size of your child's hand; the reflexive grasp will force your child to hold the object, but the hands will be more open and less fisted.

Hang objects in your child's crib, or place your child in front of dangling objects when she's in a baby seat. This way she becomes accustomed to finding objects and responding to them reflexively so that when she's ready to be more deliberate she has already learned to *expect* to find things.

Vary the textures of the objects you use. Don't use all wooden blocks or all yarn balls. Provide a range of textures, colors, sizes, shapes, and even weights.

Remember that your child's visual impairment may prevent her from going after an object she's dropped, either because she just doesn't see it, or because she hasn't yet learned that the toy exists even when she is not in immediate contact with it. So, tie toys to her high chair, infant seat, jumper chair, and walker, using first a fairly short string that practically keeps the toy in one place, and then gradually lengthening the string as your child demonstrates her awareness and willingness to go after the toy and play with it again.

When you observe that the thumb is becoming part of the grasp, and a scissors movement is developing:

Choose objects of smaller size and those that are thinner, such as teething rings, or the popular brightly colored plastic keys, or canning jar rings. The goal is to choose those things that have to be grasped between the thumb and index finger, so that the thumb is forced to participate and therefore becomes stronger.

To continue the process, look for toys that require more manipulation by the thumb and index finger:

Allow your child to feed herself by giving her teething biscuits, crackers, pieces of banana and cheese.

Tearing up magazines, catalogs, tissue paper, and toilet paper, while messy, is fun and helps strengthen the muscles in the fingers and hand.

Sticky tape can also be fun. Placed on the tip of the finger, it is difficult to get rid of and causes some funny contortions.

With the emergence of a true pincer grasp, smaller and smaller objects can be introduced. But a word of caution is necessary here, too, or a sort of "Murphy's law" for babies: "Anything that *can* go into the mouth, *will* go into the mouth."

Use small pieces of dry cereal. Some parents also introduce raisins at this point, while others fear the child may choke and don't allow them until later. It is always best to check with your doctor or pediatrician, anyway, before trying new foods.

Use toys that require filling and dumping, like dropping clothespins into a plastic milk bottle, or placing blocks in a bowl. Toys are less likely to end up in the mouth if the child knows what to do with them.

Toys with crevices or recessed parts (such as a telephone dial, a form board, or a peg board) allow exploration with the index finger.

Almost any toy with moving parts is good at this stage, too, because it helps to separate the index finger from the rest of the hand.

Turn to page 101 in the REACHBOOK

The Second Important Skill: Reaching

Reaching is an important skill for children to learn because it gives them some control over the world. When a child has learned to reach, the choices of what can be played with and even what can be eaten are much greater, and the possibilities for decision-making and problem-solving are endless. Reaching is not an end in itself; it is a means to an end — to thinking, to choosing, to interacting with the environment. Reaching can make the difference between a dynamic and spontaneous child who actively explores the environment, and a passive or disinterested child who waits for the world to be brought to him.

Like the development of grasp, reaching has a natural progression. Your child will follow the same progression, regardless of how visually or multiply handicapped he is, although you may need to look more closely at the position your child is in, or the lighting conditions in the room, or the sensory qualities of the toys you choose. What is important is the *experience* of reaching, and that you don't make assumptions about what your child can and cannot do.

Reaching to Sound

Take reaching to sound, for example. In the "Taking Off" chapter we talked a little about the theory that blind children do not walk as early as sighted children because they do not learn to reach until much later. It has been suggested that the reason for this late reaching is biological: Blind infants have to use sound to guide their reaching, but no infant — blind or sighted — can reach to sound until 9 or 10 months of age. Therefore, they have to practice reaching much longer before they understand moving in space independently — that is, walking.

It, appears, however, that this so-called biological time delay in reaching to sound may be inaccurate. For one thing, in early studies of this subject the sounds were always made directly in front of the babies, blind or sighted, when they were being asked to reach. More recent research on how babies respond to sound suggests that this is the last place you would expect a child to respond, and that they in fact respond first to sounds made to the side, and at the same level as the ear itself.

Chapter 1 also discussed the problem of expectations — if you don't *expect* your child to reach until he is 9 or 10 months old, you don't *start* teaching him to reach until he is close to that age, and by that time you have already decreased his chances of learning to reach any earlier.

So, what does this mean for your blind or visually handicapped child? It means that you start early to set up situations for him to respond to, and that his reaching to sound does not have to be delayed. You can do this by:

Choosing a variety of squeak toys, rattles, bells, and other noisemakers that produce interesting sounds, and are close in size to what the child can hold, given his grasping stage. Be careful, however, that the noise is not too scary, shrill, or loud. Sometimes, the sound will overload a child's senses and he'll just "tune out" altogether.

Making the sound at ear level on the side first. Wait for your child to turn his head toward the sound. If he does not turn his head the first time you make the sound, make the sound again and gently push his head toward that side, then bring his hand up to touch the toy, and make the sound again.

Once your child can turn his head to sounds made at the side, change the position of the sound: move it down, *below* ear level. Your child will turn his head first to the side, and then down. Again, coordinate the sound with a reaching movement by taking his hand to touch the object.

When sounds below ear level can be localized, or turned to, the next position is *above* ear level. Use the same procedures you used above. At this point, you can also start moving the sound out in front of the child.

Prompting Reaching

Remember that a visually handicapped child may need a little extra help before doing what is expected. You may need to *prompt* his reaching at first: that is, using a hand-over-hand approach, take his hand to the toy and show him how to pick it up and hold it. By doing so, you give your child *feedback* in the *entire* arm, and let him know what is expected. Gradually, you reduce the amount of prompting you give, by

Holding at and moving from the wrist; then

Holding at and moving from the elbow; then

Lightly touching the upper arm, almost as a reminder to move, without actually doing the movement yourself.

The idea is to get your child to do more and more of the movement on his own, while still recognizing that he may need a little extra help.

Children do not start off reaching exactly to the object they want. They swipe at first, perhaps succeeding in hitting the toy, but not necessarily grasping and holding on to it. Children with good vision spend a lot of time monitoring their reaching by looking back and forth from their hand to the object they're reaching for. If they miss, they know what they have to do next time to reach correctly and get the object.

Children whose vision is impaired or whose perception is affected by a multiply handicapping condition, such as a motor or hearing impairment, cannot monitor their actions quite so easily. You can help your visually or multiply handicapped child by providing some of the feedback he does not get on his own. Tell him if he *almost* found his toy, or show him how he can use two hands at once to search for an object. The more information your child has, the easier his next attempt will be.

Eventually your child will be able to reach in all directions, get what he wants, and manipulate objects in various combinations — banging blocks together, putting beads in containers, dumping things out of containers — and even feed himself.

Reaching is important for visually and multiply handicapped children because it signals two major steps: (1) that the child *knows* something is, or might be, out there, and (2) that he can go out there and get it *on his own*. It is the beginning of active exploration of the world, and of making choices and taking *responsibility*. Sure, it sounds a little off-the-wall to talk about babies taking responsibility, but, as Chapter 7, "Looking Ahead" will point out, independence training really begins long before that first day of school.

It is very easy to take everything to the blind child — and, in fact, throughout these materials you are urged to do just that — but somehow in all this parenting/teaching, you also have to build in motivation, curiosity, interest, independence, and even excitement. This certainly is not easy, but these suggestions may help:

When encouraging your child to reach for things, don't pull his arm or hand forward to touch the object. Instead *work from behind*, so the reaching movement is coming from the child and is more like pushing than pulling. (Have somebody do it to you and see how *you* feel.)

Once your child has learned to reach, place things just a little farther away than arm's length. If he misses, show him how to reach a little farther by leaning forward or stretching out his arm.

Don't reward your child's frustration by feeling sorry for him. Make him do it one more time. *Always end in success* — don't stop until he does it on his own or with your help. Task analyze each activity you're working on so that you can break it down into small enough steps that will assure your child's success without getting to that frustration level.

Reaching opportunities can be found all day, in every situation: eating, dressing, bathing, playing. Reaching cuts across all situations and is not limited to a 15-minute teaching period. Let him reach for the pile of diapers, or reach for his foot to pull off his sock, or search for the soap in the bathtub.

Severely physically impaired children may not be able to reach. But they can show desire and motivation in other ways, such as smiling or nodding the head or lifting a foot. Watch for these signals and reward them.

Make up new situations. It gets boring to reach for the same things all the time, or to reach for the sake of reaching. After a while you say to yourself, "Why bother?" All activities should be done for a purpose, not as an end in themselves.

Shifting Weight

Up to this point, reaching has been discussed in terms of a fairly still, nonmoving child — that is, it has been assumed that the child was reaching from a sitting position, or while lying on his back. But reaching from a tummy position is also significant. In order to reach and grab something when you're lying on your tummy, pushing up on your hands, what do you have to do? *Shift weight.* You have to change your base of support from being fairly evenly distributed on both hands and arms to being supported on just one hand and arm. And that is no easy task if you have not developed head and trunk balance, or rotation, or if you simply have not spent a lot of time lying on your tummy. Then again, maybe no one has ever shown you how to do it.

You may question why this weight-shift reaching is important as long as your child is reaching in other positions. Well, think about crawling on all fours: Every movement forward means lifting one hand, temporarily supporting all weight on the second hand, moving the first hand forward, placing it on the floor, then starting the whole process over again with the second hand. Children first practice this when reaching from a tummy position.

It may help you at this point to go back and reread "Taking Off" to review the motor prerequisites: balance, rotation, tone, protective reactions, reflexes. As you do, think about the interrelatedness of reaching to each prerequisite skill. For example, can a child with an ATNR reach? Does a child need balance to reach? If your child has low tone, can he still reach out and pick up something? What if he has high tone?

Turn to page 104 in the REACHBOOK

The Third Important Skill: Voluntary Release

Voluntary release is the third fine motor skill needed for further development. It refers to how children let go of what they're holding. A voluntary release is one where the child is *aware* of what is being held and what she wants to do with it. Release is deliberate and controlled by the child.

Voluntary release is a long way from the earlier stages of development when the child's grasp is reflexive and occurs automatically without any thought attached to it. Weight-bearing, a more functional grasp, and the realization that objects can be manipulated for the child's own purpose all interact to make her aware of *what* is being held and *when* it is being held.

One of the easiest ways to tell if your child has a voluntary release is to ask her to give you what she's holding. As long as she understands what is being asked (and as long as she wants to be cooperative), a child will reach out and give you the toy. Children who fling toys around without examination or inspection probably have not yet learned that objects exist, or have not yet developed an informative grasp — that is, one that allows them to get information through their hands. The chapter on "Thinking it Through" will help you understand more about what is called "object permanence," while the earlier section in this chapter will help you with grasp.

Placing things in containers and dumping them out again is a favorite preschool activity. Children who do this are showing you that they have voluntary release and are curious about how things work. However, try to distinguish between a true release and a "relaxation" release. Adults frequently encourage babies to play these dumping-and-filling games long before babies are ready because it's a good social activity. A baby who is not yet ready will grasp the object tightly in her hand, hold it over the container, and do nothing (except laugh) as the adults in the room encourage her to "Come on, now, drop the toy. Drop the toy in the bucket." Finally, the toy drops out of the hand, but *not* because the child has voluntarily released it. The toy has dropped by accident, or because the child has finally relaxed enough that her hand isn't holding as tightly any more. Don't stop playing these games with your child, though, because they do help her learn; just be sure that what you call a voluntary release is something the child controls, and not something that controls the child.

Turn to page 106 in the REACHBOOK

Some of the activities you can do to help your child develop a voluntary release include:

Doing the same activities you did to help develop grasp. Your child cannot learn to release if she doesn't learn to grasp and hold onto things. It is the gradual process of grasp becoming meaningful, voluntary, and suited to the object being picked up that refines the muscles and sensitivity of the hand to the point where something can be released on purpose.

Hand-over-hand techniques are good for demonstrating what can be done with the hands. Show your child how to stack things, fill and dump containers with sand, water, cookies, or beads, and how to share food and toys with others. You don't have to wait until her grasp is sophisticated; these kinds of activities can go on at the same time the grasp is being developed and refined.

Try placing something sticky in the palm of your child's hands, like honey, pudding, or peanut butter. This may interest your child in licking her hands, which is good for hand-to-mouth activities and for learning to eat finger foods. But it can also be used to make her more aware of the experience of opening and closing her hands. The stickiness causes the fingers to stick to the palms and exaggerates the feeling of grasp and release.

The Fourth Important Skill: Wrist Rotation

Try to imagine what it would be like if you were not able to turn your wrist: You would not be able to open a jar of coffee, or play golf or ping pong, or even drink a glass of water the way you do now. You would have to find some way to compensate for the lack of movement, either by moving your whole body or by changing what you want to do.

Wrist rotation is the ability to move the hand from one side to another and back again. It is used when eating, drinking, scissors cutting, opening jars, spreading peanut butter, and a myriad of other activities that children and adults do every day. But it does not happen overnight: As you might expect, babies are not born with wrist rotation; it develops over a period of months as grasp, reach, and release are refined and become a part of the child's routine way of doing things.

Usually you can expect wrist rotation *after* a pincer grasp and voluntary release have been developed. But another landmark for you to use to determine if your child is ready for wrist rotation is the state of rotation in other body parts. That is, you would not expect to see wrist rotation before you saw trunk rotation, primarily because of the developmental principle of inner body (trunk) to outer body (arms and legs). In fact, however, while wrist rotation first appears about the same time as walking (that is, when standing balance, trunk and hip rotation are all in place), the child practices this new skill for many months before he turns the wrist back and forth completely and easily.

Turn to page 107 in the REACHBOOK

There are no specific activities you can use to develop wrist rotation. Continue to do the activities you have been doing and be sure to include eating and dressing and other everyday chores. *You don't have to teach fine motor skills as much as you have to provide practice opportunities*. This is because using the hands is so closely connected to eating, dresing, grooming, and playing that as long as you do these, the fine motor skills will fall in place. The catch is that you *do* work on these areas; you already know that they are important in developing independence and social acceptance. Now you know that they also help your child learn to use his hands as well.

Mouthing

A word about mouthing: Many teachers have written that mouthing — a term used to describe the almost automatic movement of an object to the mouth while it is still held in the hand — occurs for a longer period in visually and multiply handicapped children. It has also been suggested that mouthing has a different purpose for blind children — more a form of sensory exploration and verification than the short-lived phase that is usually observed in all children. Blind children supposedly use their tongue almost as a third hand — to explore cracks and crevices, texture, composition, and so forth. But you as parents should understand that this is only theory and has never been proven.

This does not mean that visually handicapped children are not using their sense of smell when objects are brought up to their mouths or noses. But it *does* caution parents against making more out of ther blind child's actions than they would their sighted child's actions. Mouthing is a natural part of development; it leads to self-feeding, and it is rarely observed in children who have developed a pincer grasp and are therefore assumed to be able to secure information through their hands. Older mentally retarded and emotionally disturbed children are also known to do a lot of mouthing, even with sight. But most babies stop indiscriminate mouthing when they are able to feed themselves, and they quickly learn what goes into the mouth and what does not.

Before you decide whether your visually or multiply handicapped child's mouthing is normal or okay (or both), ask yourself:

What kind of grasp does she have? Has she developed a pincer grasp yet?

Does everything go into her mouth?

Does she feed herself with fingers, or spoon, or both?

Is she eating a variety of foods of different textures so that you're certain her mouth is receiving enough oral stimulation?

Does it seem like a bad habit? Will it be difficult to change?

Does it really bother me? Do others comment on the amount of mouthing she does?

Your answers to the above questions will help you decide if your child's mouthing poses a problem, whether it's part of her normal course of development, or whether it is happening because she needs more experiences with her hands.

Associated Reactions

Severely physically impaired children may show "associated reactions" — movements in other parts of the body that have no apparent connection to the reaching movement. They concentrate so hard on getting all their muscles working and coordinated that there is some spillover into other body parts that they haven't learned to control yet.

Of course, some people never learn to control associated reactions: Do you stick out your tongue when you're hunched over working on a very tiny, very detailed, drawing? Or when you're trying to thread a needle? Do you open your mouth while applying mascara? Do you bite your lip when hammering a nail? These are associated reactions, too. Expect to see them in your child, but don't worry about them. You should look to see if there is some way you can position your child so that there is less spillover. For example, pillows on either side of the trunk may give your child some stability so that he can reach while in a prone position without struggling to keep from rolling over.

Choosing Toys

Children who are not totally blind can benefit from toys that are brightly colored or have high contrast, as well as toys with interesting sounds. As you do your toy shopping, choose toys with the following characteristics. Note, too, that you don't have to spend a lot of money on toys; for every characteristic listed below, a common household item is listed in parentheses.

Movable parts
(telephone, clothespins)

Bright colors
(Tupperware containers, soap bubbles, beach balls)

High contrast
(checkerboards, mirrors)

Noise-making abilities
(radios, hair dryers)

Interesting textures
(wooden spoons, dish towels, sponges, pillows)

Varying sizes,
depending on your child's grasp (mixing bowls, measuring cups, pots and pans)

Different weights
(pillows, bean bags, fruits, plastic bottles)

Other things to keep in mind as you select toy items are: Buy simple things first, then more complex ones. In the case of pegboards, for example, you might first use a toy car with one peg "person" to take in and out; then a pegboard with several pegs and holes of the same size; then a pegboard with several different sizes of holes and pegs.

Choose toys that require more gross motor movement before those requiring fine, small movements, such as exercise gyms for the crib before a "Busy Box." Select small toys that can be held and manipulated in the hand before larger ones: A child has to be able to do things with a cube before she can do anything with a puzzle.

School Readiness

The carryover from your attention to hand use into the school years will be obvious. As a child's grasp changes, so does the way she holds and uses crayons, pencils, and pens. Her ability to control them also changes. Writing braille requires strong fingers that can work independently of each other.

School readiness for multiply handicapped children also means paying attention to fine motor skills. First of all, you never know what they can do, or what their potential might be, without trying. Secondly, teachers of multiply handicapped youngsters will continue to work on fine motor skills because of their importance to self-help. Your work now will pay off later.

Writing and Drawing

As in almost everything else discussed in *Reach Out and Teach*, handwriting and drawing abilities are also learned in a certain sequence. Much of that sequence depends upon what a child's grasp and release look like, as well as how much vision he has and how he thinks, or processes information, about the world. So, as you look at your child's "artwork," always remember to judge it in relation to what is going on in his overall development. For example, scribbling is perfectly reasonable for a child who holds a crayon in the fist rather than in the fingers. But by the time the child has developed complete wrist rotation, you would expect a more adult-like grasp and more deliberate markings on paper.

Drawing and marking on paper has a definite progression: First, the child scribbles up and down without wrist rotation because a left to right (or horizontal) motion is difficult, and it is not as natural a movement as up and down (vertical), which is closer to a reaching movement. Then, the scribbling becomes more deliberate and controlled so that a single vertical line can be drawn, then a circle, then a horizontal line, then increasingly more complicated figures. Eventually stick figures representing people can be drawn, but to do so, children must have a good idea of their own body, as well as an imagination, or an ability to make a *symbol* stand for something else.

These paper and pencil activities should not be forgotten for visually and multiply handicapped children. There have been many artists with severe visual impairments (Vincent Van Gogh, for example) and many who are unable to hold a paint brush in anything but their teeth! But that is not the only reason for doing these activities with visually handicapped as well as sighted children. Drawing is the first step in learning to recognize the alphabet by touch and by sight because it is the first experience in putting shapes together.

Some activities you can use to help your child learn pencil and paper skills are:

Giving the young infant a chance to explore his food and in the process, of course, to make a mess.

"Fingerpainting" with soap bubbles, shaving cream, or flour and water mixtures. Show your child how to make the movements, how to use just the index finger, and perhaps most importantly, how to clean up.

Making big, whole body movements with the arms. Sometimes it's easier to draw a circle or a vertical line if you can first exaggerate it or make it super large, then gradually get smaller and smaller until it can be put on paper.

Shapes do not just exist on paper. Choose toys with shaped parts, such as a box with holes in various shapes and shaped blocks that fit through the holes.

Point out all shapes, like round donuts, square pieces of bread, round buttons, round bicycle wheels, square rooms, etc. Explain the various shapes of the body, such as a round face, a squarish body, and so forth.

Choose fat crayons until your child's grasp is refined enough to hold the thinner crayons.

Adapt whatever writing instrument you use so that it can be held by a physically handicapped child, such as placing a foam hair curler on it, or purchasing specially made adapters.

Paint sometimes with nontoxic white glue (known as "school glue") so a totally blind child can feel his paintings after the glue dries. Add food coloring to it if your child has color awareness.

Squeezing, rolling, and patting clay and other materials increase hand awareness and strengthen fingers.

String paintings, made by dipping pieces of string in glue and then arranging them on paper, add a touch feedback to your child's artwork. Add food coloring to the glue or paste to help your child's color awareness.

Choose coloring books with simple drawings — one object on a page, at least in the beginning, until your child is more accustomed to coloring and drawing. Some coloring books even have dark black lines. If not, glue string to the lines to help define the shapes for your child.

All of your activities in the fine motor area are designed first to help your child get as much information as possible through her hands and second, to take that information and use it in a meaningful way. Your child is picking up information about the people and objects around her with her hands.

Turn to page 108 in the REACHBOOK ➡

Chapter 5

COMING ACROSS:

Daily Living and Communicating

COMING ACROSS:
Daily Living and Communicating

An area of great concern to parents has always been daily skills — those activities of taking care of yourself (dressing, grooming, eating, etc.) that, once taught to a child, allow for greater independence for *both* of you. Since one of the major goals for visually and multiply handicapped children is to provide the freedom to help them become as independent as possible, teaching self-care skills becomes very important in the preschool years.

Teaching self-care probably feels a little more familiar to you than do some of the other topics discussed in *Reach Out and Teach*. It is something that you do yourself every day, and it is something that you have to teach all of your children, whether they are visually or multiply handicapped or not. However, when the child has a visual impairment, the task does seem a bit more complicated, and even experienced parents wonder about where to begin and how to teach.

Teaching Self-Care Skills

Before looking at any of the suggestions for teaching self-care skills, it is a good idea to review the teaching guidelines and strategies that you learned in Chapter 3, "Taking Off."

Teaching Guidelines

1. **Frustation is normal**, but don't let it get the best of you. Stop, relax, and then try again. Teaching any skill, especially to your own child, can be frustrating. Sometimes it may seem to you as if your child is always wrong and you are not getting the kind of feedback that *you* need to keep on teaching. You may also see that your child is learning small steps of the whole task, but still cannot complete the task herself. It seems to be taking forever.

Remember that as a parent, you are involved on a very personal level with your child. Your expectations are high, and when your child doesn't seem to be learning you feel as though you have failed as a teacher. Your child then begins to feel that she is failing you because she is involved on a very personal level, too. Frustration builds up, and soon you may find that you don't want to work at all with your child because both of you just keep failing. You both get angry, you both yell, and nobody makes progress.

This feeling of frustration is normal for all parents. It is not peculiar to you and your visually or multiply handicapped child. Everyone who tries to teach anyone anything, including teachers, has the same feelings. The difference is that you are personally involved, while a teacher can usually step back, analyze the situation, and come up with a new approach.

Think back to new situations in your life. Can you remember your father *trying* to teach you to drive, your mother *trying* to teach you to knit, your best friend *trying* to teach you a new game? How did you feel then? Were you always calm, peaceful, and happy? Probably not. It is important to keep this in mind when you try to teach your child.

It is also important to recognize *when* you are becoming *totally frustrated*. You need to step back, breathe deeply, wiggle your toes, stretch to the sky, or do anything that will give you a minute to calm down. A screaming match will not help. Sometimes just by relaxing, your child will relax, too, and you can begin again. It is important, however, that you finish the activity in some way, so that your child does not get the idea that her protests can make you do all the work for her, or get her out of working altogether. The more this happens, the more difficult it will be to control later.

2. Remember that you are the boss. You are the adult, and adults make the rules of the house. All parents make concessions to their life-styles when children come into the family, but after the initial shock of how much time and care a child takes wears off, adults adjust and develop some kind of a schedule that makes it easier for all family members to survive day-to-day living. This sense of organization, scheduling, and who's in charge is necessary for the family to grow. It is important that your child develops this sense of adult control right from the very beginning.

3. Make your child a do-er. It may be easier and faster to do things for your child, but you risk her becoming dependent on others to do things rather than learning to do them herself. For example, you may have taught your child to put on her own socks, but it just takes her so long to do it! Most of the time, you simply do not have 15 minutes just for putting on socks, so you help a little; it is easier, faster, and she can practice doing it herself on the weekends when you have more time. The problem with allowing this to happen is that your child soon learns that if she stalls long enough, you will do it for her. Before you know it, your child is 8 years old, and you are *still* putting on her socks.

Once your child knows the steps and can participate in the skill you are teaching, let her do it herself. She will become better and faster at it. She needs to find out that she *can* do things by herself, and that you expect her to do things *for* herself and *by* herself.

Some parents have ambivalent feelings about letting their children do things for themselves. "Will she still need me? Maybe if I keep doing things for her, she will always need me." Parents want to protect their children from all of life's traps. You can make life easier for her by doing for her; after all, she can't see and that makes it harder. But she needs to try, to fail on her own, and to grow on her own. After each accomplishment she will still need parents to help her conquer the next goal. It never ends.

Teaching Strategies

1. Use common sense. Teach new skills *when* they come up and *where* they come up. You want your child to learn for a purpose, not just for the sake of learning.

2. Try it yourself. Think about how you would do something, or how you would want someone to teach you, *before* you try to teach it to your child.

3. Be prepared. Make sure you have everything you need before you start.

4. Be spontaneous. Jump on that "teachable moment" no matter when it occurs.

5. Be consistent. Use the *same* words, work at the *same* time, in the *same* place, and follow the same teaching steps.

6. Work from behind. It is easier for your child to feel the movements when you are behind him, and it feels more natural to be moved from behind than to be pulled forward.

7. Give less and less help. Start out by helping your child by placing your hands on his and putting him through the movements. Gradually, move your hands to his wrists, then his elbows, and then perhaps just lightly touch his arms, as he learns to do more and more on his own.

8. Let your child help. Give your child a chance to feel needed, whether it's choosing clothes, setting the table, or picking up toys.

9. Give enough time. Remember that it may take your visually or multiply handicapped child longer to do a task. Give him enough time to finish.

Getting Ready

The most efficient and effective way of teaching self-care skills is to do it in a natural setting (brushing your teeth at the bathroom sink instead of at the table, for example) and at a naturally-occurring time (brushing your teeth after meals and before bedtime, instead of at a time that's convenient).

Turn to page 111 in the REACHBOOK

The method you use is the same one discussed in, "Getting Started": Task analysis. Think about blowing your nose, for example. The steps might be:

1. Pull tissue from box
2. Place tissue over your nose
3. Pinch both nostrils closed
4. Close your mouth
5. Blow
6. Open your mouth
7. Wipe the area around your nose
8. Repeat steps 2–7, if necessary
9. Feel to see if your face is clean
10. Throw tissue away
11. Wash your hands

With almost any of the self-care skills, the easiest way to task analyze is to go through the motions yourself and think about what you are doing as you are doing it. Look at each step and decide which ones are critical and must be taught, and which can be skipped. In brushing your teeth, for example, it is not really important to wet the toothbrush before you put on the toothpaste. That is an individual choice. What *is* important is that somehow the toothpaste gets on the toothbrush, the toothbrush gets to the mouth, and the teeth get brushed.

Turn to page 112 in the REACHBOOK

It is also important to have everything you need to teach the skill you're working on in one place, and to keep it there all the time. This is another reason for teaching in a natural setting and at a naturally-occurring time, since the tools you will need are more likely to be there already. If toilet training takes place in the bathroom, regardless of whether or not you use a potty chair, the toilet paper, soap and water, and towels are already there and waiting.

But if toileting occurs in the child's bedroom, what happens if you forget the toilet paper? This could be frustrating for both you and your child, as well as messy. But more importantly, your visually impaired child cannot see where you go to get the toilet paper, and she is left with the "Fairy Godmother Syndrome" because the toilet paper seems to come out of nowhere. Eventually, she will have to make the transition from bedroom to bathroom for her toileting needs, and it will save time, confusion, and misunderstanding later on if you start in the bathroom in the first place.

Think, also, about your own feelings of frustration and disappointment when you started to bake brownies at 10:00 one night and discovered that you didn't have any flour. Your time was wasted, you made a mess that you had to clean up, and you didn't even get your chocolate fix. Your child can have these same feelings if you are not prepared.

Turn to page 113 in the REACHBOOK

Now that you have reviewed the teaching guidelines and strategies and are ready to start, here are some suggestions for helping your child learn feeding, dressing, and toileting self-care skills.

Eating Skills

1. Be consistent. This means eating meals at the same time every day. If mealtimes or even the number of meals varies from day to day, your child may not know what it feels like to be hungry. When meals are at the same time each day your child knows the feeling of hunger, and begins to anticipate that it is time to eat.

> **It is very important** not to give snacks to your child all day long (unless, of course, your doctor prescribes it). If you do, you will probably not have much success at mealtimes. Remember that snacks also include drinks (other than water) because they, too, are very filling.

Of course, there are days when this consistency just cannot take place. That's all right — don't worry about it. But make inconsistency the exception and not the rule.

2. Eat meals in an area designed for eating, not in front of the television, on the floor, in the family room, by the telephone, or in bed. Your child needs to learn where things belong, and it is important to teach him where food comes from, how it is prepared, where the dishes and utensils are kept, and how the dishes and utensils get clean again.

3. Prepare the eating area so that your child and you feel comfortable about the mess that is sure to be made. If your child is trying to spoon soup into his mouth and it runs down his arm on the floor and you get upset about it, he will stop trying to feed himself. If you are a person who cannot tolerate messes, your child may never learn to feed himself.

> **Before your child** comes to the table, place a plastic sheet, an old rug, or some newspapers under his chair. This will make it easier to clean up any spills or dropped food.

4. Eating is a social behavior. People need to learn the rules of eating, and this is accomplished only with other people.

> **If your child** has many feeding problems, you may choose to feed him before the rest of the family eats. But you should still include him at the table with the rest of the family during the regular meal.

5. Make your child sit upright for mealtimes. Food may slide down easier if your child is lying down, but it doesn't help him learn about swallowing and chewing.

If your child cannot sit by himself, prop him with pillows or hold him in your lap in a sitting position. The infant seats that can be adjusted to various levels are also a good way to increase your child's sitting position gradually.

6. Be sure your child is in a comfortable position in furniture that fits him. His hips, knees, and ankles should be bent; he should lean slightly forward; and his feet should touch the floor.

If your child's feet do not touch the floor, place something under the feet to support them, such as a footstool or a box. This helps him to define his space and keeps him from feeling as though he is hanging in mid-air. For multiply handicapped children this can be especially important because their feet need to be flexed to prevent them from going into extension and perhaps slipping out of the chair.

7. Avoid interruptions. Let your friends, neighbors, and relatives know when you eat meals so they do not drop in or telephone at an inconvenient time. You and your child have much to do, and interruptions in the routine will confuse your child and may not permit you to follow through on your plans. Interruptions can add to the frustration level for *both* of you as well.

8. Work as often as you can in a quiet setting. This helps your child to understand what you are saying and helps develop a calm atmosphere. This in turn helps to lower your frustration level.

9. Use the same words for plates, glasses, napkins, and different foods, and always place them on the table or tray in the same position. This will also help develop your child's anticipation.

10. Use your regular dinnerware and utensils as soon as your child is able to handle them. Plastic cups, plates, and tableware are okay when your child is learning, but he also needs to learn to use glass, silverware, and china. He will not always use plastic and paper dishes throughout his life.

There are many different dishes and silverware available that might make your teaching easier. Check in the "baby needs" section of the local drug or department store for:

Cups with a spout top or a slit that help your child move from bottle to cup without spilling.

Cups that are weighted on the bottom so that they cannot be tipped over.

Bowls and plates with suction cups to keep them anchored to the table.

Spoons and forks with bent handles to make scooping easier.

Choose dishes that are brightly colored (red, orange, yellow) to encourage use of vision and ones that are unbreakable.

Take a paper or plastic cup and tear out a section, such as shown in the illustration below. This does not crowd your child's nose, allows him to breathe, and does not block his vision.

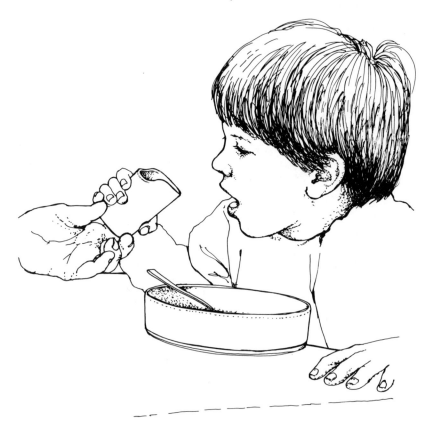

Melmac dinnerware and Corningware dishes are also good. If these are your everyday dishes, your child can learn on these and not have to switch later. If you are worried about the plate or bowl moving around, a little honey or pancake syrup on the bottom will give it more stability.

11. Make sure that the foods you give your child are nutritionally balanced. Introduce all different kinds of textures to your child, and do not give up if he spits it out, gags, or chokes. All children react this way when new foods are first introduced. Keep trying, and remember that you're the boss.

Turn to page 116 in the REACHBOOK

12. Start out with small portions so that your child can have success in finishing meals. It is important to teach that a task — any task — should be completed, and by giving your child a small portion, you build in success. It sounds much better to say, "Oh, you want more cereal!" than to say, "Finish your salad."

13. Let your child touch food when he is first learning to identify it. Carrots feel different before they are peeled than they do after peeling; they feel even more different when they are sliced, cut in strips, cooked or mashed. Your child needs to feel the different ways foods can be prepared and presented. Even though you want him to be able to identify foods, you will want to be sure he understands that *playing* with food is not acceptable.

14. Give your child enough time to eat so that he can practice being independent. Don't expect him to finish his meal in 10 minutes. On the other hand, you do not want to allow the meal to drag on for so long that you finally end up feeding him yourself out of frustration and impatience. This teaches your child to "hold out" for your help. If he does not finish the meal in 20 to 30 minutes (whatever you think is appropriate), the meal should be over anyway.

15. Teach your child to use a knife and fork once he becomes independent with a spoon. Spearing foods is more efficient than scooping, and adults usually use all three utensils. When you see a multiply handicapped adult eating with a spoon, it only makes him appear more handicapped. Start your child early.

16. Let your child participate as much as possible in preparing the meal, setting the table, and washing, drying, and putting away the dishes. These chores help develop your child's independence and his anticipation of events. Many children are also more willing to try new things if they can help out and really participate in the activity.

17. Work from behind when teaching your child to hold a spoon, scoop, drink from a glass, or any eating activity that requires a

motor movement. This helps him to feel the exact movement being made. It also provides for reassuring and comforting body contact between parent and child.

18. Reinforce your child! Tell him when he is doing a good job and that you are proud of his efforts.

Turn to page 118 in the REACHBOOK

Suggestions for Teaching Eating Skills

1. Be consistent. Try to eat the same number of meals at the same time every day
2. Eat at the same place for all your meals
3. Be ready for messes
4. Eat your meals together, as a family
5. Make sure your child sits upright
6. Be sure your child is in a comfortable position
7. Avoid interruptions
8. Keep the noise level down to normal conversation
9. Use the same words each time for foods, dinnerware, utensils, and actions
10. Let your child use the same dinnerware as everyone else in the family
11. Prepare meals that are balanced in variety and texture, as well as nutritionally sound
12. Give small portions
13. Let your child touch food, but not play with it
14. Give your child enough time to eat
15. Introduce knives and forks when ready
16. Let your child help
17. Work from behind
18. Give feedback

Dressing Skills

1. Be consistent again. Choose consistent places for dressing and undressing, such as the bedroom in the morning and the bathroom at night. This helps your child learn where it is appropriate to dress and undress.

Also think about *when* your child gets dressed and undressed. It does not matter if you eat breakfast first and then dress, or if you dress before breakfast. What *does* matter is that you use the same order each day and dress at approximately the same time each day. This helps your child to anticipate the events of the day.

2. Choose clothing for your child that is easy to manage. This may mean that your child will not be able to wear all the current styles. Bib overalls, for example, as cute as they are, are very difficult for a child to unbutton and pull down independently when she is in a hurry to use the bathroom.

When you buy clothing for your child, think about how she will be able to use it independently, rather than how stylish it is. Zippers, elastic waistbands, and velcro closings are easier to manage than buttons, and large buttons are easier than small buttons. As your child masters these easy openings, choose clothing with more and more buttons and snaps to challenge and help her achieve independence.

Choose shirt openings that are stretchy so that your child can easily put her own shirt on and take it off. The stretchy opening helps her to remove the shirt faster and doesn't make her panic because it gets stuck on her head.

When your child is first learning the steps in dressing, buy her clothes a little bit bigger than she actually needs. This makes the dressing process easier and allows for independence.

3. Keep your language consistent. Use the same words for each piece of clothing, and let everyone who works with your child on dressing know what these words are. It can be very confusing if mom talks about ''pants,'' dad talks about ''jeans,'' and the teacher talks about ''trousers.''

4. Make sure your child gets dressed each day. This helps your child to separate day from night. If this separation is not made and your child spends all day in her pajamas, she may confuse day and night — and then *you* will have a problem getting any sleep!

5. Teach dressing skills from behind the child. Place your hand over hers and guide her through the activity. As you do this, you will gradually feel her anticipate what is next and begin to do it herself. When you notice this happening, allow her to do it on her own. Eventually you will be able to back off and just help her out with verbal instructions.

Sometimes it is easier for you if you and your child dress in front of a mirror. That way, you can work from behind and still see what you are doing.

6. Talk about colors as you dress your child, and later as she dresses herself. Especially when your child is young, you are never sure how much color vision she will have. By using color words you familiarize her with the concept of color and with the words themselves, and by helping her match outfits you begin to teach her about what goes together and what does not. Maybe she will never be able to identify an orange shirt and purple pants by sight, but she *will* be able to tell you that they don't go together.

7. Let your child help and actively participate in the purchase of and daily selection of her clothes. And show her where to put her dirty clothes when she takes them off and how to fold and put away her clean clothes. While you're at it, show her where the washer and dryer are, too.

8. Give your child enough time to accomplish the skills by herself. Get her up a little bit earlier in the morning if you need to so that she has time to dress herself.

9. Use common sense. Dressing helps your child develop a sense of time. Certain clothes soon begin to mean that certain activities will be taking place. Putting on a jacket, for example, usually means that you are going outside. If your child learns to put on her coat without going outside, it will be difficult for her to understand *why* she has to learn to put on something that only makes her hotter, and she will probably resist doing so.

Suggestions for Teaching Dressing Skills

1. Be consistent
2. Choose easy-to-manage clothes
3. Use the same words for each piece of clothing
4. Make your child get dressed every day
5. Work from behind
6. Talk about colors
7. Let your child help
8. Give your child enough time to dress independently
9. Use common sense

Toilet Training

Most people recognize that toilet training is a long-term process. Childen can be dry two or three days in a row, and then have a day where they wet or soil themselves two or three times. Everyone has bad days, but somehow when those days are associated with toilet training it seems to be a major battle of wills just to get through the day. Patience and consistency in how you handle these days will make all the difference in how quickly your child becomes toilet trained. Remember these guidelines:

  1. Frustration is normal
  2. You're the boss

In order to begin toilet training with your child, he must be able to hold urine, or stay dry, for 1½ to 2 hours. If he cannot do this, he will not know the feeling of a full bladder, and it is this full bladder feeling that leads people to the bathroom. If he does not know the feeling of a *full* bladder, an *empty* bladder will not mean very much.

Toilet training is more than using the toilet. Keep in mind as you are teaching that it also means:

  Recognizing that full bladder feeling
  Finding the bathroom
  Pulling down pants
  Urinating or having a bowel movement in toilet
  Wiping
  Pulling up pants
  Flushing toilet
  Washing and drying hands
  Leaving the bathroom

Many parents have found the following suggestions helpful:

1. Keep a schedule of your child's toilet habits for at least one week, using the forms included for that purpose in your REACH-BOOK. Check your child every half-hour and write down if he is wet or dirty. After a week, look at the schedule and try to choose a time when it looks as though your toilet training will be most successful. For example, if your child is always wet at 8:30 A.M., you would toilet him at 8:15 A.M. Your chances of success will be much greater if you can build on your child's natural signals.

Turn to page 119 in the REACHBOOK

2. Give your child extra fluids if no optimum time is apparent from your schedule. This will help him to develop that full bladder feeling. Take him to the bathroom shortly afterwards, and see if he will urinate. Hopefully, he will soon associate that full bladder feeling with sitting on the toilet and not having that full bladder feeling any longer.

3. Do not let your child wear diapers during the daytime once you begin toilet training. Rubber pants, disposable diapers, and cloth diapers all keep a warm, comforting feeling close to the skin, and your child will not know the discomfort of being wet or dirty. There will, of course, be accidents. But your child will not know he is having an accident unless he can feel it.

You will need to be particularly patient at this time. Treat accidents calmly. Tell your child about it, let him feel the outside of his pants, clean up, and then go on about your routine.

4. Toilet training belongs in the bathroom. It may be easier for you and more convenient for your child to keep a potty chair in the kitchen, but most people do not urinate in the kitchen. Your child needs to know the proper place to accomplish all self-care activities.

5. Make sure your child's feet are flat on the floor when he is sitting on the toilet. If his feet don't touch the floor, place a footstool, board, or box under them. It is uncomfortable to be hanging in mid-air, and it can be frightening to have to balance over an open toilet.

6. Stay with your child when he is on the toilet. You want to be there to praise his success as it is happening, not after the fact. Besides, he may find it confusing if you leave the bathroom, return, find that he has urinated, and *then* praise him. From his point of view, you could be praising him for sitting still while you were out of the room.

7. Let your child know that this is not playtime. Toilet training is serious business, and your child is sitting on the toilet for one purpose only — not to play in the sink, read a book, be read to, or play with toys.

8. Do not keep your child on the toilet longer than 10 minutes at the most. If he does not urinate or have a bowel movement, he simply does not. He is not holding back on you. And if he does seem to wet himself right after you've left the bathroom, take it in stride. Be patient, and work on your timing.

9. Use a reward for successful toileting that is highly motivating for your child and *only* used when he urinates or has a bowel movement on the toilet.

Some tricks that might add to your child's success include keeping the bathroom cool rather than cozy warm so that your child doesn't enjoy spending a long time in it; pouring warm water over your child's genital area; placing your child's hand in water (but not to play); and running water from the faucet.

Suggestions for Teaching Toileting Skills

1. Be consistent in the words you use to describe toileting acts
2. Keep a schedule to find out when your child will be successfull
3. Give extra fluids to help your child know the feeling of a full bladder
4. Keep your child in underpants during the daytime
5. Do your toilet training in the bathroom
6. Make sure your child is properly positioned on the toilet, well balanced and with his feet supported
7. Stay with your child when he is sitting on the toilet
8. Let your child know that toilet-time is not playtime
9. Keep your child on the toilet for 10 minutes only
10. Choose a reward that is given only for successful toileting

---

Learning to Communicate

Learning self-care skills is certainly important for developing your child's independence. But an area that is critical for *all* your child's learning, and for her ability to get along with others, is communication.

Children begin communicating at birth, regardless of whether or not they are visually or multiply handicapped. Cries, gurgles, laughs, lip smacks, and babbles are basic forms of communication which later develop into a language system that can be either verbal or nonverbal. The best communication teachers have always been parents; you teach your children how to use words and language, and even how to "talk" without words, through your daily interactions with your child. Everything you do — hugs, kisses, touches, hand gestures, facial expressions, body postures, and eye gazes — are part of the entire communication process, and your child is learning just by being near you.

Often, when parents discover that a child has a vision problem or other handicapping condition, everything seems to focus on the problems. Natural ways of communicating are lost because it doesn't seem like you are getting through. The critical question you need to ask yourself is, "How would I talk with my child if she were not visually impaired? Would I act any differently?

If this is your first child, listen carefully to how your friends talk with their children, and try to use them as models for the way you talk with your child. Also listen to what children of your child's age who are not visually impaired are saying, and talk about similar things and interests with your child. Talk with your child about things, events, and people in natural environments. Just as you toilet train in the bathroom because that is the most logical place to use the toilet, so, too, should you talk about rolling a ball to your child when you have a ball to roll.

The first few years of communication — both exposure to language and practice of language — lay the basis for all further language learning. Your child will use this foundation and apply it to new situations. If your child is older and seems to be experiencing some problems in the language area, you can try teaching her by using some of the suggestions included in this chapter for younger children. Just like in every other area of development, language builds on what is already in place. If your child is having feeding problems, chances are she will also have speech problems — because the same muscles that are used for grinding and chewing food are also used for speech. But her *receptive* language — what she understands when someone else speaks or gestures — can be highly developed.

If you think that your child has a serious language problem, you should contact someone qualified to evaluate the situation. Your pediatrician can usually refer you to a speech and language clinic, or your early childhood program may have a speech pathologist on staff. Although speech and language development is one area that varies widely among children, it never hurts to check with someone else if you are concerned.

Turn to page 125 in the REACHBOOK

First Communications

Babies begin communicating from the moment they are born. Some mothers have even said that their babies communicated *before* birth by the way they moved around in the womb. During the first month of life, most babies will respond to the human voice and to touch by quieting. Most of the sounds they make are crying sounds, although they also make throaty noises. Parents soon learn to distinguish among their baby's various cries, noises, and movements. They know which cry or movement means hunger, which means tired, which means wet, and which means pleasure.

Sometimes parents of a visually or multiply handicapped baby may anticipate their child's needs a bit too much, and not allow their baby to cry or show through other behaviors what he wants or needs. While you should not let your child cry or struggle endlessly, try to remember that cries, movements, and other behaviors are basic forms of communication in the early months, and your child has to learn to express himself even in this simple way. Try not to overanticipate your child's needs, but do be responsive to his basic effort to communicate.

Cooing is an exciting stage of communication during the first few months. Typically, it begins when the parent and baby gaze at each other. The baby makes a cooing sound, and the parent imitates the coo, sometimes without being aware of doing so. Sighted babies raise their eyebrows and open their eyes widely while waiting for the parent to respond. It is during this period that parents and children first enter into a communication partnership of *turn-talking*. Turn-talking is really the springboard of communication; all other communication takes off from here. Everyone takes turns — listening and talking, talking and listening — when they are with another human being.

When a baby is visually impaired, however, he may not be able to look at his parents. The feedback that parents depend on is therefore missing. Mothers, fathers, and the visually impaired infant will need to depend more upon what they hear and feel than on eye gaze in order to get the feedback they need to play the cooing game and to turn-talk. Your visually or multiply handicapped child *will* learn to turn-talk and to coo, *if* you give him lots of auditory and tactual feedback and make it a fun, relaxed time.

During the first few months of life, your child, like all children, will spend a lot of time listening to what is going on around him. He recognizes familiar voices and knows when the uncle with the deep, gruff voice is visiting, even if it is only occasionally, because the voice is different. In addition to coos, he is now able to gurgle at the back of the throat, to chuckle, and to squeal. Happily for you, he soon will begin to cry less and use other vocalizations, gestures, and movements to communicate.

Your child is also learning to socialize when he is communicating with you. Many babies soon begin to babble in strings of sounds, making vowel and consonant sounds as they get older. Turn-talking becomes even more obvious during this period because babbling seems to be infectious: The more the baby babbles, the more the parent talks (and babbles!) back.

Turn to page 126 in the REACHBOOK ➤

Although it is not known exactly how important a role vision plays in learning to talk, it is known that older babies with normal vision pay particular attention to adults' mouths as they are talking. Take your child's fingers and place them on your lips as you babble to each other. This will help him to associate the sounds with you and your lips.

Give your child lots of opportunities to touch the people he cannot see very well. This will help him begin to associate familiar voices with familiar touch and familiar odors.

Sighted babies turn to sound sources soon after birth. This is one way that they begin to associate voices with people. Children who are visually impaired can also turn to sound, but in the beginning they may need to be shown where the sounds are coming from. This is done by pairing touch with the sound. For example, when you walk into a room, be sure you identify yourself by telling your child who you are, and let your child touch you. Your routine might go something like this: "Hi, Timmy. Here's mommy, I'm home from work. Let me give you a big hug!" If you then open the closet door to hang up your coat, your child will hear the closet door opening and closing. Tell him what you are doing. Your child needs to hear explanations of those things that most children understand by using their vision and watching events occurring around them. If you carry your baby in a sling, he can also "help out" as you open and close the closet door.

Although your child certainly does not understand everything you say when he is still an infant, remember that children understand words and other communicative behavior long before they begin to talk. When your child is visually impaired, you need to talk *more*. Your words must substitute for what cannot be seen.

Name your child's toys as he plays with them, no matter how young he seems. And expand on just naming by saying things like, "Oh, that's your sound ball. It's soft and round and fuzzy. And you can shake it, too. Listen to the bell when you shake your sound ball in your hands." If he drops the ball, teach your child how to search for it with his hands. Don't let the sound disappear into nowhere.

At first, you may feel like a chatter box because it seems like you spend so much time talking. Many parents report, however, that talking with their child helps them to relax, forget about their child's vision problem, and to focus upon the many ways that their child communicates *without* vision.

Try not to spend all your talking time just naming objects and toys. You also want to point out similarities, remind your child where he saw or touched the object before, and show him how he might use it. *Make connections.* It is not easy for your child to do this himself because he cannot see the connections, but your conversations will help him put the pieces together.

Ask less questions and give more answers. Adults tend to ask children, particularly those who are not yet talking, a lot of questions, maybe because the adult then answers the questions in his own head. But your young, visually or multiply handicapped child needs the answers. Avoid using the question method until your child is in law school.

Quiet time is just as important as listening time. Don't you get exhausted when you're with a non-stop talker? You can exhaust your child with your non-stop talking, too. Worse yet, your child may tune you out altogether and just not listen.

The Second Stage: Imitation

As your child babbles more, she will begin to *imitate* sounds. This is the signal that your child has reached the next stage of communication, and that she is beginning to understand more of what you are saying.

Your child will begin to *anticipate* things that happen in her daily routine. If you give her a favorite blanket, she knows it is time for a nap. It is helpful to associate objects or clothing with things that happen every day . For example, a plastic plate might be used only at snack time, and a particular sweater might be the signal that it is time to go outside and play in the sandbox.

If given the opportunity to associate such things with events, the child who does not yet talk (and even the child who *cannot* talk) will communicate a message when she brings you her sweater: She is telling you that she wants to play in the sandbox. *Communication does not always mean words.*

It is exciting when your child says her first real word. Just remember that some children, sighted and visually handicapped, are listeners for a long time before they learn to talk.

Turn to page 128 in the REACHBOOK

While your child may learn to say "da-da" and "ma-ma" during this stage, children usually use more gestures and nonsense sounds than they do understandable words. They begin to imitate intonation — the rise and fall of your voice. If you say, "Are you hungry?" your child will often babble back with the same intonation (notice how your voice rises at the end of a question?). And while your baby may say "da-da" it is quite possible that for her "da-da" has a variety of meanings, such as food, daddy, or *any* man she sees or hears. But don't take it personally.

During the early part of the imitation stage, your child will learn the meaning of *no*. Other behaviors you might see during this stage include looking in the right direction when someone says, "Where's daddy?" and pointing at a toy she wants. She will also make a calling sound, such as "ga!" to get your attention.

While sighted children learn to use gestures and pointing naturally, without being taught, you may have to let your visually impaired child *feel* gestures if you expect her to learn to use them appropriately.

   When you go to pick your child up, lift her arms upward first, say "up" at the same time, and *then* pick her up.

   Teach pointing by using the child's body to play games. For example, you might say, "Where's your nose?" and then help your child touch her nose with her hand or finger. Later, play the game on *your* body by having her point to your nose, ears, hair, mouth, etc.

A sense of self is important, but it is also necessary to develop an awareness of other people and things outside the self. Show your child that a toy is within arm's reach: Take her hand to the toy and then show her how to reach in the right direction without your help. You are playing language, motor, and cognitive games all at the same time — teaching words and at the same time making your child aware of her body, your body, and objects around her. You will find more information on body and self-awareness in Chapter 6, "Thinking it Through."

While visually and multiply handicapped children need help in learning how to point, it is a critical part of both language and fine motor development. Teaching pointing will not only help language growth, but will help your child orient herself in space.

Turn to page 129 in the REACHBOOK

The Third Stage: Expanding Vocabulary

As your child continues to grow and learn, he will begin to recognize the names of important people, pets, and objects in his life. You began this process months ago when you named people and things for your baby. During this stage you should continue naming things, allowing your child lots of opportunities to feel the things and people that you are talking about.

When you are labeling in this way, think about the many different ways we see things. For example, your child's kitty cat is not always dry and it is not always sleeping. If the kitty comes indoors after getting caught in a rainstorm, let your child *feel* its wet fur. Food also takes on a variety of different visual and tactual characteristics. Your child needs to understand that an egg is an egg, whether it is in the shell, raw (hopefully in a bowl and not on the floor), fried, scrambled, hard-boiled, or baked in a cake. Many visually and multiply handicapped children develop incomplete ideas of everyday things in the environment because it is all too easy to forget to show them that an object can be the same object even when it looks and feels different.

It is particularly important that a visually handicapped child's language, both internal (what he understands) and external (what he says), is *reality-based*. What does an elephant mean to a totally blind child? He can *smell* it; he can even touch *parts* of it; but he will never be able to put all those parts together to get an idea of how enormous an elephant really is. Help your child by:

Using concrete examples. Whenever possible, use the real thing. A plastic mammoth with long, pointed tusks does not mean a whole lot (particularly when it is an extinct animal).

But if your child can touch and explore a live turtle, the meaning of phrases like "turtleneck" and "hiding in a shell" will have more meaning.

One of the first words children learn is *no.* Your child needs to hear you say "*no*" when he does something wrong or he will not learn to use the word himself. If he doesn't learn to stop whatever he is doing when you say "*no*," it may one day result in his getting hurt. Don't be afraid to tell your child no; there are ways you can do it without damaging your child's self-concept or curiosity. When he learns to say no himself, he has begun to use words meaningfully to control the environment.

Turn to page 130 in the REACHBOOK ▶

Most children during this stage also love to listen to nursery rhymes and children's songs. Records or tapes can be used by your child to give you some free time, and you can feel reassured that your child is practicing a very important part of language learning. But it is always better to listen to recordings with your child and to sing along with the rhymes or songs. Nothing replaces *your* personal contact, so, as often as possible, read to your child yourself and use recordings only as a backup.

A little listening can go a long way: Many older visually and multiply handicapped children isolate themselves from their families by listening to radios, stereos, Talking Books, and other recordings. Remember, communication requires at least two people, and even the finest machine cannot replace a human being.

Turn to page 131 in the REACHBOOK

Do not forget to talk about your child's clothing. Identifying and naming the various pieces will not only help your child learn language, but will reinforce your training in self-care. You should also talk about where your child's clothing is kept, where it is put when it is dirty, and where and how it becomes clean again. From your child's point of view, a closet is an open space where he can feel only the bottom of his jacket. Show him the pole, the hanger, any hooks, and demonstrate how high they are. You are not only teaching your child words, you are teaching ideas and concepts. If you involve your child in getting his jacket, if he feels that he is part of the activity, then he will be motivated to learn the appropriate words.

Use simple sentences with your child when teaching the names of objects. Using the example above, if you give your child the hanger, say something like: "Here's the hanger. Someone's jacket is on the hanger. It must be your jacket. Let's take the jacket off of the hanger. Then you can wear it."

Talk to your child normally and naturally. Sometimes parents get so involved in labeling that they sound like a recording: "Hanger. Yes, that's right. Hanger." Always listen to what you are saying and ask yourself, "How would I say this if my child were *not* visually impaired?" Then, allow him to feel what he cannot see.

Toward the end of this stage, a child's speaking vocabulary increases to around 20 to 50 words. Toddlers begin to put two words together to express an idea, such as "milk gone" or "more cookie." They know the names of most things in their home environment, they watch television, and they listen to stories. They have come a long way from that first word, both in understanding and in using language to communicate.

Turn to page 132 in the REACHBOOK

Continuing Your Child's Communication Growth

The communication strategies you have been using are useful throughout your child's preschool years. In fact, throughout your child's growing years, you will need to name and describe new objects and events, while allowing your child as much opportunity as possible to experience them directly. Talk *with* your child in give-and-take situations. Although parents are the primary teachers of language and communication during the early years, be sure your child also has an opportunity to communicate with children her own age, through play and sharing activities. Sighted children begin to socialize with other children and adults at about the same time as their independent nature begins to flourish, and one of the first ways you will notice this is through your child's games and play; her refusal to share a toy with a playmate (and the playmate's subsequent reaction) is a good example of both communication and independence. Interacting with other people in a positive manner is important not only to the development of your child's independence, but to her continued language learning. Independence training and social interaction are greatly facilitated by communication skills, and vice versa; and whether your child is able to speak or not, she still must be able to *communicate*.

Visual Impairment and Language Learning: Some Problems

There is much about language learning that is still a mystery, even to researchers who specialize in the study of language. The struggle that deaf children have in learning to communicate suggests that hearing plays a vital role in language learning, but it is not known how critical a role vision plays. Some visually handicapped children do have problems. As parents, you should be aware of some of the difficulties that your child might encounter.

Language Delay

Many visually handicapped children experience a delay, or slowing down, in learning new words, usually around the *end* of the second year. Children of this age basically talk about the toys, pets, and people they are involved with. Sighted children are curious about what they see, and what they see motivates them to touch. Because your child cannot see, or cannot see clearly, you need to motivate her by bringing people and things to within her arm's reach, or by taking her to those items that cannot be moved. Your child needs first-hand experiences, not second-hand stories.

Throughout your child's life she will need oppportunities to talk about the things and people she interacts or comes in contact with. Although you might expect and witness delays in learning new words, you can help to minimize them by providing your child with a variety of experiences with you, other people, animals, and objects — being sure all the time to talk *with, not at,* your child. The more variety the better because generalizing (applying one experience to others) can be misleading. One totally blind child, for example, who was going sailing with her parents, stood on the dock and asked, "Is this the hickory-dickory-dock?" Her knowledge of "dock" did not fit her current experience. The next time she runs into "dock" (such as "pad*dock*"), she will have something new to think about.

Turn-Talking

Talking *with* your child means that you give him chances to talk to you, too. As you recall, turn-talking occurs first at the cooing stage. Communication requires taking turns, an interchange of listening and talking in which each person has a chance to make his needs known and to be responded to. When a child is slow to answer, you might feel that you have to fill in and provide the words for him. But don't. Visually and multiply handicapped children may need a longer time to respond; give them the time they need, and do not try to anticipate what they are going to say. Even children with normal vision will continue to point to toys they want instead of using the words they know if parents are too quick to respond. Let your child have time to ask for things before you step in.

Another problem develops in the later years with turn-talking. Once they have a command of language, some older visually impaired children tend to monopolize the conversation themselves. You need to teach your child to take turns at listening, too. Make him aware of how many people are participating in a conversation.

Teach your child to turn toward the person who is speaking. When your child is young, you can begin doing this by helping him turn his head in the direction of sound. Later, once you are sure you have his attention, be sure he faces you as you speak. This is a critical communication and social skill that will help your child throughout life and make it easier for people to talk with him as well.

Echolalia

Echolalia simply means that the child is acting like an echo, repeating what she hears. Most children are echolalic at some point, usually around the stage when they are putting more and more words into sentences. Some visually impaired children maintain this stage of echolalia beyond the time when they should have outgrown it.

Echolalia can be an indication that your child does not understand what has been said. Simplifying your language — using shorter sentences, and giving only one direction at a time, for example — may help your child get through this problem. If you are concerned that she seems to repeat more than other children her age, consult with your doctor. Your doctor will know what other children are doing and whether your child might benefit from seeing a speech and language pathologist.

Children Who Do Not Speak

Some visually handicapped children, because of their additional disabilities, never learn to speak. Even though some children are not able to talk, *all* children communicate. As parents, *you need to be responsive to all types of communication* — cries, smiles, gestures, facial expressions, body movements. Even though your child may not be able to speak to you, you should continue to speak to him. A teacher or language specialist can help both you and your child learn *other* ways to talk together. For example, a child who has both hearing and visual impairments can communicate with you using sign language and finger spelling, and a child who has motor impairments can use a communication board that has been specially designed with tactual cues.

Although visually and multiply handicapped children may seem to have more problems in language learning, remember that sighted children, too, can be delayed, echolalic, and unable to speak. Difficulties in language learning are not necessarily caused by visual impairment, and it should *never* be used as an excuse for your child's communication problems.

Keep this in mind. Talk with your child as if she were *not* visually impaired, and give her lots of time and opportunity to touch and interact with things and people she cannot see. *You* can accomplish more than any specialist who may work with your child just by being you and being a parent. All children learn language and learn to communicate in some way because they have superb teachers — their parents.

Notes on Additional Reading

Just as development proceeds in many directions at the same time, many of the readings mentioned in Chapter 1, "Getting Started" and the other chapters of *Reach Out and Teach* touch upon communication and daily living skills. The following readings deal with these subjects more specifically.

In *Raising the Young Blind Child: A Guide for Parents and Educators*, by Kastein, Spaulding, and Scharf, Chapters 1, 12, and parts of Chapter 9 deal with the development of language, while Chapter 3, 10, and 14 deal with skills of daily living. This is also the subject of Chapter 5 in *Show Me How: A Manual for Parents of Preschool Visually Impaired and Blind Children*, by M. Brennan. *Tune In!* by Yates, is a guide for developing listening skills, which must be mentioned here because of its importance in the development of language. *Talk to Me: A Language Guide for Parents of Blind Children*, by Kekelis and Chernus–Mansfield, deals with language more directly. There is also an article, "Traditional Nursery Rhymes and Games: Language Learning Experiences for Preschool Blind Children," by Blos, which may be helpful. Finally, *Preschool Learning Activities for the Visually Impaired: A Guide for Parents*, from the Illinois Office of Education, contains many suggestions related to daily living skills, and so does the more recent *Workbook for Parents & Teachers: Teaching the Visually Impaired Preschool Child 2–5 Years Old*, by J.S. Galante.

For the child with cerebral palsy, *I Wanna Do It Myself*, by C. Gimbel and K. Shane, pages 48–66, deals with activities of daily living, as do Chapters 5 through 9 in *Handling the Young Cerebral Palsied Child at Home*, by Finnie; Chapter 10 deals with speech problems.

For the child with severe hearing impairment, Chapter 6 in *Understanding the Deaf-Blind Child* by S. Freeman deals with communication and Chapter 7 deals with daily living skills. *Leisure Time Activities for Deaf-Blind Children*, by L. Mikalonis, will also help to develop communication and self-care skills at home, while *A Practical Guide to the Training of Low Functioning Deaf-Blind*, by M.J. Watson and J.L. Nicholas, provides suggestions for a team effort of parents and professionals working towards these goals.

In *Beginning with the Handicapped*, by V. Hart, Chapter 2 deals with self-care skills, and Chapter 5 with communication for children with various severe multiple handicaps. Similarly, in *A Comprehensive Program for Multihandicapped Children: An Illustrated Approach*, by S. Jegard et al., Chapter 4 deals with communication, and Chapter 8 with self-help skills.

Finally, useful suggestions may appear in the quarterly *National Newspatch* from the Oregon School for the Blind. For additional information on all of these publications, see the Bibliography at the and of this HANDBOOK.

Chapter 6

THINKING IT THROUGH:

Knowing Oneself and Understanding the World

THINKING IT THROUGH:

Knowing Oneself and Understanding the World

Sensory Development

Almost everyone is taught as a child that there are five senses: touch, taste, smell, hearing, and vision. You probably memorized this list and can now recite the names of the five senses if someone asks you. But you have probably spent very little time thinking about what these senses actually mean in terms of *how* you receive information from the world. They have become so automatic that you are not even aware when you are using them.

How would you describe someone you met at a play group? You might say that the person was tall, heavy set, smelled like onions, and when he walked by you his arms felt very hairy. Or you might describe one of your parents as being soft, chubby, full of laughter, and smelling of lilacs. See how you used those five senses to put together descriptions of what your environment is like? You relied on some more heavily than others to form images and associations about the people around you.

Turn to page 133 in the REACHBOOK

Now that you know your child is blind or visually impaired, what does this mean for his sense of vision? What kind of adaptations or changes need to be made in order for him to understand the kind of information that is usually given by vision?

People often think that a visually handicapped person's other senses are automatically sharper. But this is not necessarily true. Visually handicapped children (and adults) require experience and specific training in order for their other senses to become more helpful.

This chapter will look at these five senses, discuss how they develop in children, and talk about some ways you can help your child get the most out of using all of his senses. As you read, remember that how *you* experience any given situation may not be how *your child* experiences the same situation. You, because of your vision, your age, and your experience, are able to put together all the pieces of sensory information you have, evaluate them, and come up with one conclusion or one thought about the situation. Your child may not be able to do this: He may know all the bits and pieces, but not know how to put them together. Or, he may have one sense that is so strong and so overpowering that it is difficult to gain any information through the other senses. Then again, your child might be able to put all the pieces together, but his interpretation may not be the same as yours. Try to keep these ideas in mind because they may help you avoid misunderstandings, and keep you from making assumptions about what your child is and is not able to do.

Smell and Taste

Typically, the senses of smell and taste give a child the smallest amount of informatioin about the world. Smell can, however, be a powerful learning tool to a visually impaired child. You should try to make the best use of your child's sense of smell from her earliest days by doing things like:

Always wearing the same perfume.

Labeling unique smells in your home environment (e.g., onions) and always using the word "onions" when they are in use — fried, soup, raw, sliced, or diced.

Walking into the kitchen and saying, "Oh, we are having chicken soup tonight."

Always rely on *your* sense of smell to point out smells to your child.

Turn to page 135 in the REACHBOOK

Taste may be very different for your child to use to obtain information. Often, visually and multiply handicapped children do not seem to like food and mealtimes in general, and they refuse to try new textures and flavors. However, there are many occasions when your child can be using her sense of taste *without* eating, such as sucking her thumb, licking a toy, or kissing mommy who has on lipstick. All of these experiences involve taste, and you will help your child be aware of her sense of taste if you use words to explain those taste experiences to her.

The sense of taste may indeed cause battles, but your child needs to try and have words for as many tastes as possible — sweet, sour, salty, tart, bland, spicy, bitter, etc. These experiences at an *early* age help your child in her willingness to try new foods. (See Chapter 5, "Coming Across," for more information on eating skills.)

For both smell and taste, it really is not important to know *how* they develop. What *is* important is that you give your child as many experiences as possible with these two senses.

Turn to page 137 in the REACHBOOK ➤

Touch

The sense of touch is a very important one for visually impaired children. You may also hear it referred to as *tactile development* or *tactual development*. Touch means not only use of the hands and fingers for information but use of *any* part of the body, such as feet, head, lips, arms, and even tummy.

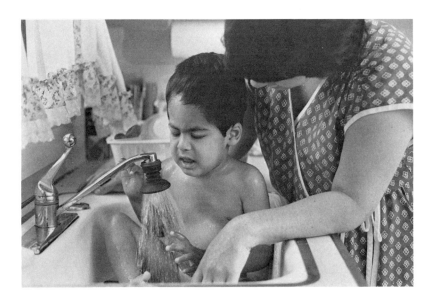

Tactile Defensiveness

Your child may be quite happy to touch things himself to gather information but not allow you to touch him to give him information. This is something called *tactile defensiveness*. It is important that you:

Keep touching your child.

Use a firm touch instead of a light one (sometimes your light touch can feel more like tickling and actually be upsetting to your child).

Make sure that many different people touch and caress him.

Dress him in a variety of different textures (smooth, silky, cotton, corduroy, denim, fuzzy, etc.).

Allow him to touch different foods, toys, fabrics, and people.

Teach him to search in a systematic way. For example, always moving his hand from:

top to bottom, then from
left to right, then from
the lower left diagonally to the upper right, then from
the upper left diagonally to the lower right, and then
around and around in circles that get increasingly larger
and larger.

The sense of touch and how your child uses it will be affected by how much vision he has and how well he uses it. At times, when your child feels threatened because the activity is new and he is unsure of what he is doing, you may find that he uses old ways of tactual exploration before he explores an object visually. He is trying to compare the new information with his old memories. While this is fine, and shows that your child is thinking, be sure that he does not use touch exclusively and deny the use of his other senses.

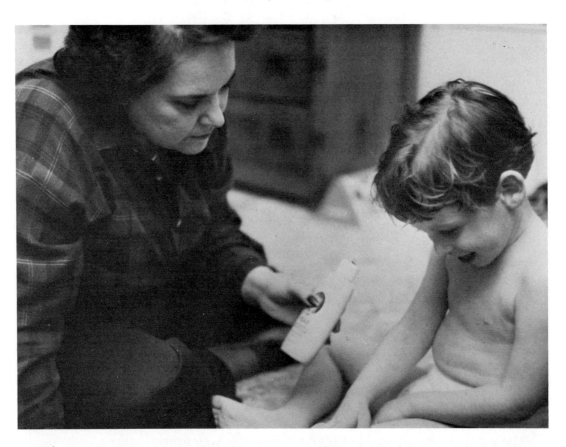

Turn to page 138 in the REACHBOOK

Vision

Your child's visual perception of the world progresses in an orderly manner. It does not happen overnight, but improves over time as your child becomes better able to interpret, or make sense of, whatever vision she has. Knowing this sequence will help you to decide what you need to work on next, and to determine how much vision she actually is able to use.

In the past, visually handicapped children were taught *not* to use their vision: They were blindfolded, taught braille, and made to use their hands for exploration regardless of how much vision they had. School-age children were placed in "sight-saving" classes. As more and more was learned about the visual system, however, people began to wonder what children were supposed to be saving their vision for. Scientists who studied vision in animals, for example, found that the amount of light that entered the eye affected the growth of the visual area of the brain, and that animals who were raised in total darkness were *unable* to see once they were brought into a lighted environment, in spite of the fact that nothing was physically wrong with their eyes.

Educators of visually handicapped children began to reexamine their teaching methods, and it soon became apparent that visually handicapped children could be *trained* to use their vision better, even though their actual *amount* of vision did not change. It was their ability to *interpret* what they were seeing that made the difference.

One point to remember about your child's vision is that the only way you can be sure she cannot see is if she does not have eyes. Otherwise, you should be constantly checking to see *if* she can use her vision, *how* she uses it, and *when* she uses it. It may be that she is able to use her vision in some situations but not in others, depending on the lighting conditions, time of day, and how tired she is.

The best way to find out about a child's use or potential use of vision is to observe her and to interact with her in all kinds of situations. Your child will not always show a doctor or teacher all of the things she can do, particularly in a strange setting like a clinic or doctor's office. (Refer back to the "Questions You Should Ask Your Eye Specialist" and the "Questions Your Eye Specialist Should Ask You" in Chapter 2 for ideas on how and what you can find out about your child's vision.) Remember, too, that the word "blind" does not necessarily mean that your child can see nothing; don't let these labels scare you, and don't let them affect your judgment.

Turn to page 139 in the REACHBOOK

To ascertain your child's stage of visual skill development, it is easiest to look at how most children learn to use their vision. For children who have normal vision, this is not a conscious process; it just happens. But children with visual problems often need to be taught how to develop a skill, and then how to move from one skill level to another.

The Visual Response Continuum

There are nine general principles that describe how children respond visually to their world. Each principle is a continuum, or range of responses, starting with the most basic or minimal response, and leading up to the highest level of response that can be expected. Individual children will respond at any point along each continuum and will usually be at different points in each. Visually and multiply handicapped children will follow each continuum to a greater or lesser degree — that is, they may respond at one end of the continuum, but have difficulty moving to the other, or be *unable* to move to the other end because of their eye condition.

As you observe *your* child's response in each continuum, you might want to refer back again to Chapter 2, "Talking it Over" and to your eye specialist's answers to your questions.

Awareness ► Attention ► Understanding

A child will be *aware* of lights and people or objects before he will pay attention to them, and before he can *understand and interpret* what it is he is seeing. This explains why an infant will close his eyes when the lights are turned on, but does not recognize his parents until he is older.

Lights ► People and Objects

A child will react to lights before he will react visually to the faces of his parents and to his toys. Infants will focus in on lights, but they will not pay attention to the toys in their cribs until they are older.

Fixation ► Tracking

A child will *fixate*, or focus, on lights and people or objects before he will be able to follow them as they move. Children have to be able to maintain their focus without moving their eyes before they can focus *and* move their eyes at the same time.

Near ► Far

A child will respond to lights and people or objects that are close to him before he responds to those that are farther away. A baby's ability to focus at different distances depends on the ability of the lens of the eye to change shape (and thus focus), and on the ability of the muscles of each eye to work together to focus at the same point. Like the muscles responsible for gross motor skills (see Chapter 3, ''Taking Off'') and fine motor skills (see Chapter 4, ''Picking Up''), the eye muscles at first are fairly tight. With use, they become more flexible and can adjust to focus at greater and greater distances.

Peripheral ► Central

A child will respond to lights and people or objects located in the outer portions of his visual field (the periphery) before he responds to those in his central field. This explains why infants sometimes do not seem to see a toy placed directly in front of them, but do seem to focus on it when it's slightly off-center.

Familiar ► Unfamiliar

A child will respond visually to those things in the world that are familiar to him before he responds to something new, or unfamiliar. Eventually, he will *prefer* to look at new things. This explains why babies seem to avoid looking at anyone other than their parents in the first couple of months and then seem fascinated by new faces.

Parts ► Wholes

A child will look at *parts* of faces and objects before he can see the *whole* face or object *all at one time*. When being cradled in the arms, for example, newborns are actually looking at the hairline or eyes of faces — places of high contrast — and not seeing the entire face. Later, they begin to see the *whole* face and not just the parts. This explains why babies don't recognize their parents as being different from anyone else until they are 5 months or older.

Simple ▶ Complex

A child will respond first to simple patterns before he will respond to more complex patterns. Younger babies will first prefer to look at things that are plain and simple, such as one toy of one or two colors — a quilt of solid color patches; a soft, fuzzy patchwork ball; a stuffed panda; a music box mounted on the crib slats. Later, mobiles, crib gyms, and busy boxes become more interesting to look at. This also explains why a rattle placed on a patterned crib sheet may not be seen — because there is too much complexity in the visual field, and the child is not able to separate the *figure* (the toy) from the *ground* (the sheet).

Large ▶ Small

A child will respond to large patterns and objects before he responds to smaller ones. So, he will pay attention to a large ball before he pays attention to a small ball. For example, if you show a young baby two checkerboards of different sizes but of the same color and number of squares, he will look longer at the larger checkerboard. Later he will prefer the smaller one.

Depending on the eye condition, the large to small continuum may not apply to children with visual impairments. If there is a field loss, a large object may be so large that all the child sees is one solid color with no lines or contours. If the child has a central loss, a small object may be missed altogether. Check your eye specialist's answers to questions number 7 and 8 from Chapter 2, "Talking it Over."

How to Make Use of this Visual Response Continuum

This visual response continuum has value to you as a parent only insofar as it helps you to understand what your child is seeing and how you might help her to see more. The activities suggested below do not guarantee that your child will use her vision better, but they will give her the best *chance* of learning to use and benefit from her visual sense.

To summarize the visual response continuum:

Awareness ► Attention ► Understanding
Lights ►People and Objects
Fixation ► Tracking
Near ► Far
Peripheral ► Central
Familiar ► Unfamiliar
Parts ► Wholes
Simple ► Complex
Large ► Small

To use this continuum, observe your child and decide what you think she responds to in each category. Your REACHBOOK will help you.

Turn to page 140 in the REACHBOOK

Following are examples of how you might use what you now know about your child's vision to facilitate development of visual skills.

If you find that your child seems to be *aware* of lights but does not *track* or *follow* them, you would start your activities by:

Working on **fixation** or focusing
   (Fixation ► Tracking)

on **unmoving lights**
   (Lights ► Objects)

presented **close** (7–9 inches) to his face
   (Near ► Far)

and slightly **off-center**.
   (Peripheral ► Central)

If your child seems to *focus* on and know you, *tracks* or follows you with her eyes when you walk away from her, but doesn't look at the toys in her crib, then:

Work on **fixation** or focusing
   (Fixation ► Tracking)

on **one large toy**
   (Lights ► People and Objects)
   (Simple ► Complex)
   (Large ► Small)

presented **close** to her body
   (Near ► Far)

in a crib with **solid-colored** sheets, or when lying on a solid-colored blanket on the floor.
(Simple ► Complex)

Once she looks at or *focuses* on the toy in this situation, then:

Move the toy slowly.
(Fixation ► Tracking)

When she *follows* the toy, then:

Move the toy
(Fixation ► Tracking)

farther away.
(Near ► Far)

Once your child is able to track a toy that is not close to her face, then you could:

Try **fixation**
(Fixation ► Tracking)

on **another toy.**
(Familiar ► Unfamiliar)

As you can tell, there is no set formula for how you use this continuum, except to think of all the response possibilities as *guidelines* for your activities and expectations.

Turn to page 143 in the REACHBOOK

Other suggestions for working on your child's visual awareness and understanding include the following:

Look for some signal that your child is aware of light, such as turning her head, quieting, a change in her breathing rate, or a smile. But just because she does not give you a signal does not mean that she cannot see the light. The light may not yet have meaning for her, or it may be so stimulating (too bright, too intense, or even too painful) that she has learned *not* to react.

Observe your child in different emotional situations — known vs. unknown; stressful vs. unstressful; when she feels well vs. when she feels ill; when she has just awakened from a nap vs. when she's tired. Your child may respond differently depending on how she feels.

Observe your child's reactions in different kinds of lighting — colored, indirect, fluorescent, reflected, flashing; and when the source of light is coming from different directions — behind her, in front of her, over her left shoulder, over her right shoulder, from above.

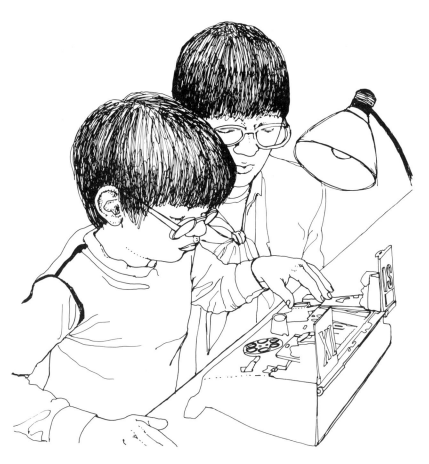

If your child has seizures, use one of the "Cause-Action Consequence" pages from your REACHBOOK to see if any particular lighting situation seems to set off a seizure. There is disagreement among medical and educational professionals about whether or not any type of light (fluorescent, flashing, black light, etc.) can set off seizures. Ask your teacher, doctor, and eye specialist for their opinions, but *your* observations will give you the most information.

Give you child as many sound, touch, and smell clues as possible. For example, when daddy comes near, daddy should say something like, "Hi, big girl!" (or whatever nickname daddy uses). Then have your child feel daddy's face (maybe a beard, mustache, bald head, glasses, or five o'clock shadow). Talk about daddy's smell (oily from the car, like fresh grass after mowing the lawn, musky from his aftershave). Daddy should look at his child and encourage his child to look back.

You will need to talk about all these characteristics of people and objects so that your child will begin to associate objects, people, their names, and their sensory characteristics with whatever visual image she can see.

Just as you teach your child to look at and get clues from things close to her, teach her to use all the clues she can from people and objects at a distance. Play games with her to find things. Keep moving these objects farther and farther away, or into more complicated situations, such as partially covering a red ball with a blanket. You might find that she is able to find the red ball when it is 3 feet away, but if you put a patterned blanket partially over it, she cannot find it — perhaps because the pattern is too confusing, or because she cannot separate out figure-ground information (the ball looks to her like it is part of the blanket).

These kinds of games will give you much information on how, when, and where your child can see. Always include different people (children as well as adults) in the games you play to increase your child's awareness.

Your child may prefer small objects over large ones because she can get the whole picture. For example, she will prefer a small rattle to a teddy bear because a rattle has more visual meaning — she can see it all at one time. To your child, the teddy bear may be just a big patch of brown fur.

When your child looks at faces she begins to realize that she is not the only one in the world. She needs many visual (as well as other sensory) experiences with people in order to develop her body image and the separation of her body from other bodies. (Body awareness and self-awareness are discussed in more detail later in this chapter.)

Watch for your child to begin looking at small objects both near her and far away; she will visually scan the crib, room, and playpen for favorite objects.

Help your child to get the large picture of the object and to find the same object in different situations by helping her to use her hands.

Use puzzles to help your child put two or more pieces or objects together to make a whole. Your child needs this phase of visual development to develop problem-solving skills. Begin with simple puzzles of two, three, and four pieces, and gradually build up to more complex puzzles of several pieces.

Work with your child on matching objects (such as two shoes), matching objects to pictures (such as a child's shoe to a picture of a child's shoe), and then matching pictures to pictures (such as a picture of a child's shoe to a duplicate picture, and then a picture of a child's shoe to a different picture of a shoe).

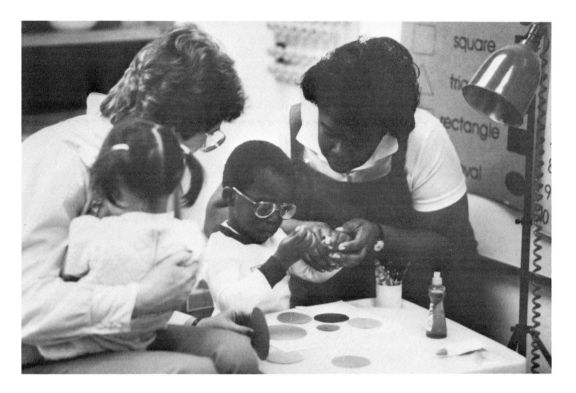

Visual–Motor Skills

As you think about your child's use of vision, remember to think about how the eyes are constantly moving. Think about your own eyes: You look up, down, sideways, and you do not move your head in order to do this.

When working on tracking or following moving objects, you might have to hold your child's head still so that he follows with his eyes only. Be sure to hold the light about 8 to 12 inches away from him, and make sure the light source is not too strong (penlights are better than flashlights). Cover the light with cellophane or transparent plastic in his favorite color. Encourage your child to use his vision, and provide opportunities for him to follow moving objects in everyday situations — following the spoon at mealtimes, watching the spaghetti disappear into brother's mouth, following you as you leave the room and then peek around the corner of the door.

Expect your child to be able to track *horizontally* first (from left to right and right to left), then *vertically* (from top to bottom and bottom to top), then *diagonally* (upper right to lower left and upper left to lower right), and then *in a circle*.

Work with your child on finding the most comfortable distance and location possible for any of your play and learning times. Your child's ability to pay attention to activities may be governed by *how long* he is able to maintain his focus. Let your child decide how long is good for him, then give him a break and go on to something else.

Give your child opportunities to use both sides of his body by thinking of activities that require him to cross over from one body side to the other. At the table, place the salt shaker on his right side, have him pick it up with his right hand, and give it to his sister sitting next to him on the left. Or if your child has a motor impairment on one side of his body, try placing his favorite toys on that side so that he has to reach to get it with his other hand.

Give your child a variety of experiences where he "looks and then gets":

> "Oh, do you want your bottle? Here it is. That's right, you looked at your bottle. You can have a drink now. Here it comes. Boy, that tastes good!"

Think of how every experience and every activity of the day can be used to promote reaching and at the same time develop your child's use of vision.

Place objects into containers and help your child to find them. Use bright or high contrast colors, such as raisins in a yellow plastic bowl, or oranges in a paper bag.

There are many activities you and your child can do on a daily basis that involve using both visual and motor skills:

Ball play. Roll, catch and throw balls of various sizes, colors, and weights. Do this inside, outside, standing up, sitting down, with two people, three people, four people — any way you can think of.

Building. Stack blocks or dishes; use big cardboard blocks to build a play space; make bridges.

Stringing. Beads are available in many different sizes, shapes, and colors. (Buy them from a craft store if they're too expensive at the toy store; or you can use pasta from the grocery store.) As your child gets older, you will want him to string his beads to copy a string of beads that you have made, and later to copy a string of beads from a picture.

Drawing. Use crayons, paints, pencils, felt-tip pens, and chalk for: scribbling; copying circles, squares, and triangles that you make; drawing people and pets; learning to write your child's name.

Cutting. At first your child will only chop with scissors, so let him chop away on old magazines and catalogs. Let him cut open a bag of chocolate chips when you bake; let him practice on a large square outlined in thick black lines.

Pasting. Use colored tissue paper, construction paper, 3-dimensional objects like pasta shells and buttons, and simple pictures from magazines and catalogs.

Climbing. On chairs, sofas, stairs, jungle gyms, sliding boards.

Kicking. Large and small balls, while standing in place, while running.

The purpose in all these activities is to help your child gain understanding from his visual world. But your child's vision by itself is not enough for learning; it is how *all* the senses work together that is important. Regardless of how much vision your child has — even if he only has light perception — he needs to use it in conjunction with his other senses to get the most benefit.

It is probably tempting to spend a lot of your limited time working on helping your child to use his vision more effectively. Unless you continue to work on *all* sensory areas, however, any visual improvement could be wasted. Try to keep your child's visual development in perspective, and build sensory awareness and attention into all your everyday interactions with your child.

Hearing

Hearing is the sensory area that many people think is most important for a visually handicapped child. While it is also believed that blind people have better hearing *because* they are blind, it is not necessarily so. Hearing, like all the other senses, needs to be developed.

Children are well known for getting colds and ear infections that can affect their hearing. If hearing is your child's main way of learning, then you will need to watch for colds and any changes in the way she is using her hearing. It is sometimes difficult to spot hearing problems because:

1. They are not as visible as, say, an eye problem;

2. There are so many other things going on with your child that it is easy to overlook; and

3. Children do not themselves know if they are not hearing, so they cannot tell someone about it. (You may remember how an elderly relative was losing her hearing, but she seemed to be the only person who didn't know it.)

Observe your child's use of hearing so that you will be able to spot a possible ear infection before any damage is done to the ear. And be sure to check with your doctor, an audiologist, or a speech and language pathologist if you have any concerns about your child's hearing.

Turn to page 145 in the REACHBOOK

Your child's *use* of her hearing develops in much the same way as her vision. The guidelines below will help you understand how children learn to use their hearing, and should help you to focus in on what your child is doing.

Awareness

A child usually gives some signal that he is aware of sounds in his environment — his sucking movements might stop; his breathing pattern or rate might change; he may turn his head to one side; or he might stop all movement and get very still. All of these are signs that the child is aware of a change in the environment. At first, the response may only be to gross sounds, such as the vacuum cleaner, loud music, or door slamming. Generally, however, even very young children will respond to the sound of a human voice. So, look for an awareness of voices, loud noises and, gradually, responses to more ordinary household noises like the clock's ticking, the coffee pot's perking, and water running in the shower.

Your child may be confused by all the sounds usually present in your house, and thus may choose not to pay attention to any of them. Your job will be to alert him to the sounds, tell him what they are, and make him more comfortable and relaxed with them.

Most children learn by observing where the sound is coming from, such as talking comes from mouths, music comes from stereos, doorbells come from a box in the hallway or a buzzer on the door, and so forth. Because your child cannot see very well, you will need to help him understand the *origin* of sound, as well as the sound itself, because it will help him make connections with his other experiences:

"Yes, you're right. That *is* the water running in the kitchen. Your brother is running the water in the sink so he can do the dishes. When you get a little older, *you* will wash the dishes, too."

Turning to Sound

Once your child has shown you in some way that she is aware of sound, the next step you would expect is that she would try to *find* the sound, usually by turning her head. At first, your child's search might seem random, but as she gains experience she should be able to turn directly to the source.

Help your child turn her head in the right direction by placing your hand on her cheek and pushing gently but firmly.

Try to give as many opportunities as possible to turn to sound throughout the day. If you make turning to sound simply a routine that you repeat over and over, your child will lose interest very quickly and not repeat the action. Then it will appear that she has not yet learned to turn to sound, when she actually has learned that turning to sound has no purpose.

Show her that turning to sound *does* have a purpose by *taking her hand to the sound.* You will probably do this anyway when you are giving your child reaching opportunities. Use toys that have other sensory qualities, such as a two-color squeeze toy that has interesting textures and makes sound with very little hand pressure.

Turning to your voice can be particularly rewarding if you give a kiss when your child does it.

Localizing Sound

Once your child has shown that he can turn to sounds, he will begin to turn to sounds no matter where they are. Remember the sequence for reaching to sound that was discussed in Chapter 4, "Picking Up?" Children follow that same sequence in localizing sound:

1. Ear level, on the side
2. Below ear level
3. Above ear level
4. In front

If your child is multiply handicapped and cannot turn his head to localize sound, look for eye movement to sound. And even if your child is totally blind, he will turn his eyes to sound, at least in the beginning. If he is not reinforced, however — that is, if you don't give him any feedback that yes, it was good to turn his eyes toward the sound — he will not continue to do it.

Try different sounds at different distances to see which sounds your child likes best and how far away the sound is when he no longer seems to respond. You want to use his favorite sounds on bad days when you know he needs a lot of motivation.

If your child does not seem to respond the first time, make the sound last a little longer. Sometimes visually and multiply handicapped children need a longer time to figure out where the sound is coming from, or their response is delayed because of other problems.

Check to be sure your child's response is the same at both ears. If it is not, check with your doctor to see if there is an ear infection in the ear that seems to be less responsive to sound. Everyone has a side that he likes or uses more than the other, so you might find that your child simply has a preference.

As in all other activities, localizing sound is not an exercise done in isolation. Every sound is an opportunity to find out more about your child's ability to localize, so look for his response when playing, eating, dressing, walking outside, and reaching.

Meaning to Sound

Your child will learn more about sounds if you are sure to name the sound for her and to point out its other sensory qualities. The sense of touch is important here because as a sound is made a vibration is given off. The information gained from the vibration is helpful to your child in identifying the sound in other situations.

Remember that often the word for a sound has many different meanings. Take "bell," for example. There is a telephone bell, the doorbell, the church bell, the alarm clock bell, the school bell, the bicycle bell, and so on. You need to be specific about the words you use so your child does not get confused. Think what it would mean to you if you had just learned about the bell that rings when someone is at the door of your home, and then one day when you are in the park with your mom, she tells you about another bell — but you know you are not at home, and you don't hear anyone talking to your mom. The second bell was a bicycle bell, which *you* might be able to see, but your child cannot. Use the words "*doorbell*" and "*bicycle bell*."

Using Sound in the Environment

When you are teaching your child about the meaning of sound, you are usually concentrating on one sound at a time. There are actually several sounds being made at any one time, but you have *chosen* the sound that you want to tell your child about. Your child will also need to learn how to pick out the important sounds — those that will give him the most information — and to ignore the sounds that do not give meaning. This skill will become critical when your child is learning to move about in the environment. If he tries to pay attention to all the sounds in the environment, he may not hear the car coming.

Before your child gets to this step, you should have started to help him distinguish one sound from another. For example, the television may be playing when you call his name. Does he hear you call him and does he show you, either by turning or some other signal? Or do you have to touch his shoulder to make him aware that you called him?

When you start working on this, make sure that the new sound you are introducing is very different from the sound that is in the environment. Gradually work your way up to sounds that are not much different, and play games such as "What made that sound?" and "Can you find the _____?" to see if he can identify the source.

Different sounds can be important one time and not important the next. For example, the sound of the refrigerator's humming is not important if you are in the kitchen eating a meal. But if the refrigerator is located next to a down staircase without a door and you are crawling around on the kitchen floor, the sound of the refrigerator can be *very* important — it can signal that you are close to a dangerous area.

Turn to page 146 in the REACHBOOK ➤

Body Awareness

Body awareness is the child's first step toward developing an idea of who she is and what she is capable of. It is an important part of sensory development, although it is not strictly sensory because it involves almost every aspect of a child's learning.

When babies are first born, they are almost victims of their own reflexes and of the sights and sounds around them. It takes a while to sort all of that out and to gain a little control over the movements they make. But even then, there is little evidence that young infants know that their body is anything different or separate from their parent's bodies, or even from their cribs. At that point, the entire world is there to satisfy *their* needs.

The first time a baby gives a sign that she recognizes that her body is something separate and apart from the rest of the world is when she notices her hand. It can be quite funny to watch: The baby catches a glimpse of her hand as it moves by, seemingly coming out of nowhere and taking her by surprise, and then she holds it there, in mid-air, staring at it! Many developmental checklists and formal tests use this hand-staring as a milestone of behavior because it signifies the child's first awareness of her own body and the beginning of her efforts to control what she does with it.

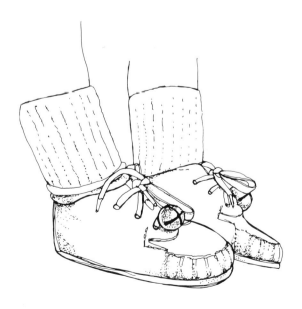

For a severely visually handicapped child, or for a multiply handicapped child who has motor impairments, this milestone may never occur. (You can't stare at your hand if you can't move it within your line of vision.) But the behavior, sorting out your body from the rest of the world, is still important. Other ways of building body awareness in visually handicapped children, include:

Tying jingle bells to her shoelaces and to her wrists so that everytime she moves she hears the bells ring. Later, as her motor skills get better, she will feel the bells when she plays with her feet and fondles her hands. Also, try sewing the wrist bells to the top of a baby sock so that you can slip them on and off easily.

The massaging activities you read about in the "Picking Up" chapter are also good for body awareness.

Almost any activities from Chapter 3 help children to develop a sense of their different body parts. Weight-bearing on the hands and on the legs and feet is particularly good — when the body has to fight against gravity, it literally feels the weight. Try it yourself by holding a potato in one hand and a gallon container of milk in the other: Which arm feels it the most? Which one are you the most aware of?

Name the different body parts as you smooth on powder or lotion:

"Doesn't this powder smell good? I'm going to put some on your leg. And now, I'll rub some on your tummy...It feels good on your tummy, I bet."

"Oh, do you want some lotion on your hand? Okay...now rub it on your other arm."

Take your child's hands to touch the different parts of your body, starting perhaps with the parts of your face (nose, mouth, eyes, ears, hair), and then moving on to other parts. Always name the part ("Daddy's nose").

This is an exception to the larger-is-better rule. If you take your little child's hand and put it on your big arm, her concept of your arm will not be much better than if you just talked about your arm without trying to show her. But she can feel all of your nose at once (usually), even in her tiny hand. Talk about your arms and her arms, but do not expect that she will understand until she has the little parts down first.

Finger games and nursery rhymes often use body parts and are just as valuable for visually handicapped children as they are for sighted children.

Your child should know all her body parts, including elbows, knees, ankles, and wrists, before moving on to what is sometimes called *body orientation*. This means that the child is aware of her body in terms of various spatial concepts, or body planes. For example:

Front/Back
Sides
Top/Bottom (such as top of head or bottom of feet)
Middle

Equally important is your child's ability to place her body in various positions in space. This is an activity for the older child, but it will tell you a great deal about how much she really understands about her body and how she visualizes, or maps out, the rest of her world. Ask her to:

Put her left side against the wall.
Put her back on the floor.
Kiss you on the cheek.
Put her right hand on her left elbow.

Make a game of it by being silly:

"Put your head on the chair seat."
"Touch your knee to your chin."
"Use your right hand to take off your right shoe and put it on your right ear."

Body awareness is a gradual process that takes place throughout your child's infant and preschool years. While babies are usually able to point to their body parts, most children have difficulty with right and left even in the first and second grade. No matter how long it takes your child to show body awareness, you can expect to see:

First, an awareness — for example, when she gets quiet and listens to the bells on her shoelaces;

Second, that she can point to a few, and then many, of *her* own body parts;

Third, that she can point to a few, and then many, of *your* body parts;

Fourth, that she can show that she knows front/back, top/bottom, and sides of her body;

Fifth, that she can position her body in terms of other things in her environment;

Sixth, that she can show you the right and left side of *her* body; and

Seventh, that she can point out the right and left side of *your* body.

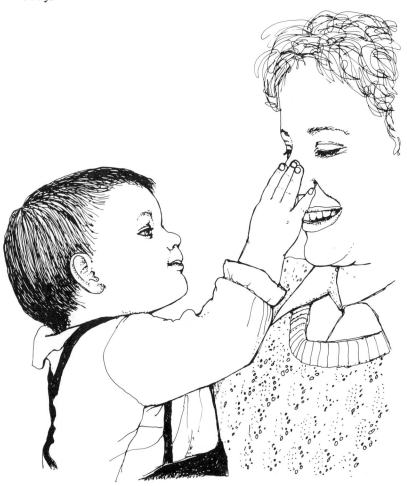

Turn to page 147 in the REACHBOOK

All the activities discussed so far in this chapter have been concerned with *sensory development*. This is also called *perceptual development* because it involves how a child *perceives* the world — how she receives information about the world from her senses. What a child *does* with that information — how she puts bits of information together, how she thinks, and how she makes decisions

— is called *cognitive development*. The rest of this chapter will discuss just how your child gives meaning to the world she lives in, and what you can do to help her learn.

Cognitive Development

Like the other areas discussed so far in this chapter, cognitive or intellectual development follows an orderly process. It is believed that visually handicapped children follow the same process and sequence' of cognitive development as sighted children, although visually handicapped children frequently score poorly in this area on developmental tests. The problem is that many of the test items require vision in order to be scored correctly.

You should understand that your child's score or developmental age on a test of mental development is not necessarily an accurate assessment of her ability or potential. In general, tests *estimate* a child's abilities and always have a margin of error — that is, the score obtained can be either an *over*estimate or an *under*estimate of the true score, because so many factors (how the child feels, what happened before the test, what the weather was like, etc.) interfere with how a child performs on any one day. When the child is visually or multiply handicapped, however, the problems are compounded: Test items that require vision cannot be used because they are not fair to the child; if the items are adapted so that vision is not used, there is no assurance that the same thing is being measured and therefore the adapted item may require more or less of the child than the original item did; and visually handicapped children are even more affected by environmental changes, such as an unfamiliar room, unfamiliar adults, or stormy weather conditions, because they have fewer clues to reassure them.

Sometime during your child's preschool years, she will be tested by a psychologist or educational specialist, either to determine whether she is eligible for an early education program or to assess her present level of functioning. When these results are discussed with you, ask the following questions:

What was the name of the test or assessment used?

Is this a standardized test? A test that has been standardized has been developed by administering the test to hundreds of children of different ages, finding out how many pass each item at what age, and then determining the average performance of the group. It is the average performance that your child is measured against.

If so, what type of children was the test standardized on? If the test was not standardized on visually handicapped children, the average performance is not the average performance of visually handicapped children, but of some other group of children. The test is unfair to your child and cannot give an accurate picture of your child's strengths and weaknesses. This is called *validity;* a test is valid for use with visually handicapped children if it has been standardized on visually handicapped children. The Education for All Handicapped Children Act of 1975 requires that children be assessed with valid instruments.

And if so, what is the test's reliability? The reliability of a test refers to the likelihood of obtaining the same results if it is given again within a short time period. A good test should have a reliability of at least .70 — which means that 70 percent of the time you will get the same results — but .85 or .90 is better.

Who administered the test to your child? The Education for All Handicapped Children Act requires that a child be tested by someone who understands and has had experience with children like her. This means that the person who tests your child should be knowledgeable about visually or multiply handicapped children. Because there are relatively so few visually handicapped children, few professionals have had the kind of experience that meets this requirement. If the person who tests your child has not, ask to have your child tested by someone who does, or ask for a teacher of the visually handicapped or an orientation and mobility specialist to help administer and interpret the test.

Because it will be difficult to find a test that gives an accurate picture of your child's performance, try to look at themes within the test results. It might help to ask yourself questions like:

What are her strengths?
Where does she need more work?
How can I help?
How does she put her world together?
How does she solve problems?
How does she group things together, or understand relationships between and among play objects?
Does she apply old ideas — things she's learned before — to new situations?

Sensory Integration

As parents, you want to help your child learn the necessary skills for thinking and problem solving, regardless of how much vision he has. This means that your child must be able to *integrate*, or use together, all five senses at the same time, and then be able to draw meaning from each event that happens in the environment. Many of the activities discussed earlier in this chapter will continue to facilitate cognitive development, particularly where very young children are concerned, because problem solving begins with being aware of and attending to sensory information.

During these early months, involve your child in as many experiences as possible. Tell him what is going on around him, since you are still not sure what he can see and what he cannot. When he reaches out and hits the mobile on his crib, you should say, "Oh, your hand hit the toy. Listen to the bells." In this way, your child will begin to make the connection between the movement he made and the sound that followed.

One important consideration for you as you begin to think about your child's mental development is his environment and, in particular, his bedroom. Many of the things that are found in children's rooms are there because they are visually appealing to the child *and* to the adult. Because your child is visually impaired, however, you want to decorate his bedroom so that it has the potential for learning. A mobile that is not at the right height for either seeing or touching is doing more for mommy and daddy than it is for baby; be sure your child is not just seeing the bottoms of feet when he looks up at his mobile while lying in his crib. If sunlight shines brightly through the windows, you will want to put up curtains and maybe even place your child's bed *under* the window so the sun is not in his eyes. Containers for your child's toys help give him some structure. A sound-making object kept in the same place at all times could become a *landmark* for your child, such as the ticking of a clock placed right next to his bed, or a floor board that creaks whenever anyone steps or crawls onto it. Your child will be more secure in a room that is both predictable (always the same) and practical (one that meets his needs).

It is important to stress again that for a visually handicapped child learning does not necessarily occur incidentally. Your visually or multiply handicapped child will need every opportunity to pick up on events and relationships that help him to understand the world. You are a vital link in the whole process, and will be better able to help your *child's* understanding if *you* know a bit more about the process of cognitive development yourself.

Turn to page 148 in the REACHBOOK

Object Permanence

Object permanence means that you know something exists even if it is not in sensory contact with you. For example, you know that there is a bottle of soda pop in the kitchen even if you are in the bedroom and neither see, smell, taste, nor touch it. It is there, nevertheless. But babies do not automatically know this, which explains why young babies don't seem to care when you leave the room, while sometime before they are 1 year old, all babies suddenly get extremely upset at your leaving. The younger babies do not yet realize that you are the parent and, frankly, they don't miss you because they don't know what a good thing you are. The older baby *does* know what a good thing you are, and when you leave that room, she *knows* it. She is not quite sure yet that you will come back, but she knows that you exist.

This realization is much harder for blind and visually handicapped children because the loss of contact is so sudden. If you have vision and your bottle is being held by your parent instead of in your own hands, you can still *see* it. Or, if your sister is shaking your favorite rattle, you can *hear* it and *see* it. But if you are visually impaired, your bottle or rattle is literally *in* your hands one moment and *out* of them the next. You cannot rely on your vision to show you that your bottle is still there; and even though you might *hear* your rattle, you cannot rely on your vision to *confirm* that the noise you hear is really your favorite toy.

While object permanence is not acquired overnight — it is the sum total of a child's experiences over a period of time — it is easy to see how good vision makes the whole process easier. Vision maintains sensory contact with people and objects for just a little longer. Without good vision, it is almost like having a fairy godmother who makes things appear and disappear at will, without any logic or reason controlling when or why it happens.

The Fairy Godmother Syndrome

This Fairy Godmother Syndrome makes it particularly difficult for blind and visually handicapped children to learn object permanence. The way you talk to your child, tell him what is going on around him, and set up learning experiences for him will go a long way toward helping him learn that there is a world outside of his own body.

Turn to page 149 in the REACHBOOK

You know that your child is learning object permanence when he shows you that he is aware of something when it is no longer touching him, making a noise, or producing an odor. If he is talking, he might ask for his bottle. If he is not yet talking, look for behaviors such as:

Dropping a toy and picking it up again.

Searching for toys with his hands.

Making a squeeze toy squeak, even though it's new and he hasn't held it before.

Discovering the warm air coming from the heater vent and crawling back there the next time he has a chance.

Crying when you leave the room.

If he has enough vision, "discovering" himself in the mirror.

Getting excited when he hears the sound of his jack-in-the-box.

Sparking Your Child's Mind

You cannot make cognitive development happen. The most you can do is provide the chance for your child to make connections in her own mind — kind of like providing the spark that will cause her thoughts and actions to catch fire. "Sparks" that you can use to help her learn object permanence include things like:

Remembering the teaching strategies you learned in Chapter 3,

Use common sense
Try it yourself
Be prepared
Be spontaneous
Be consistent
Work from behind
Give less and less help
Let your child help
Give enough time

(You may want to review these strategies before reading further.)

Using your child's name. This helps her understand that *she* is permanent, too.

Giving your child clues when you approach and walk away from her, such as telling her, "Here I come!" and "I'm going out to the kitchen now," using a perfume or aftershave that will announce your approach and linger after you have gone, and bringing her hand up to touch your face.

Showing your child how to go after something that has dropped, such as a toy that she has been playing with. Tying her toys to strings, as suggested in Chapter 4, will also help your child learn that objects exist even when they are out of her hands, particularly if you use very short strings at first so that they are only slightly out of reach.

Filling and dumping containers with your help. This activity is one of the ways children "practice" object permanence: One minute they are holding a block or other small toy in their hands; the next minute, it's gone — out of touch and, if the container has a lid on it, out of sight. Then, by reaching in or dumping over the containers, the toy reappears. Children usually do not do this on their own until they understand object permanence, but you can introduce it early to show your child that toys *can* come back again. Soon, she will learn that she can have some control over when her toy disappears and when it reappears — and realize that the toy exists *all* the time, and not just when she's playing with it.

Playing ball with one of the balls that have a continuous beeping sound in them. As you roll the ball back and forth with your child, she will have continuous contact with the sound, as well as tactual feedback from catching and rolling the ball and the communication reinforcement from playing with you.

Trying not to be a fairy godmother. Think about how the world seems to your child and resist the temptation to bring everything to her. While many of the activities suggested in *Reach Out and Teach* do involve bringing the world to your child, you must guard against doing it too often. Make getting things she wants somewhat of a challenge — make her work a bit. Remember, you want your child to be a "Do-er" and not a "Done-to-er."

Object Constancy

Object constancy is also part of the framework that supports your child's cognitive development. It means that your child *knows* an object is the *same* object, even if it *looks* different. A simple example of object constancy would be the difference between what you look like when you get up in the morning, and what you look like when you get dressed up for a special occasion — you *look* different, but you are still the *same* person.

Another way to understand what object constancy means to your child is for you to take a cup. Hold it in your hand, examine it, and then place it on a table located across the room. Go back and sit down in your original spot. Now, look at the cup. Does it look any different?

You probably said, "No, it doesn't look any different. It's the same cup." Look again. The cup across the room looks *smaller* because it is farther away. *You* know it is the same cup because (1) you were the one who put it there, and (2) you have *learned* that objects look smaller when they are farther away than they do when they are close to you. You have *learned* about object constancy. But imagine the difficulty for someone who does not have vision: How will he know that is the same object? Even if it makes a sound, the sound is going to be different when it is farther away, and he won't be sure that it is the same object unless he can get over there and check it out. And if he has a motor impairment, how will he do that?

Generalization

On the surface, object constancy may sound a lot like object permanence. But there is an important difference: Object permanence is knowing that objects exist when they are not immediately available, while object constancy is recognizing the similarities in those objects. And the ability to identify similarities and likenesses (and eventually, differences) is necessary to *categorize* the world: to think about it in a systematic way. Your ability to understand that there are many different *kinds* of cups, all of which share certain things in *common* (e.g., containers with handles), allows you to store the *concept* of cup in your mind, instead of storing the image of many different cups. You don't need to learn "coffee cup," "measuring cup," "teacup," or even "cupped hand," because your knowledge of "cup" allows you to *generalize,* or *apply old ideas to new experiences.*

This is why, of course, object constancy may be a difficult idea for your child to learn. The opportunities for making these associations are limited when your interactions are limited simply because you do not see very well. That is why it is important for you to provide as many of these opportunities as possible. Again, there are no magic formulas for doing this. If you have been following the suggestions found throughout *Reach Out and Teach,* you are already on your way to helping your child acquire object constancy.

Turn to page 150 in the REACHBOOK →

Consistency is again the key word: You must use the same word for the same person, object, or action. This will help your child understand that the beeping ball is still the same thing even when it is being bounced by her brother and the sound is softer and higher-pitched.

Many of the same activities you learned in the earlier section of this chapter on sensory development can also be used to help your child learn object constancy. Pointing out smells, tastes, and tactual qualities (round, soft, hard, sharp, etc.) will help your child learn that there are common properties shared by many different objects.

Give your child two of the same objects — two blocks, two balls, two shoes. Let her know that she has two of the same thing.

Be sure to point out what to you seems obvious. For example, the clock in the hallway outside your child's bedroom chimes all day long. When your child is in her bedroom it sounds very near. When she is in a different part of the house, however, it sounds different. So, when the clock chimes, point it out: "There goes the hall clock again." And call it the "hall clock" even when you are right next to it.

These are just some of the activities you can use to help your child with object constancy. As with all activities, however, you do not have to sit down and *teach* object constancy; the idea behind the activities — what it is like for your child who *cannot automatically* see the similarities in the world — is what is important, and you can use this idea all day long.

Knowing Oneself

Many of the activities given in the earlier part of this chapter for increasing body awareness depend on the child's knowing that he is a person. It may seem strange, but it is possible to point to body parts when someone asks you to without being aware that you are a separate and individual person. Children can be taught to point to body parts if you practice it often enough; use the same words each time, and praise them or give them food as a reward, in much the same way that animal trainers train lions to jump through a hoop of flames. But self-awareness involves something more.

The difference between body awareness and self-awareness is almost like the difference between perceiving and knowing — body awareness is knowing that you have a body, while self-awareness is knowing that your body is distinct and separate from all the other bodies in the world. Self-awareness also means that you know that you have some control over your life. Up to this point, everything was done *to* you by someone else; now, with self-awareness, you realize that *you* can do things and that the amount of help you need from others will change.

Another way to understand self-awareness is to look again at object permanence. If you remember, a young visually handicapped child at first does not realize that his toys or bottle still exist when they are not in direct contact with him. That is, when he is nursing or drinking from a bottle, he is very much *aware* that the nipple is there and that his hunger is going away. But he does not *automatically know* that the nipple is there when he is not nursing. If babies could talk at this stage, you would not expect them to ask for their bottle. You would expect them to respond when the nipple was placed to their lips, yes, but to the baby (and particularly to the visually handicapped baby), it is still like having a fairy godmother.

You have probably decided by now that self-awareness and object concept are very closely related — and you are right. Obviously, a baby could not recognize himself as an individual person if he were not able to sort out all the other events in his life. Look for your child to have an object concept first, and then look for the behaviors that tell you that he sees himself as an individual person, capable of acting on his own, such as:

Dropping a toy from his high chair, waiting for you to pick it up and return it to him, and then dropping it again. (This is a great game for most babies, called "See-Mommy/Daddy-Run.")

Crying when you leave the room.

Handing you a wind-up toy that is no longer moving and expecting you to wind it up again.

Starting to crawl on all fours, or to walk.

Having temper tantrums, particularly as he gets older. (The "Terrible Twos" got that reputation for a reason.)

Wanting to do things himself, without your help.

If he has some vision, looking at himself in a mirror. If the two of you look into the mirror together, he can point to you and to baby.

Each of the above behaviors happens at different stages in a child's life. Do not expect your child to do them all at once, but if he does even one of them, that is your clue that he knows, or is beginning to realize, that he is an individual.

Turn to page 151 in the REACHBOOK

You can help your child's development of self-awareness by:

Talking to him by name. Use his name, and wait for him to respond, whether he responds by quieting, or getting excited, or by turning his face toward you.

Gradually expecting him to do more, or to make more of his needs known. For example, if all he has to do to be fed is to cry, he will quickly learn that crying is the way to get what he wants. But this does not require a lot of effort on his part. It means that he is in control of the situation, but it does not mean that he is learning how to think and devise new ways of interacting with his world.

Placing his toys slightly out of reach. In other parts of *Reach Out and Teach* you were told to position your child so that he would easily find things to touch and manipulate, such as being sure the jungle gym in his crib was within easy reach, or sitting him in a cardboard box or inner tube with some of his favorite toys around him. This is fine, and like all activities, it has its time and its place in your child's life. But if the world is brought to you all the time, you do not have much incentive to go out and find the world. Your child would stand a good chance of becoming a "Done-to-er" instead of a "Do-er."

It's okay to make him work a little bit for what he wants. And it gives him a sense of satisfaction and a feeling of accomplishment to be able to do something one day that he was not able to do the day before. By setting up these situations early on, you are helping your child develop good habits that will last him well into the future.

Cause and Effect

Reach Out and Teach has emphasized the need for visually and multiply handicapped children to grow into "independent childhood," where they make some of their own decisions, take responsibility and, in general, become "Do-ers." Your child's ability to do this, however, is based on the ability to understand cause-and-effect relationships.

Understanding cause-and-effect relationships means understanding that *actions cause reactions,* or that if you do something, something else will result. For the baby, it means realizing that she can have an effect on the world and that she has some control over it. It is the basis for all future learning and is critical for a child's later problem-solving ability. (Problem solving is discussed later in this chapter.)

You can start teaching your child about cause and effect even in the crib:

Place crib toys low enough so that your baby can accidentally hit them. Try to choose toys that provide some type of sound feedback, so that every time she hits it she will *hear* a result. Soon she will begin hitting on purpose.

Place a music box in the crib that can be activated by pulling a string. At first, take your child's hands to the string to show her how it works. When she wants to hear music, she will have to pull the string.

The American Printing House for the Blind (APH) will soon have a "sound mat" available that is made of brightly colored squares of materials that make a sound when pressed or stepped on. The sound can be adjusted in both loudness and duration (for example, from 3 seconds up to 60 seconds of music). While it was designed to be used as an incentive for movement, it is also an excellent tool for teaching cause and effect.

You do not have to wait for the APH mat, however. Some of the crib and playpen pads available today will do the same thing. There are also toys, such as a soft plastic piano "keyboard," that you can place under your baby's feet so she can create her own "music" by kicking.

Inflatable toys with jingle bells inside are also good cause-and-effect tools. Or make your own by putting jingle bells into a plastic Zip-loc bag, blowing air into it, and sealing it shut. Again, your baby will be able to make a noise by hitting or kicking it. *But do not leave your baby alone with this toy* unless you cover it with fabric (use a pillow cover that closes completely) — it is still a plastic bag, and if it deflates, it could be dangerous for your baby.

Multiply handicapped children are usually able to understand cause and effect without too much difficulty; it just may take a little longer. Older children who have not yet learned cause and effect can be helped by doing activities such as:

Using wind-up toys. There are many brightly colored, active toys on the market that will repeat actions when wound up. Most children love to watch them. While the wind-up part might be too small for a child to do herself, you will know she understands the cause-and-effect relationship if she:

Hits or bats at the toy after it has stopped moving; or

Hands the toy to you after it has stopped, as if to say, "Wind it up again, please."

Finding other toys which encourage cause-and-effect concepts, such as toys that talk when a string is pulled; jack-in-the-boxes; busy boxes, and even sorting toys, where a shaped block is put through a hole and then magically appears somewhere else.

Teaching your child that she can use words or gestures to get something. For example, if she wants a cookie, she will need to *say* "cookie," gesture towards the cookie jar, give you the sign for cookie, or point. The idea is to get her to realize that *she* must do something before she gets a result.

Building towers of blocks, bowls, cookies, and other items that your child can knock over.

Remembering the Fairy Godmother Syndrome — the world does not just appear and disappear to your child. The more relationships you build in by preparing your child, telling her what is going on, and waiting for her to show an interest, the more you are working on cause and effect.

Cause and effect is also sometimes known as *means-end* behavior. The basic concept is the same — you get something or cause something to happen by doing something. You can often show your child the real meaning of cause and effect or means-end behavior without really knowing it; for example, the cause-action-consequence analysis discussed in Chapter 2, "Talking it Over," pointed out how your actions might unknowingly be teaching your child that crying is the way to get what she wants. In such a case, your child has a knowledge of cause-and-effect relationships, but that knowledge is not really very useful. It will not work in every situation or with every individual she meets, *and* it is always dependent on someone else. The real value of understanding cause and effect is in knowing that *you* can have an effect on the world, that you no longer have to wait for the world to come to you. It also results in *motivation, curiosity,* and a *desire* to go out and meet the world head-on.

Turn to page 152 in the REACHBOOK

Remember that cause-and-effect learning also does not occur in a vacuum. You want to build these learning experiences into all your interactions with your child, all day long. The important thing is for you to realize *how* you can do this — by providing opportunities — and *why.*

Cause-and-effect learning is not just a cognitive process. You can also use it in your sensory awareness activities. For example, blowing bubbles: Here, your child can learn that blowing air through his lips makes a bubble that is pretty, that floats through the air, that reflects light, and that bursts if you touch it. He has learned a variety of sensory characteristics as well as learning about his own abilities to make things happen.

Learning to use a straw is another cause-and-effect experience that has invaluable rewards, especially if you start with thick milkshakes. You may need to start teaching this by holding your finger over one end of the straw while it is in the cup to keep the milkshake in the straw — because you will then take the straw out of the cup and place the other end (the one that was *in* the cup) in your child's mouth. Hold the straw up at first so the milkshake can just slide down into your child's mouth. Next time, hold your end of the straw a little lower, then a little lower again, until it is almost horizontal. When you get to that point, your child will have to do some of the work (sucking) to get the milkshake out of the straw. Then, gradually, lower your end of the straw until you can actually leave the straw in the cup. This requires your child to do more and more of the work in order to get the milkshake.

Problem Solving

All of the activities you have been working on are leading up to your child's ability to solve problems on his own — by analyzing a problem, thinking of possible solutions, and then carrying through on his own. A child who moves the chair over to the kitchen counter that has the cookie jar on it knows how to solve problems — he realized:

1. That he wanted a cookie;
2. That cookies are kept in the cookie jar on the kitchen counter;
3. That he could not reach the cookie jar;
4. That he could *climb*;
5. That he could push the chair over to the kitchen counter and *then* climb up on it; and
6. That this was the only way he was going to be able to get the cookie without having to ask you for it.

But this is an example of advanced problem solving; you would have noticed other types of problem solving way before this. *Reach Out and Teach* contains many activities to encourage problem solving even by your young infant.

For visually and multiply handicapped children, however, problem solving is sometimes difficult to learn because their visual problem limits their ability to see the possibilities and alternative ways of solving problems. In the cookie-snatching example, your visually handicapped child would only have reached those conclusions if:

1. He knew where the cookies were kept (in the cookie jar);
2. He knew where the cookie jar was kept;
3. He had climbed up on the chair before;
4. He knew that he could move a chair over to the counter; and
5. He knew that by moving the chair over to the counter and climbing up on it, he would be able to reach the cookie jar.

How is a visually handicapped child going to know these things if he cannot see them? Right — through experience. You will need to show your child how to do things like moving the chair over, and you will need to combat the Fairy Godmother Syndrome yourself by telling your child *where* the cookies are, *showing* him where they are, allowing *him* to reach in and pull a cookie out of the cookie jar, and having him *help* you put the cookie jar back on the countertop. Only in this way will your child gain the experiences needed to put events together and come up with a new way of doing things.

Some problem solving takes place when your child is learning cause-and-effect relationships — he is learning that his actions can make a difference. Other ways that you can help your child learn problem-solving skills include:

Covering his face with a cloth or scarf. If he pulls it off himself, great! If not, take his hand to the scarf and show him how to pull it off.

Hiding his toys. If you use a toy with a sound-making ability, it will be easier at first. Partially cover a music box with a scarf or towel, and tell your child to find the music box. He may go right to the music box and pull it out from under the scarf. If not, show him how he can pull the scarf off and find it. As he learns this, try covering a sound toy completely with a scarf. Can he still find it?

These hiding games can be changed by covering *your* face with the scarf, or placing the sound toys *inside* of something else, such as a shoe box or a mixing bowl. As your child gets better at finding the toys, turn the box or bowl upside down so that the sound toy is not visible. Your child will then have to turn the box or bowl over in order to find his toy, and that requires a different kind of thinking ability.

Playing guessing games as your child grows. "What do you think this is?" Show him parts of things that you already know he recognizes. Your child can show you by a gesture or word that he knows or recognizes the object. Start off with familiar items like his bottle, pacifier, favorite toy, blanket, cracker, fruit, cup, car keys.

Remembering to include common household activities. Your child's returning to the kitchen cabinet where you keep mixing bowls or plastic containers is a sign that he has learned to occupy himself. He remembers where objects are kept, and he realizes that he can get to them and have some fun!

Stacking activities are also problem-solving activities because they help your child learn that something different can be made by putting things together. Remember not to limit your stacking games to blocks only. There are many things you can use — bowls, plates, cups, cans of food, cookies, bars of soap, etc. — and many useful activities you can accomplish (putting dishes or groceries away, for example).

Showing your child that by pulling a string, his toy will come to him. Many toys are made to be pulled along behind a child while he is walking. But even if your child is not walking, he can learn that when the toy is out of reach, he only needs to pull a string to get it.

Using tools, objects that allow you to obtain a second object (such as the chair that was used to get to the cookie jar). But even before this stage, you can show your child how to pull on a blanket or napkin to pull things closer to him. Don't just give him a piece of a banana, for example. Place it on a napkin and show him how he can pull the napkin over close enough to reach out and pick up the banana himself. Or, if your child is sitting or lying on the floor (on his tummy, of course!) place a sound toy on a blanket that is touching his hand. If he pulls on the blanket, he gets the toy.

Nesting toys teach your child how things fit inside one another. There are toys on the market made for nesting and stacking such as barrels, blocks, and other stacking-type toys, but you can also use pots and pans, bowls, and other objects around the house.

The toy being used by the child in the illustration below teaches him a variety of skills:

Stacking

Nesting

Cause and effect: if he gets all the spheres on correctly, he can push a lever and they all pop off

Problem solving: there are several spheres of different sizes that must be put together so that a whole sphere is made, with the smallest one on the top and the largest one on the bottom

Use of two hands: one to guide his activity, the other to actually do the activity

Remember that problem solving is not an end in itself. Your child's ability to do things on his own will be greatly enhanced by the opportunities you give him to make his own decisions and to see the connections in his world — on a daily basis, and not in a structured learning time. As he grows and learns more about the world, problem solving will seem more like a habit than a cognitive process, and when your child enters school, it will be second nature to him.

Mulitply handicapped children, too, are problem solvers. Even if your child kicks over a glass of milk or cries for your attention, *that is problem solving* in its earliest forms. Your job is to help your child get beyond this problem-solving-by-causing-problems stage to a more *active* problem-solving stage, by using words or gestures to indicate his needs and wants.

Categorization

Object constancy was discussed earlier in this chapter as a mental process that allows children to see similarities in the world. It is the similarities that form the basis for *categorization,* or *classifying* things according to their:

Physcial attributes: how they look, feel, smell, or sound.

Group membership: class of things to which they belong, such as all animals, all people, all fruits.

Function: how they are used — for eating, wearing, playing with.

Association: how they fit together with other objects to accomplish a task or fulfill a need — for camping, traveling in the car, preparing a meal.

In its simplest forms, categorization begins with matching:

Ask your child to pick out an object that is just like another object — for example, two cookies, two shoes, two spoons. Do this by:

1. Placing two entirely different objects in front of your child;

2. Handing her a third object that matches one of the two in front of her; and

3. Asking her to find another one that is the same as the one she is holding.

Observe whether your child does this simple matching by sight or by touch. In multiply handicapped children, look for a shift in eye gaze, pointing, or a gesture to show you that she understands.

If your child has enough vision to recognize pictures in a book, ask her to match a real object, such as a spoon, with a picture of a spoon. There are many children's books available with clear, simple photographs made out of thick, nondestructible cardboard. When you look for these in the book store, also check out the amount of glare as well. If there is a lot of glare from the shiny surface but it is the only book available, be sure that you hold the book in front of your child so that you can tell how much glare she is getting.

Match by size: do the same activity, only have two objects of the same size, such as two juice glasses and one iced tea glass, or one large cookie and two small cookies.

Match by color: start out with the same objects of the same color before you try different objects of the same color.

Match by shape: circles are understood first, then squares, and then triangles. Many puzzles, formboards, and other 3-dimensional toys are available today. Expect your child to be able to match the real, 3-dimensional object first, then match to a picture, and finally to match pictures of objects to other pictures.

Match by sound: use film containers, plastic bowls with lids, pill boxes, or other small containers; and fill them with rice, sand, beans, beads, water, etc. Show your child how to shake the containers herself, and ask her to choose the two that sound alike.

Match by texture: your child should be able to tell gross difference first, such as wood, glass, plastic, china, and fabric. Later, you will want to use things like rough wood and sanded wood, or corduroy and silk, to encourage her to use her fingertips.

Turn to page 153 in the REACHBOOK

With all your matching activities, always use this sequence:

1. Give your child two objects that are the *same*. Your child has to understand *same* before she can understand different.

2. Give your child two objects that are *not* the same. Be sure she can tell you things are not the same before you go on with your matching activities.

3. Give your child one object, and ask her to find a second object that is the same as the one you gave her. Let her choose between two objects the one that matches and the one that doesn't.

4. Give your child two objects, and ask her to find an object that matches one of those in her hand. Let her choose from two objects, only one of which actually matches one of the objects you gave her.

5. Give your child two objects, and ask her to match the objects to those that are in front of her. This time, both of the objects in front match the two objects she is holding; she only needs to match them correctly.

As your child gains more experience in matching, you will use it in other activities, such as drawing, sorting, and comparing. When comparing, you will be asking her to choose an item that is longer or shorter, bigger or smaller, harder or softer, etc., depending on what you are doing. But before you can expect this type of categorizing ability, you have to be sure that your child is able to understand the similarities and can match by the basic attribute (long, short, big, small, hard, soft, and so forth). *Remember that similarities are recognized before differences.*

As your child's classification abilities increase, you will begin to see her sort things in her own mind, first by how things appear. Calling all men "da-da" is a classic example. You may also see her refer to an animal she has never seen before as an animal she is familiar with; for example, the first time a city-raised child sees a cow, she may call it a dog because that is what she is used to, and both dogs and cows have four legs, two ears, and a tail. Later, she will recognize that the animals are different but still belong to the same general classification of "animals," or that all men are *not* her daddy but still are people.

At the higher levels of categorization, children are able to group things *by their functions*. Where a younger child might be able to match two spoons, for example, the older child will be able to put together a knife, fork, and spoon as "things you eat with," and ignore the shoe that does not belong because a shoe is not used for eating. Later, children learn to group by *association*; this time, a spoon, fork, plate, cup, and napkin might be put together because they are all objects having to do with dinner. Or an airliner ticket, suitcase, and traveler's checks might fit together because they all have to do with taking a trip. At the association stage, a child is connecting everything she has ever learned.

Symbolization

Symbolization is the ability to have one thing *stand for* someting else. All the words on these pages are symbols: a word stands for something else. Symbolization is more abstract, but it is necessary for a child's mental development.

The development of language — speech, sign language, and the written word — is only one form of symbolization, but it is probably the one you will first notice in your child. Pictures are also symbols: they stand for the real thing. Many children at first try to pick up the object in a picture. For example, they see a piece of

candy in a book and try to get it off the page. In some cases, this may be a perceptual problem, whereby the child actually sees the candy as a 3-dimensional object, as if it were real; but usually, this is a developmental stage that all children go through. Until they recognize that symbols exist — that the picture of candy takes the place of an actual piece of candy — they will continue to try to lift things off the pages of books. Expect your child to be able to do this at about the same time as you observe her showing an understanding of language.

Imagination

Children must be able to symbolize before they can *imagine*. Unless you understand that symbols exist, that one thing can stand for something else, you cannot separate yourself from real life to play, make up stories, or predict what might happen. This is frequently an area of difficulty for blind and visually handicapped children because they cannot separate their bodies from their experiences quite so easily. You may find that if you give your child a doll or stuffed animal, he does not play with it the way sighted children do. Remember that sighted children can *see* the doll's face and *see* that it looks like a human face. For a blind child, the doll's face neither feels nor smells like a human. Imagination is, nevertheless, *possible* for visually handicapped children; it just takes a little while longer. The communication strategies you are using from Chapter 5 and the thinking activities found in this chapter will help your child develop his imagination.

Counting is also part of the symbolization process. Unless you understand the meaning of *one*, you cannot look at a group of things and sort them out, one by one.

Begin early to ask your child to give you ''one'' toy, ''one'' cookie, ''one'' sock. If he hands you more than one, take only one. And use numbers in your everyday conversation.

Reading is also symbolization. Children first learn an internal language, then a spoken or signed outer language, and then learn that a written (both braille and print) language can stand for the words and ideas in their head. Again, your daily interactions with your child will make this giant step easier.

Point out words on containers, in books, at the store, riding in the car. Depending on your child's vision, he may be able to see many of the words you point out, and the idea of written communication will gradually come across.

Sighted children are bombarded with letters and words almost from the day of birth. Visually handicapped children may have a more difficult time seeing them, and totally blind children will not see them at all. When you see that your child has language, and when you know that he is using his hands for information purposes, begin to put braille or large-print letters and words into his environment. For example, have a teacher make braille letters for you that can be placed on the blocks your child plays with, over the printed letter that is already there; that way, he can get both a visual and a tactual idea of letters. Make labels for your child's bed, dresser, closet, door, table, chair, stove, refrigerator, etc., and put them where your child can touch them. Give your child as much early exposure to the written word as possible.

As you go through *Reach Out and Teach* and, hopefully, as you go back through these pages time and time again, try to keep your perspective. These suggestions and ideas were written to give you some support in your parenting activities, but they are not the *only* way you can do things. Use these materials for what they can do to *help* your family and your blind, visually handicapped, or multiply handicapped child, but *don't use* the parts that are not helpful to you, or which do not fit your particular situation, or which make you feel like you are working all the time and never have any time to just enjoy your child.

There is more to parenting than teaching: There is also love, joy, hope, and tears; good days and bad days; hard times and easy times — for *all* of you.

Notes on Additional Reading

A lot of material on the development of the mind and the senses will be found in the books or chapters listed for the "Getting Started" chapter. One of these, *The Road to Freedom: A Parent's Guide to Prepare the Blind Child to Travel Independently*, by R. Webster, deals with these two aspects of development in relation to the child's ability to understand and move about in the world. It is mentioned again here because of the importance of this achievement for visually impaired people.

Tune In! by V. Yates, is concerned with developing blind children's ability to listen, and to use what is heard to understand the world around them.

In *Raising the Young Blind Child: A Guide for Parents and Educators*, by S. Kastein, I. Spaulding, and B. Scharf, Chapters 5, 9, and 15 deal with sensory development and skills, and Chapters 6, 11, and 16 with learning through play at each of three levels of development — the infant, the toddler, and the young child.

For the multiply impaired, *I Wanna Do It Myself*, by C. Gimbel and K. Shane, pages 34–37 deal with sensory stimulation, and in *Handling the Young Cerebral Palsied Child at Home*, by N.R. Finnie, Chapters 15 and 17 deal with psychological evaluation, learning and how to encourage it, and play. For the severely handicapped, *Beginning with the Handicapped* by V. Hart, Chapter 4 presents suggestions for encouraging both perceptual and conceptual development; *A Comprehensive Program for Multihandicapped Children: An Illustrated Approach*, by S. Jegard et al., Chapters 5, 6, and 7 contain specific activities and suggestions for the development of auditory, visual, and tactile skills, and awareness of taste and smell. In *Understanding the Deaf-Blind Child*, by P. Freeman, Chapter 9 deals with development of perception and ideas about the world needed for moving around in it, and Chapters 11, with learning and play.

Play is very important for this whole area of development. *Preschool Learning Activities for the Visually Impaired: A Guide for Parents*, by the Illinois State Board of Education, contains many suggestions for 3-, 4-, and 5-year-olds. Another occasional source of good ideas is the quarterly *National Newspatch* from the Oregon School for the Blind. Finally, regarding toys and things, there are *Picture Books for the Blind* from Philomel, which are in both braille and inkprint and have textured "pictures"; and the catalogs *Toybrary: A Toy Lending Library for Parents and Children*, from the Nebraska Department of Education, which is for the handicapped in general; and *Toys, Games and Your Child's Vision* from the American Optometric Association, which may be helpful if your child has a fair degree of usable vision.

Check the Bibliography for sources and additional information.

Chapter 7

LOOKING AHEAD:

The School Years and Beyond

Growing up and away
Independence training
Body image
Making decisions
Educational placement options
Educational aids
Vocational preparation
Sexuality
Case histories

LOOKING AHEAD:

The School Years and Beyond

One of the most important decisions that parents help their children or young adults make is, "What will I be when I grow up." This statement is also true for the visually and multiply handicapped child and young adult. In and of itself, this decision is extremely difficult for everyone concerned. In the case of a visually or multiply impaired person, the decision may take on such monumental proportions that sometimes it is delayed until it is too late, or it is never discussed at all. With all that has to be accomplished with this child, it seems that the decision about "what I will be when I grow up" is too far away. There is too much to do *now*. While this is true, the advice given by young and not so young visually and multiply impaired adults is: *Begin the process early, and be aware that there is strong evidence to support the argument that most visually and multiply handicapped adults can achieve independence and live a life of their own away from their parents.* That life might be in their own homes with their own families, or in a group home with other adults, but the time for your children to leave home will come sooner than you think.

Independence — what a wonderful concept. To most of us it means being on your own and making your own decisions. This is actually the goal of education: to make a child as independent as possible after the child leaves school. So, too, is this the goal of education for those who are visually or multiply handicapped.

In order to look at the process that will make your child as independent as possible, we will look at three educational periods: the preschool years; the elementary school years; and the junior/senior high school years. You will look at decisions that need to be made, things that need to be done, and some of the questions that need to be asked during these three periods. Many of these areas remain the same in each of the three sections; they are just expanded upon and, as the child gets older, talked about with the child at a more conscious and direct level. Other areas need only to be looked at during a given time.

Turn to page 155 in the REACHBOOK

The Preschool Years

This is probably the most difficult time to think about what your child is going to do in adulthood, but it really is the time to *begin*. The problem is that most parents do not know where to begin and are not sure if, at this very emotional time of their lives, they even *want* to begin. You are not the only parents who have had these doubts; but, by following the suggestions in Chapter 1, "Getting Started," about locating community resources and finding a pre-school program, you have already begun the process of training your child to be independent.

Since you have already explored the services available and have made some plans based on what is available to you, there are other areas that you need to think about in order to start your child on the road to independence.

Self-Care

With the preschooler, one area you will need to concentrate on is self-care — teaching not only *how* to do tasks such as dressing and eating, but the finer points of these skills. From the beginning, you can lay the groundwork for your child's eventual independent decision making: the selection of clothes that look good together (by matching colors, using textures or braille tags, if necessary); use of not only a spoon, but a knife and a fork; keeping the food on the plate when eating; putting clothes away; and many more. It is the attention to detail, begun very early, that is going to make your child independent.

Body Image

Another area you need to focus on is body image. As you have read in other parts of *Reach Out and Teach*, this can be particularly difficult for children who are visually or multiply handicapped. You need to look at such things as:

Posture: Some blind children tend to keep their heads down with their chins on their chest, or their shoulders slumped forward. Sometimes they don't know what to do with their hands. Remind your child to stand straight and to hold up his head. Remember, if you can't see yourself in a mirror, and you can't see how other people do it, it is hard to know *how* you should hold your head unless someone *shows* you how. Show him, too, how to fold his arms, or how to stick one hand inside a pocket to look casual.

Mannerisms: Often blind children have repetitive behaviors, such as finger-flicking in front of lights or eye-poking, that are annoying or disruptive for other people to look at, and may cause people to be afraid to interact with your child. Check in the chapter called ''Taking Off'' for some ideas about how to stop these mannerisms from becoming a habit. If you are visually handicapped, you don't know it looks funny unless someone tells you.

Movement: Movement is the ability to move around indoors and outside as independently as possible. Your child will not always have you there to hold him or to hold his hand. He needs the chance to move around by himself and build his self-confidence and self-control.

Conversation: Visually and mulitply handicapped children need to be able to *share* information as well as to find out information. Too often, we forget that visually impaired people do not have the same opportunity to initiate normal conversation that occurs when meeting someone on the street since they are dependent on the sighted person to speak first. Teach your child to greet others when in need of help. (For example, if you couldn't see the guard at the entrance to the bank, how would you know someone was there who could give you directions?)

Appearance: Without seeing how other people dress or act, it's difficult to figure out what you should do yourself. Teach your child how to present himself to other people with hair combed, shirt tucked in, pants zipped, and face, hands and nails clean.

Appropriate places and times: Visually handicapped children also need to be told when activities are appropriate, and when they are not. It is okay to fix your slip in the ladies' room, for example, but you don't hike up your skirt when standing on the street corner. Masturbation or self-exploration of the genital area also has a time and a place, and so does picking your nose. But someone has to tell you about these fine points because your visual impairment does not allow you to observe when others do it, or to gauge other people's response to *your* actions. How many times did your mother's raised eyebrow remind you to chew with your mouth closed?

Body language: A lot of the way we communicate with people is through gestures and facial expressions. This is another area where visually handicapped children are at a disadvantage because they can't always pick up on the twinkle in someone's eyes when being teased, or the set of a jaw when someone is serious or angry. Neither do they necessarily realize that you shouldn't smile when someone else is crying, or that making funny faces is not always amusing. Unless, of course, you tell them. It's a two-edged sword, though: While children should be taught when they shouldn't do something, they should also be taught when it's okay to do something. Smiles, frowns, grimaces, and pointing all can add a lot to the way people talk together. Used at the wrong time, they make people stand out; but when not used at all, people stand out just as much.

Problem Solving

Another important area to concentrate on during the preschool years is problem solving; that is, allowing and encouraging your child to take an active part in making decisions. In interviews with many visually and multiply impaired people one thing came through loud and clear: *Let* me make a mistake; *let* me succeed; *let* me get hurt; *let* me have choices; *let me have freedom.* But, you cannot just hope that at age 18 or 21 the visually or multiply handicapped young adult will know how to make her own decisions.

You were taught all during your childhood, and so must both visually and mutliply handicapped children be taught. You can begin at this age by allowing the child to explore the environment alone, without mommy and daddy always being right there to say, "Watch out for the radiator," "Don't trip on the rug," "Don't put that in your mouth," "Be careful, it's hot." You have to give your child choices, even in the preschool years: "Would you like juice or milk?" "Do you want to wear the blue or red sweater with those pants?" "Is it hot or cold outside?" "Would you like to eat breakfast first, or get dressed first?"

Being able to make choices gives the child a chance for problem solving. Of course, in the preschool years, it is at a very simple level, but as the years go by your child will be a much more active participant in making decisions about both the present and the future.

Even the most multiply impaired child has a choice; she just needs to express it in a different way. Wait for your child to give you some indication of that choice, whether it's an eyeblink, a smile, a movement of the toe, or some other sign that is special to your child.

While other parts of *Reach Out and Teach* have cautioned you against asking a lot of questions, this is one situation where it is okay. With very young children, begin with questions that require only a yes/no answer:

"Do you want some milk?"
"Are you ready to take a nap?"

When your child gives you a response to this type of question, move on to questions that require a one-word response. Be sure the response you are looking for is part of your question:

"Do you want to wear the red shirt or the green shirt?" ("red")
"Do you want to take your nap now or later?" ("later")

And as your child shows you that she can respond to this type of question, you can start giving more complicated choices:

"What do you want to drink? Milk, juice, or water?"
"What shall we do next?"

The areas of self-care, body image, and problem solving are all going on at the same time, and they should all be worked on at the same time. Nothing develops in isolation.

Turn to page 158 in the REACHBOOK

Elementary Years

Some time prior to your child's entering school, a decision will be made about which school your child will attend. This decision should be made knowing what kinds of services are available in your hometown, what family situations need to be worked out, and what kind of program your child needs. There are several ways visually or multiply handicapped children go to school, depending on their individual needs. While school districts may have different names, the basic types of classes available to your child are:

Regular classroom: Your child attends the same school and the same class he would have attended if no one had ever said, "This child is visually impaired." In this case, he requires very little outside help and functions just like other children in the classroom.

Regular classroom with itinerant or resource support: Again, your child is in the same school and same classroom, but in this case he receives a little more help. For varying amounts of time — again according to how much help your child needs — he leaves the classroom to work with an itinerant teacher (one who travels around from school to school), or a resource room teacher (one who has a special classroom in the school that children come to as needed). The teacher provides materials to be used in the regular classroom, such as brailled homework assignments, and otherwise works very closely with the regular class teacher.

Special classroom in the regular school: Your child is in a classroom with other handicapped children, but the class is located in a regular elementary school. Here your child gets the consistent help of a special education teacher, but there still are chances to get to know the nonhandicapped children in the school — usually at lunch, art, music, and physical education. Itinerant and resource support specifically for those who are visually handicapped may also be available.

Special class in a special school: Here your child attends a school with other handicapped children, but still lives at home. The school may be located right next door, or it could be a two-hour bus ride away. The classroom could be noncategorical (the students have many different handicapping conditions, but all function at a similar level), or categorical (the students are all visually handicapped).

Residential school: Many states have a school for the visually handicapped that accepts visually and multiply handicapped children from all over the state. One advantage to this type of placement is that the children get intensive help from specialized teachers.

None of these placements are set in stone. The important thing to remember is that your child should be able to move in and out of these placements according to his needs at *any particular point in time*. In the elementary years, your child may need a lot of help when he first enters school, and less help after he has acquired good reading and writing skills.

Your child's needs are not the only consideration, however. The school's ability to meet those needs are also important. Generally, public schools are required to provide all of these placements in one form or another under the concept of "least restrictive environment"—meaning that the farther you get from a regular classroom in the regular school, the more restrictive, or limiting, the placement is. But the quality of those programs can be affected by how many other children need the same services, or how many (and how good) the teachers are. While a classroom in a regular school may be less physically restrictive than one in a residential school, the regular class might actually be *more* restrictive — both socially and educationally — if your child cannot get the help he needs.

Your child will need options and flexibility in the elementary years. Start now to find out what is available in your school district and remember that the same "good practices" described in Chapter 1 for preschool programs also apply to public and residential schools.

Questions for Parents

Regardless of whether your child is in a regular elementary school with or without itinerant or support services, a special class with or without itinerant or support services, or a residential school program, similar questions need to be addressed.

1. Now that my child is of school age, what agencies are available to provide help?

2. What kinds of support services are available to my child in school?

3. What kinds of technology (from low vision aids to the Kurzweil Machine, which transforms printed material into spoken language) are needed for my child?

4. How do I go about obtaining this technology?

5. What kinds of outside activities should my child be involved in? (There are laws that prevent your child from being kept out of extracurricular activities and sports.)

6. What medical problems will affect my child's participation in school activities? Is there any help with the cost of these long-standing problems?

7. Is my child getting the right kind of education? Is he being taught everything he should be?

8. Are the skills my child is learning appropriate for his age level?

9. What kinds of services are available for me, the parent?

10. How do I find an advocate (helper) who can guide me through all the pitfalls on the way to independence, so that all the steps are thought about, discussed, and acted upon in order to accomplish that goal at the proper time?

Turn to page 159 in the REACHBOOK

Your Child's Educational Rights

Your child has a legal right to a free and appropriate public education. Depending on the laws of your state (see Chapter 1, "Getting Started"), the school must follow certain rules in order to assure that your child is educated as he would be if he were *not* handicapped. Your child's visual or multiple handicap should not prevent him from getting the education that is best suited to his particular needs. This right is guaranteed by Section 504 of the Rehabilitation Act of 1973, which states that no handicapped individual shall be discriminated against under any program or activity that receives Federal financial assistance. This applies specifically to public elementary and secondary schools, which must provide a "free appropriate public education to each qualified handicapped person..., regardless of the nature or severity of the person's handicap" (45 Code of Federal Regulations Part 84.33(a)).

In 1975, President Gerald R. Ford signed the Education for All Handicapped Children Act (Public Law 94-142). The Act was reauthorized and amended slightly in 1984 (Public Law 98-199). It is basically a funding measure that offers additional money to state departments of education and local school systems to help cover the increased costs (for teaching staff, books, or other materials) of educating handicapped children. If your state receives any of these funds, your local school system *must* follow the guidelines and rules required by the Act. The only exception is if your child's age is not within the age range that your state legislature has designated as ages when children must attend school ("mandatory school age"). This is usually 4, 5, or 6 years old to start school and 18 to finish school. Some states will educate handicapped children from birth to school age, and from 18 to 21 years (some even extend to 25 years of age). But once your child is the age when your state provides special education, the school system must:

Enroll your child in school.

Evaluate your child fairly at least every three years. This includes:

Obtaining your permission.

Using tests that are valid — that is, designed to be used in the manner in which they are being used (see Chapter 6, "Thinking it Through").

Being sure that the person or persons testing your child are qualified to do so.

Using more than one test.

Testing your child in his native language or other mode of communication (such as braille or large type).

Using a multidisciplinary team — that is, medical, health, educational, social, and other professionals who can evaluate all your child's needs.

Including at least one professional who is familiar with your child's handicapping condition(s), whether it is blindness, low vision, cerebral palsy, hearing impairment, emotional disturbance, etc. If your child has more than one handicap, the professional must either be involved in the evaluation itself or on the team that interprets the results of the evaluation.

Develop an Individualized Educational Program (an IEP) geared to your child's strengths and weaknesses that:

Is written at a meeting attended by a team of people, including you, your child's teachers, a school administrator, a member of the evaluation team if your child is being evaluated for the first time, your child (if he is old enough), and anyone else you want to be present.

States:

- your child's *present level of functioning* (what he does now);
- *annual goals* (what he should be able to do a year from now);
- *short term objectives* (what he needs to learn to accomplish his annual goals);
- *standards or measures* for determining when these objectives are met (*criteria for evaluation*); and
- *length of time* it should take to meet these objectives.

Indicates which *related services* your child needs and how often he will receive them. Related services refers to physical therapy, occupational therapy, transportation, catheterization, low vision examinations, speech and language therapy, psychological services, recreation, medical and counseling services, and anything else that will help your child benefit from his educational program.

Specifies how much time your child will spend in *regular education* classes — that is, classes with nonhandicapped children.

Is used to determine your child's *placement* (the type of class and educational program he receives).

Is *updated* at least once a year.

Provide a continuum of educational placements, or a variety of classes and options that range from least restrictive (a regular class with nonhandicapped children) to most restrictive (a special class of handicapped children in a school of handicapped children). (See earlier discussion of educational programs in this chapter.)

Make every effort to assure that your child attends his neighborhood school.

Obtain your written permission before placing your child in a special education program.

Provide a system or procedures that both you and the school must follow if you disagree with or have a complaint about the evaluation, placement, or IEP for your child, including:

Paying for a second evaluation by professionals of your choice;

Setting up a meeting or hearing where an impartial judge — or someone who has no involvement with either you or the school — can listen to both sides of the story and make a decision that is fair to your child and based on his needs;

Telling you what steps you can take if you still are not satisfied, or what steps the school will take if it is not satisfied, including appealing to the state education department;

Keeping your child in his present placement (or if he is just entering school, placing him in a temporary class that you agree to) until the issues are resolved one way or the other;

Not changing your child's educational program (including anything that is written in the IEP) without notifying you and obtaining your permission; and

Giving you a written list or statement of all these procedures, known as your "due process rights," specifying:

- how much time you have to challenge a decision or to complete each step; and
- who can provide you with legal assistance.

Provide an education, including books, materials, and equipment, for your child at *no cost to you.*

> Key Ideas Behind the Education for All Handicapped Children Act of 1975
>
> *Free, appropriate education,*
> Based on the *individual* child,
> Determined by a *fair evaluation,* which
> Includes *parents* in the planning process,
> Provides *all educational and related services* that the child needs,
> *Specifies how and what* the child will be taught,
> *Fits the placement to the child,* and not the child to the placement, and
> *Guarantees the due process of law.*

Turn to page 160 in the REACHBOOK ➤

Learning Aids

How will your blind or visually handicapped child get along in school? If you do not have a visual impairment yourself, it is probably hard to imagine how your child will be able to keep up with the other children in reading, writing, and mathematics. But there are several aids and devices that your child may be able to use, and

more and more are being developed all the time. Even computers are available today with braille, large print, and talking terminals.

Some of the aids your child might use in school are listed below.

Optical Aids

Glasses with special prescriptions:

Bifocals, prisms, contact lenses, or other lens combinations may be prescribed for a child with visual limitations to use at all times or only for certain activities.

Tinted lenses may have to be worn both indoors and outside if light hurts a child's eyes.

Magnifiers: Either held in the hands or placed in spectacles, magnifiers make the size of the image reaching the eye larger. (With some eye disorders, magnification does not help; see Chapter 2, ''Talking it Over'' and check with your doctor.)

Telescopic aids: These are small telescopes (hand-held or placed in spectacle frames) that your child can use to see the chalkboard and class demonstrations.

Nonoptical Aids

Nonoptical aids are devices that are not individually prescribed, and may or may not be designed specifically for the visually handicapped.

Visual Aids

Bookstands: These help to keep your child from tiring by bringing the work closer to her eyes.

Felt-tip pens: Usually preferred in black, and available in varying widths, these make a bold letter or diagram that is easier to see.

Acetate: Usually preferred in yellow, though available in various colors, acetate placed over the printed page tends to darken the print as well as improve the contrast of the background paper.

Lamps: With variable intensities and positioning, lamps can provide the additional or dimmed illumination that your child may need.

Large-type books: For comfort or for those children who cannot read regular print at close distance even with an optical aid, large-type is often helpful.

Bold-line paper: If your child finds it difficult to see the lines on regular writing paper, bold lines of various widths are available in several types of paper.

Page markers and reading windows: These may be especially helpful if your child finds it difficult to focus on a word or line of print.

Tactual Aids

Braillewriter, slate, and stylus: A braillewriter is a manually operated, six-key machine that types braille. The slate and stylus, used to take notes, are easily carried in a pocket or on a clipboard. The slate is a metal frame with openings through which braille dots are made with the aid of a pointed stylus.

Raised-line drawing board: This is a rubber-covered board on which the blind child can draw or write on acetate sheets with a pen or similarly pointed object, and feel the lines "raised up" as they are made.

Cubarithm slate: This aid enables the blind child to do mathematics using standard braille characters. Cubes with raised braille notation fit into square holes in a waffle-like frame.

Abacus: This device, invented by the Chinese, is useful for learning math.

Raised-line paper: This paper (writing paper, graph paper, etc.) has raised lines to help a child to write script "on the line" or to make graphs.

Templates and writing guides: Made out of cardboard, plastic, or metal, these are open rectangular forms that allow signatures or other information to be written inside the opening.

Auditory Aids

Cassette tape recorders: Your child can use a tape recorder to take notes, listen to recorded books, or to talk out her writing assignments.

Talking books and other recording programs: The Library of Congress (Talking Book program) and other organizations provide free library services to visually handicapped persons, offering a wide variety of text books and leisure reading on records and cassettes. The Library of Congress lends special Talking Book record and cassette players to visually handicapped persons. Many religious organizations provide recorded religious education materials. Some of these, as well as the Talking Book program, are listed on pages 45–53 of the REACHBOOK.

Variable speed attachments: Attached to a tape recorder or Talking Book machine, these can be used to change the speed at which a student listens to tapes, thereby speeding up or slowing down the rate of listening.

New Technological Advances in Electronic Aids

Talking calculators: These hand-held calculators speak each entry as it is made, and then give the calculated answer. They are capable of performing all the computations of a nonadapted electronic calculator. (Earphones are available.)

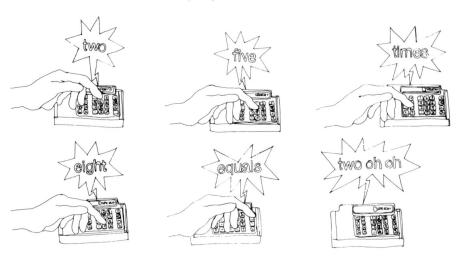

Kurzweil reading machine: This computer reads print aloud (again, earphones are available) and is found in many large libraries. It is possible to interface the Kurzweil with the electronic braille and other computers so that written material can be immediately translated into braille or recorded for later use.

Electronic braille: These machines (there are several different manufacturers) allow braille to be stored on and played back from cassette tapes, without paper. Textbooks may soon be available in cassette form, thus eliminating time-consuming braille and large-print preparation of manuscripts to assure that the visually handicapped child has access to the same books as all other students.

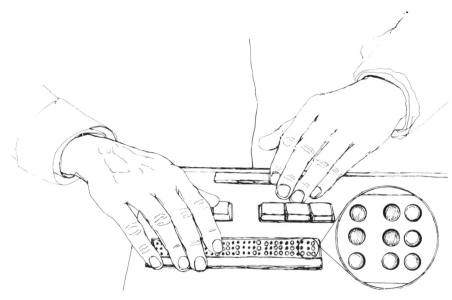

Optacon: This "Optical-to-Tactual-Converter" transforms print into letter shapes of vibrating reeds that can be read tactually. It is portable, lightweight, and permits access to the printed word when more advanced technology is not available (such as in the local library). Special attachments are available for reading computer screens and for mounting on a typewriter.

Closed circuit television: The closed circuit television electronically enlarges print material onto a television screen. Contrast and illumination can also be altered.

Viewscan: This is a lightweight reading aid for low vision persons that converts printed material into a light image up to 64 times bigger than the original.

Computers: The range and variety of computer adaptations currently on the market are huge, and new products are being developed daily. Almost any personal computer can be used by a blind or visually handicapped child with the addition of a voice synthesizer, braille terminal, large-print terminal, or an electronic braille device. Soon, blind and visually handicapped students will routinely learn word processing instead of typing.

Independence Training

At the elementary school level, you will find yourself paying increasing attention to your child's growing independence. If all goes well, your visually handicapped child will emerge from his elementary years as a fairly self-sufficient teenager who can take responsibility for his own actions, and who is interested in and concerned about others. You started this process in preschool, when you helped your child learn to feed, dress, and toilet himself; when you gave him choices; when you taught him the importance of good grooming; and when you told him about body language and self-expression. Now that he is in school, you can continue this independence training by focusing on his:

> **Manners.** Children who are polite and considerate of others are usually well-liked by adults and peers. A visually handicapped child has difficulty seeing the effects his actions have on others, so he can miss an adult's look of disapproval when he interrupts a conversation, or his grandmother's look of relief when he gives up the reclining chair and offers it to her. As your child gets older, you should expect him to be aware of other people's feelings — but you may also have to point out to him when he could be more polite, and when his thoughtfulness would be important to someone else.

> **Fashion sense.** Today's elementary school children can be quite sophisticated in their style of dress. They can also be hopelessly critical of peers who don't wear designer jeans, or cowboy boots, or school sweaters. A visually handicapped child will have to rely on both you and his classmates for information on the latest styles. If you have older children, ask them to keep your visually handicapped child up to date, or touch base with your neighbors and other parents. Most of the time your visually handicapped child will learn what's "in" and what's "out" by listening to what the other kids say, or by being teased for what he's wearing. While you certainly do not want continually to buy the latest fad for your child, you do want him to learn that his appearance can make a difference in how he fits into society.

> **Creativity.** The difficulty with all this is that you can spend so much time focusing on how other people react to your child and how your child can fit into the mainstream of society that

your child's creativity and self-expression can be stifled. Somehow you must help your child sense the boundary between social acceptance and individuality. You will probably be safest dealing with such questions in the context of your own family: Would you allow *any* of your daughters to wear blue nail polish? Would you allow *any* of your sons to shave his head?

Humor. Help your growing child to laugh and to see the funny side of events. It can be both maddening and embarrassing to find out that you have on socks of two different colors, but it can also be funny. And if your child can learn to laugh at himself, he will develop a skill that will last a lifetime and will help others to feel comfortable around him.

Health. With children who are at risk for illness, it may be difficult for you to understand that they can have some control over their own health status. But think about how you feel when you've had a bad day at work — your entire body feels "down," and you feel tired and depressed. Or sometimes you come down with a cold right after a major holiday that you've spent days getting ready for. Physical reactions to stress are not uncommon, and you will want to look for signs in your child — fatigue, fever blisters, irritability, loss of weight — that may mean he's working too hard or that he's worried about something at school.

You also want to insure your child's health by insisting on physical exercise. Because a by-product of a visual impairment is often a decreased tendency to move about in the environment, many visually handicapped children associate movement with purposeful, required activities, such as walking to school or taking physical education classes. They cannot experience the exhilaration of running, or the satisfaction of lifting weights, unless someone has given them the opportunity to try it. Make sure that your child doesn't sit on the sidelines during physical education class because the teacher thinks his visual impairment precludes his participation in all activities. With training by understanding adults, visually handicapped children can and do participate in many sports: swimming, gymnastics, track and field, weight lifting, skiing, ball games (with beep baseballs, etc.), and martial arts. The more active your child is, the healthier he will be in body and mind.

Dependability. As children get older, they should become more responsible for themselves. This means being on time for school, following a schedule, keeping appointments, completing homework assignments, and following through on promises. Watches and clocks are available with braille and large print numbers, and talking timepieces are becoming more common. These will help your child pace himself. Teach your child to write down homework assignments and to review them before he leaves school. Otherwise, he may not have the books he needs at home. (Braille and large type books are usually large and heavy. Nothing is more frustrating than carrying the wrong one home!)

Communication skills. As your child learned to communicate, you taught him about turn talking and facing the person who is speaking. In the elementary years, you will want to continue working on his listening skills, as well as working on the quality of his voice: Is he too loud, too whiny, too nasal, too soft, too monotonous, or too mumbly? Tell him how he can improve, and stress the importance of good communication for social interaction. Sometimes, children may not be aware of a waxy buildup in the ears or an ear infection that reduces hearing acuity and affects their voice quality. If your child's speaking voice seems to be a problem, check with a speech and language pathologist for structural abnormalities or a hearing loss (either temporary or permanent).

Handling his handicap. Visually handicapped children learn in the primary grades that they are somehow different from the other kids. This can be devastating at first, or it can be a source of pride. Most children have a natural tendency to tease peers who are different, but they also have a natural curiosity — so your child's special equipment or books can be interesting and exciting to classmates. And depending on how teachers and parents handle it, the other kids might want a special education teacher of their own and actually be jealous of the special attention your child receives.

But it is inevitable that at some point your child will not want to be different. Then his handicap can become a source of embarrassment or frustration, and you will need to muster all your common sense to help your child through this period. Your child will need to make up his own mind about his visual impairment, and face such questions as:

How limiting is it?

What *can* I do?

What *can't* I do?

Am I challenged to try new things, or am I afraid to try?

Do I talk about my visual impairment, or do I ignore it?

How can I adapt or modify my environment at home and school so that my visual impairment is not a handicap?

When should I ask for help, and when can I do it myself?

Am I using my visual impairment to make other people feel sorry for me?

Am I using my visual impairment to avoid work, or even to avoid people?

Are there situations when my difficulties seeing could put me or others in danger?

Your child's answers to these questions will change over time, but he must begin to look at these issues in his elementary years, when you are around to help.

What if my Child is Multiply Handicapped?

If your child is multiply handicapped, you will continue preparing her for independence. *How* you prepare her, and what you prepare her *for* will depend on the extent of her handicapping conditions. For example:

If she is severely handicapped, independence training could mean finding a way to make her food and toileting needs known to other people — by signs, communication boards, or a consistent grunt or other vocalization.

If she is mentally retarded, manners, health, fashion sense, humor, dependability, creativity, and communication are still important, but perhaps you will not expect her to learn as fast as a child who is only visually handicapped.

If she has cerebral palsy or a motor impairment, you may have to take an active role in meeting her health and physical activity needs because realistically she might not be able to do it herself. Communication skills, humor, fashion sense, creativity, manners, and dependability are still important, however.

If she is hearing impaired, the quality of her speaking voice may always be an issue, and you will need to help her deal with people's reactions and continue trying to communicate. If she

needs to use sign language and fingerspelling, your whole family will want to learn, too, so that she does not feel isolated and so that you can increase her communication skills in general. You will have to insure that her educational program meets both her visual and auditory needs.

Throughout the elementary years, whether your child is multiply handicapped or only visually handicapped, your goal as a parent is to prepare her for moving away from you in spirit as a teenager, when she will naturally want to be more independent, more in charge, and more adventurous. You can make this time less traumatic for both of you if you start early, move gradually, and use love, kindness, foresight, and understanding.

Junior High and High School

Choosing a Career

Junior and senior high school are the final stretch, and it is here that the panic really sets in. "What will my child do after school is over? Is there anything available? Who will help?"

If you have been working through the years on all of the previously mentioned materials, then, hopefully, the panic will leave quickly and you will be able to step into action. In most states there is an agency that deals with visually impaired adolescents and their vocational needs. The rules and regulations differ among states, but a good rule of thumb is that you should make contact with them by your adolescent's 16th birthday. It's not a bad idea to start when your child is 12 years old since the process takes a while, and the earlier you begin, the better your chances that services will be there when you need them.

For some of you it will not be necessary to contact a separate agency because you will already be receiving some services from an agency that takes care of both educational and vocational matters. You must, however, make sure that the flow from one kind of service (educational) to another kind of service (vocational) is carried through.

Turn to page 164 in the REACHBOOK

During these years your adolescent will have to assume many responsibilities if she is to achieve independence. She will need to actively explore the kinds of work opportunities possible for visually or multiply handicapped adults. One way she can do this is to contact other visually impaired adults in the community to find out how they made it through the process: What advice would they give?

Another way of finding out what job possibilities exist is to consult the *Dictionary of Occupational Titles*. This book is available in most public libraries, in guidance counselors' offices, and probably in the agency that is serving your child. The National Consultant in Employment at the American Foundation for the Blind maintains a listing of jobs held by blind and visually impaired people that will give your adolescent an idea of what other people have done.

Once your adolescent makes a decision about the type of job that most interests her, that job will need to be explored in other ways:

Does this job require vision?

Can you be partially sighted?

What modifications can be made that will allow a visually or multiply handicapped person to pursue this job?

What related aspects of this job could she do that do not require vision?

Can another approach be substituted?

The young adult needs to secure good counseling about the vocational market during this time. Again, depending on the school situation, this can include guidance counselors, vocational rehabilitation counselors, itinerant teachers, relatives, professionals in the field, and other visually impaired adults. The vocational counselors will talk to your adolescent, give vocational testing, discover abilities and aptitudes (what she is good at), and counsel her as to what jobs are available.

Your adolescent will also need to visit actual work places for the occupations that are of greatest interest to her. She needs to discuss the kind of training needed, the cost of training, the job prospects, the salary, the restrictions caused by a visual impairment, the benefits offered, and how long the job will last. She should have all the facts and figures before deciding upon a career goal.

One way your teenager can get a good idea about the world of work is to do just that — get a part-time job after school or work in a work-study program sponsored by the school. You have been laying the groundwork for good work habits by teaching her to be on time, have a neat and clean appearance, call when she's going to be late, and keep working until the job is done. There is nothing like holding a job to really understand what work is all about and to experience the independence that a little pocket money brings.

Turn to page 165 in the REACHBOOK

Independence Training

Also important during this time is that your adolescent refine skills such as independent travel (cane, dog guide, bus, subway, etc.), reading (including braille, large print), the use of technological devices and low vision aids), and recreation. Recreation is an important area to devote some time to because it provides the skills needed to use leisure time effectively.

Also, remember that your teenager, like every other teenager today, will have questions about dating and sexuality. These subjects may be hard for you to talk about, but if *you* can't, be sure your teenager can talk to someone. And start early to help your child pick up on the little things that go on in social situations, like:

"**She's flirting** with you — I can tell by the sound of her voice."

"**Why does she giggle** when you talk to her? Well, because she likes you, and she's a little bit self-conscious."

"**Teenage boys whistle** and yell at girls on the street because they *like* them, and they haven't learned yet how to show it without being silly. Don't be upset. Just ignore them — they will stop soon enough."

"**Don't be embarrassed** that you dropped some food on your blouse. Be glad someone told you so you could wipe it off before anyone else saw it."

It used to be that girls had to wait to be asked for a date. In today's world, both boys and girls do the asking. But imagine how difficult it is for blind, visually or multiply impaired youths to ask for a date when they can't use facial expressions to judge whether they will be accepted or not. And then to have to say, "Great, can you drive?" or "My dad will drive us." Privacy and independence are hard to come by when you are forced to rely on others. It is important to give your child a perspective on these issues:

> **"Yes, there are** some things you will always need help with, but that doesn't mean you're any less of a person."

> **"If you want,** I'll teach you how to walk from Sue's house to the movies; then you can ask her again when you feel you can do it by yourself."

Extracurricular and religious activities are a good way to meet other young adults. No matter how visually or multiply handicapped your child is, he can still help out by taking tickets, helping to clean up, being the disc jockey, and serving on committees. But he has to try, and prove to himself and others that he can do it.

Your teenager will naturally be curious about her body and about the opposite sex. She is somewhat limited, however, by how much she can get through her senses. If you grew up without a visual impairment, you know that most of your ideas about men's and women's bodies came from looking at real people, at pictures, maybe even at statues. Past a certain age in our society, it is impolite to get too close to people or to touch certain parts of their bodies, so what is a visually handicapped person to do? You can *tell* your teenager about puberty, menstruation, and sex, but words do not help much when your curiosity and your feelings are all mixed up. How do you, as parents, handle it?

> **First, get some help.** There are several groups who have dealt with this issue before and can help (blind adults, Planned Parenthood, Sex Information and Education Council of the United States).

> **Take advantage** of your child's preschool years. It is perfectly natural for mothers to bathe with their young sons and fathers to bathe with their young daughters. It could also be your child's only opportunity to learn about the body in a healthy manner.

> **Do not be put off** by your young child's or teenager's questions. Answer them as best you can and as naturally as you can. If *you're* embarrassed, your child will be.

> **As early as possible,** tell your child he is bright, handsome, or strong. Let him know that these are qualities people like, and that *he* has them.

> **Let your child know** that there are some things that aren't done in public: picking your nose, scratching in the groin area, and fixing a bra strap, to name a few. Impress upon your child that even though he can't see others, others can see him.

Give your child privacy. It's hard enough to kiss someone for the first time, let alone when you're being watched. Dating and kissing or "making out" for visually impaired teenagers are not much different from the visits prisoners have with their families under the watchful eye of guards: You know someone is there, you know they are watching, and you're afraid to show your feelings or make a mistake.

Independence for your visually impaired teenager means trust and confidence for both of you. Hopefully, you will be able to put all of these things in place, realize that there is no one perfect answer, and allow your child opportunities to be free. Then both you *and* your child will achieve independence.

Turn to page 168 in the REACHBOOK

Case Histories

To some of you just beginning the process, this idea of your child achieving independence and functioning in the work force seems a long way off. Let's look at some visually impaired and multiply handicapped adults and their stories.

Barbara

Barbara is a 21-year-old young adult, born totally blind. Barbara discovered very quickly that if she were going to "succeed and become someone," she had to control her life. Barbara attended a residential school for visually impaired children in another country and was taught, along with her own determination, that you had to be a fighter and be willing to take risks. Barbara decided in junior high that she wanted to be a teacher, not necessarily a job that visually impaired people are encouraged to seek. Because of her determination and ability to pound the pavement, answer all advertisements, and interview in any town, her perseverance won out. Barbara was employed in a special school teaching language. Getting in the door and her real love for handicapped children encouraged Barbara to pursue a master's degree in teaching visually impaired youngsters. Today she is a student at a university finishing her degree.

Barbara believes that the greatest treasure any parent can give a child is the ability to become independent. She feels strongly that parents of handicapped children have to allow their children to be "normal" and, like all parents, to know when to let go. Parents have to let their children participate in social activities, date, and have normal sexual experiences. Barbara also feels that visually impaired children and adults and their parents must have contact with other visually impaired children and adults.

John

John is a 30-year-old visually impaired man who, early in his life, was identified as mentally retarded. John attended a special class for retarded children with support services from an itinerant teacher for the visually impaired. At 16, he registered with a state vocational agency and a comprehensive plan was developed for his future.

When John finished school, he attended the state's rehabilitation center for twelve months. During this time his employment interests and skills were explored, a position secured, and training for the position accomplished. John has been employed as a maintenance man in a local factory for 10 years, and he is considered by his employers to be a valuable, conscientious employee.

He lives in his own apartment (three rooms) takes care of all his personal needs, participates in a social life, and actively contributes to society.

John's advice to parents whose children are identified as "not quite right" is to make a plan. John feels that because of the cooperative effort during his educational years, he was ready for work and is now very happy with what he does.

Susan

Susan is a visually impaired 30-year-old woman working as a secretary in a federal agency in Washington, D.C. She went to special classes for visually handicapped children in a regular elementary school and to a regular high school with itinerant services. Susan was not encouraged to become a secretary because others thought she would be "too slow." Susan worked hard with her high school teachers and itinerant teacher of the visually handicapped, and later developed many ways of adapting the tried and true ways so that she could accomplish the role of secretary. Again, it was Susan's independence and her parent's ability to let her try — even though they knew she might suffer — that allowed her to reach her career goals.

Susan offers much the same advice as Barbara. In addition, she feels that much too much time is spent telling the child with limited vision what she cannot do because of her impairment, and not enough time spent telling her what she *can* do because she is an individual.

Tom

Tom is a 27-seven-year-old young man who spent his educational years in a residential school for the visually impaired. While he was in school, he was considered a "slow learner" and, therefore, participated in a nonacademic, vocational track. But Tom was always a real dare devil and enjoyed all kinds of activities that involved some risks. He always seemed to be challenging the fact that he was visually impaired.

After graduation from school, Tom went back to his home in Texas and went to work for his father, who works in the oil business. Today, Tom's job is to plant dynamite charges — a very dangerous job that most employees would not do, but one that nevertheless needs to be done. Tom has been trained thoroughly, knows the danger, but enjoys the thrill of doing something that is risky. As Tom says, "I am really needed."

Tom lives in a condominium with other visually impaired young men who are employed in the area. The condominium was purchased by a parent organization so that their children could be independent, yet supervised.

Tom's advice to parents is, "Take a chance — be happy."

Bob

Bob is a 27-year-old totally blind accountant employed by a publishing firm in a major city. He was educated in a residential school until the ninth grade and then attended his local high school so that he could specialize in mathematics. Bob attended a local college and received his master's degree in accounting.

Bob has found the new advances in technology, such as the Optacon and Kurzweil Machine, to be of great benefit to him. He feels that he can function totally independently in his given career choice. With an ironic smile, Bob tells his story: When he was an infant the doctors told his parents they should let him die, but advised that if he lived, they should put him in an institution. *His* advice to parents is, "Don't set a limit on your child. Have expectations. Believe your child will accomplish something."

These are but a few of many stories about visually handicapped people. There are sucesses and there are failures, just as there are in everyone's life. But, the lesson to be learned from the lives of these individuals is to believe in your child's capabilities and try to help him first to discover, and then develop them. Who knows what you will accomplish, if you can just — REACH OUT AND TEACH.

Turn to page 171 in the REACHBOOK

Notes on Additional Reading

You may want some additional help in making the most of the present and looking ahead to your child's future. Some of the following publications may be useful: *Take Charge! A Guide to Resources for Parents of the Visually Impaired*, by D. Nousanen and L. W. Robinson, will help you locate all kinds of services and information. Chapter 4 in the *Handbook for Parents of Preschool Blind Children*, by I. Davidson, et al., deals with the same kind of needs, but the actual resources listed apply mostly to residents of Ontario, Canada.

At the preschool level, *Mainstreaming Preschoolers: Children with Visual Handicaps*, by L. Alonso, et al., is a book you might share with the teacher or other professional working with your child. It will also give you an idea of what your child should be getting in a preschool program.

Also dealing with the early years, *The Road to Freedom*, by R. Webster should be mentioned here because it is so strongly oriented to the future independence of the blind child through good mobility.

Taking a longer view, *Can't Your Child See?*, by Scott, Jan, and Freeman, Chapters 8, 9, 10, and Chapter 6 regarding multiply handicapped children, and *Our Blind Children*, by B. Lowenfeld, Chapters 8 through 11, and Chapter 12 regarding multiple handicaps, follow the child from nursery school through adolescence. Both deal mainly with the blind child. The sections on multiply handicapped children cover all aspects in a single chapter.

Where Are They Now? A follow-up study of 314 multi-handicapped blind people, former pupils of Condover Hall School, by S.O. Myers, is a large volume presenting an enormous amount of information on the adult life of multiply handicapped visually impaired persons in a variety of settings. It is definitely for the stouthearted, but the personality of the author should be a help. Both Freeman and Myers write about Great Britain, so that conditions may not correspond exactly to those in the United States. However, in Myers' book there is such a wealth of personal material that this is only a minor drawback.

For an extensive discussion of severely and multiply handicapped children in the United States, see *National Parent Conference on Education of Children Requiring Extensive Special Education Programming* (Proceedings edited by S. Machalow), Parts I, III, and IV. While Myers presents case histories, this book discusses issues and strategies in more general terms. It is not easy reading, but it is clearly written and honest.

In an entirely different vein, *To Race the Wind*, by H. Krents is an autobiography of a young lawyer blind from birth and a very readable account of personal experiences. The same may be said of the article, "Growing Up Virtually Blind: A Self-Report," by E. Crowley.

Finally, *Exceptional Parent* is a magazine in which concerns for the future of handicapped children are often discussed from various points of views.

For additional information on all of the above, please see the Bibliography section of this HANDBOOK.

Bibliography

All the items in the Bibliography are listed alphabetically (1) by author for books and articles, and (2) by name for journals and magazines. When a book was published by an agency without an author's name, the agency is listed as the author. All journals and magazines are listed at the end of the Bibliography under periodicals.

In most cases, each item is shown as available from the publishers. A few are out of print, but are available as photocopies from the Educational Resources Information Center (ERIC), a decentralized nationwide network of clearinghouses, which collects and disseminates documents in education. In ordering from ERIC make sure you give them the ED number listed for that item. Prices have been shown when available, but these are subject to change and many may already be out of date. ERIC charges about ten cents per page for photocopies.

You need not necessarily buy these materials. You should be able to borrow practically all of them except, of course, the periodicals. Some may be available at a library near you. Failing that, the M.C. Migel Memorial Library at the American Foundation for the Blind, 15 West 16th Street, New York, New York 10011, telephone (212) 620-2159, has most of these publications in its collection. They may be borrowed in person, by mail, or by telephone if you live within the continental United States. They may also be borrowed on inter-library loan in Canada. As many as four titles may be borrowed for a three-week period.

To give you as much information about these publications as possible, the following information has been included:

1. Whether it is mainly for parents, or for both parents and teachers (this is shown in order of importance);

2. Whether it deals mainly with the blind, *B*; visually handicapped (low vision), *L*; multiply handicapped, *M*; or deaf-blind, *D* (again in order of importance; for example an *M* followed by *B* would mean mainly about multiply handicapped but some information useful for the blind); and

3. Which chapter(s) in *Reach Out and Teach* this publication relates to. You can check back to the Notes on Additional Reading for each chapter for some additional comments.

The subjects covered in the seven chapters are:

Getting Started: Introduction to parenting a handicapped child, teaching your child at home, and locating community resources.

Talking It Over: Family mental health, coping, and self-concept.

Taking Off and *Picking Up*: Gross and fine motor development.

Coming Across: Communication/language development and skills of daily living.

Thinking It Through: Sensory and cognitive development.

Looking Ahead: Educational and independent living perspectives, from preschool to adulthood.

You can use this to locate material on a particular subject. If you are looking for something on language development, for example, check the items under "Coming Across" and read the descriptions in the Bibliography and Notes on Additional Reading for that chapter to find which publications may be most appropriate to your needs.

Most appropriate for:
P — Parents
T — Teachers

Main focus on:
B — Blind
L — Low vision
D — Deaf-blind
M — Multiply handicapped

Bibliography

Publication and Author	Available From:	Cost	Most	Main	Relevant to "Reach Out and Teach" chapters:	Description
Mainstreaming Preschoolers: Children with Visual Handicaps, L. Alonso, P.M. Moor, S. Raynor, C. von Hippel & S. Baer DHEW publication #(OHDS) 78-31112	Superintendent of Documents U.S. Government Printing Office Washington, DC 20402		T P	B L	Getting Started Looking Ahead	A Head Start publication, discusses mainstreaming, visual handicaps and their effects on learning, planning environments and teaching, parent-teacher partnership and resources. Illustrated, 127 pages.
Toys, Games and Your Child's Vision American Optometric Association	American Optometric Association 243 N. Lindbergh Blvd. St. Louis, MO 63141		P	L	Thinking It Through	Flyer with suggestions on eye care and age related list of toys and activities. 3 pages.
Touch Toys and How to Make Them Rose Barquist and Eleanor Timburg	Information: Eleanor Timburg 3519 Porter St., N.W. Washington, D.C. 20016 To order: Touch Toys P.O. Box 2224 Rockville, MD 20852		P T	B L M	Getting Started	Presents various toys for visually impaired and blind preschool children and gives directions for making them. Drawings, 77 pages.
"Traditional Nursery Rhymes and Games: Language Learning Experiences for Preschool Blind Children" Joan W. Blos	American Foundation for the Blind *New Outlook for the Blind* June 1974, Vol. 68 No. 6 pp. 268-275		T P	B L	Coming Across	Suggestions for a sequence of language related activities using songs, rhymes and stories that need no pictures to be enjoyed and understood.
Show Me How: A Manual for Parents of Preschool Visually Impaired and Blind Children Mary Brennan	American Foundation for the Blind 15 West 16th Street New York, N.Y. 10011 1982	$4.00	P	B L M	Getting Started Coming Across	One of the AFB Practice Report Series. Provides rationale and instructions for activities enhancing development in various areas for ages 0 to 5 and suggestions for social and daily living skills. Contains listing of agencies and organizations and bibliography. 47 pages.
"Growing Up Virtually Blind: A Self-Report" Eileen Crowley	*School Psychology Review,* 1980, **9,** 391-395. National Association of School Psychologists 1511 K Street, NW, Suite 927 Washington, DC 20005		P T	B L	Talking It Over Looking Ahead	Describes the author's life experience from premature birth to adult life as employed professional.
Handbook for Parents of Preschool Blind Children Iain Davidson, et. al	The Ontario Institute for Studies in Ed. Publication Sales 252 Bloor St. West Toronto, Ontario M7A IL2 1976		P	B	Getting Started Looking Ahead	After discussing reactions to and nature of blindness, concentrates on practical suggestions. Separate chapter on community resources. Photographs. 97 pages.
Move It Richard Drouillard and Sherry Raynor	American Alliance Publications P.O. Box 870 Lanham, MD 20706 1977	$3.75	P	B L	Getting Started	Sequel to Raynor's and Drouillard's *Get a Wiggle On.* Basic suggestions for parents of blind and visually handicapped children. Cartoons, 93 pages.

Most appropriate for:
P — Parents
T — Teachers

Main focus on:
B — Blind
L — Low vision
D — Deaf-blind
M — Multiply handicapped

Publication and Author	Available From:	Cost	Most	Main	Relevant to "Reach Out and Teach" chapters:	Description
"Developmental Needs in Blind Infants" Rebecca F. Dubose	American Foundation for the Blind *New Outlook for the Blind* Feb. 1976, Vol. 70, no. 2 pp. 49-52		T P	B	Getting Started	Discussion of the special developmental needs of blind infants and training procedures that parents can provide.
Workbook for Parents & Teachers. Teaching the Visually Impaired Preschool Child 2-5 yrs. old Joseph S. Galante	Buffalo Public Schools Duplicating Office Buffalo, New York 1981	free	P T	B L M	Getting Started Talking It Over Coming Across	Two introductory sections on (1) vision and (2) the family, followed by 14 sections of detailed suggestions for learning in various areas. Drawings, 80 pages.
A Handbook for Parents of Deaf-Blind Children Jeanne Esche Carol Griffin	Department of Education Instructional Materials Development Center Michigan School for the Blind 715 W. Willow Street Lansing, MI 48913	Free	P	D	Getting Started	Elementary text about deaf-blind infants and toddlers giving guidance for stimulation and development. Drawings, 24 pages.
Parenting Preschoolers: Suggestions for Raising Young Blind and Visually Impaired Children Kay Alicyn Ferrell	American Foundation for the Blind 15 West 16th Street New York, N.Y. 10011 1984	Single copy free	P	B L M	Getting Started	Helps parents with the questions raised by early development of their child and gives direction to parents at a time when critical decisions must be made. Photographs, 28 pages.
Handling the Young Cerebral Palsied Child at Home N.R. Finnie (2nd ed.)	E.P. Dutton 2 Park Avenue New York 1975	$6.31 paper $9.95 cloth	P T	M	Talking It Over Taking Off Picking Up Coming Across Thinking It Through	Primarily for parents. Describes motor abnormalities in cerebral palsy and techniques and equipment to counteract them. Not intended for visually impaired. Illustrated, 337 pages.
Understanding the Deaf-Blind Child Peggy Freeman	Heinemann Health Books 23 Bedford Square London WC1B3HT 1975		P T	D	Getting Started Talking It Over Taking Off Picking Up Coming Across Talking It Through	Author is mother and teacher of multiply handicapped. Emphasis on early years and parent/teacher cooperation. Detailed information and suggestions in all areas of development. 126 pages.
I Wanna Do It Myself Carol Gimbel & Karen Shane	Elwyn Institute Educational Materials Center Elwyn, PA 19063	$2.25	P	M	Getting Started Taking Off Piking Up Coming Across Thinking It Through	Gives suggestions for activities to be used in homes of multiply impaired children with emphasis on cerebral palsy. Cartoons, 67 pages.
The Visually Impaired Child; Growth, Learning, Development Infancy to School Age Carol Halliday	American Printing House for the Blind 1839 Frankfort Avenue Louisville, KY 40206 1971	$1.25	P T	B L	Getting Started	Delineates visual impairment and discusses child growth with reference to the visually handicapped. Contrasts development to that of sighted child. Photographs, 87 pages.
Beginning with the Handicapped Verna Hart	Charles C Thomas 2600 South First Street Springfield, IL 62703 1974	$8.95	T P	M B	Taking Off Picking Up Coming Across Thinking It Through	For parents and teachers of severely handicapped young children. Identifies what to teach and how to teach it using a task analysis approach in various areas of functioning. 128 pages.
Infant Stimulation: A Pamphlet for Parents of Multihandicapped Children Sandra Hoffman	Kansas University Medical Center Lawrence, Kansas 1973 (attn.: S. Hoffman)	single copies free	P	D	Getting Started	Explicit directions about motor development activities and training, also for the other areas of sensory stimulation. Illustrated, 22 pages.

Publication and Author	Available From:	Cost	Most	Main	Relevant to "Reach Out and Teach" chapters:	Description
Toy Workshops for Parents: Bridging a Gap. Baby Buggy Paper No. 201 P.L. Hutinger et al	ERIC Document Reproduction Service P.O. Box 190 Arlington, VA 22210 1978 ED 180173		P T	L M B	Getting Started	Three papers describe a home based program for rural handicapped and high risk infants and toddlers. The development of toy workshops to help parents construct materials for their children is described.
Preschool Learning Activities for the Visually Impaired: A Guide for Parents Illinois State Board of Education	ERIC Document Reproduction Service P.O. Box 190 Arlington Heights, VA 22210 1972 ED 074677	$10.00	P T	B L	Getting Started Coming Across Thinking It Through	Games and activities to develop skills and abilities of the preschool blind child. Photographs. 102 pages.
A Comprehensive Program for Multihandicapped Children: An Illustrated Approach Suzanne Jegard, Loye Anderson, Carol Glazer, and Witold A. Zaleski	National Institute on Mental Retardation Kinsmen NIMR Building York University 4700 Keele Street Downsview, Ontario CANADA M3J 1P3 1980	$23.50	P T	M	Getting Started Taking Off Picking Up Coming Across Thinking It Through	A workbook for parents and childcare workers involved with multihandicapped and mentally retarded children. Presents procedures and directions for stimulation and development based on knowledge of developmental sequences and related to realistic expectations. Illustrated, 146 pages.
Raising the Young Blind Child: A Guide for Parents and Educators S. Kastein, I. Spaulding, and B. Scharf	Human Sciences Press 72 Fifth Avenue New York, NY 10011 1980	$14.95	P T	B L	Talking It Over Taking Off Picking Up Coming Across Thinking It Through	Organized into three parts dealing with the infant, the toddler and the young child. Within each age range areas of development are discussed with suggestions on how the parents can help the child to develop and learn in day to day situations. Photographs, 208 pages.
Talk to Me: A Language Guide for Parents of Blind Children Linda Kekelis and Nancy Chernus-Mansfield	Blind Children's Center 4120 Marathon Street Los Angeles, Ca 90029-0159	Parents free others $1.00	P	B	Coming Across	Practical suggestions based on an understanding of communication and the effects of blindness from infancy through preschool. Tells parents what to do and why and even how to make it fun. Photographs, 12 pages.
To Race the Wind Harold Krents	G. P. Putnam's Sons New York 1972		P	B	Looking Ahead	Autobiography of a young congenitally blind lawyer and musician. 282 pages.
Before and After Zachariah Fern Kupfer	Delacorte Press 1 Dag Hammarskjold Plaza New York, NY 10017 1982	$12.95	P T	M	Talking It Over	Story of a family with a profoundly retarded child, written by the mother. Highly personal presentation. 241 pages.
Our Blind Children Berthold Lowenfeld (3rd Edition)	Charles C Thomas 2600 South First Street Springfield, IL 62704 1971	$11.95 paper $17.75 cloth	T P	B	Getting Started Talking It Over Looking Ahead	Addressed to parents. The book follows the blind child from birth through adolescence, discusses teaching methods and answers some questions frequently asked by parents. Some photographs, 244 pages.
National Parent Conference on Education of Children Requiring Extensive Special Education Programming Proceedings Steve Machalow, Ed.	U.S. Department of Education Special Education Programs 1982		P T	M D	Talking It Over Looking Ahead	Examines the needs of severely handicapped students and services (or lack of them) from preschool to adult age. Emphasis on parent's role and collaboration with educators. Focus on student's eventual functioning as an adult and the Individualized Education Program (I.E.P.) as one of the means of achieving this goal. 159 pages.

Most appropriate for:
P — Parents
T — Teachers

Main focus on:
B — Blind
L — Low vision
D — Deaf-blind
M — Multiply handicapped

Publication and Author	Available From:	Cost	Most	Main	Relevant to "Reach Out and Teach" chapters:	Description
Some Children Are More Special Than Others. . .A Guide to Mattel Toys for Parents of the Visually Handicapped Child. Mattel, Inc.	Toys for Special Children Mattel Toys, a division of Mattel, Inc. 5150 Rosecrans Avenue Hawthorne, CA 90250 1980-1		P T	B L	Getting Started	Catalog of selected Mattel toys with suggestions for their use with visually handicapped children. Illustrated flyer, 6 pages.
Leisure Time Activities for Deaf-Blind Children Lillian Mikalonis	Joyce Motion Picture Co. 18702 Bryant St. P.O. Box 458 Northridge, Ca 91324	$20.00	P T	D	Coming Across	The manual provides nearly 100 separate projects, game learning experiences, and other leisure time activities for parents and others to use with deaf-blind children. Illustrated, 122 pages.
Homemade Toys and Activities for Mother and Child Margaret Miller	Mott Children's Health Center Educational Department 806 W. Sixth Avenue Flint, MI 48503	$2.25	P	L M B	Getting Started	Intended for use by parents in collaboration with teacher or other specialist. Toys for motor development and visual and auditory stimulation. Many ideas can be applied to visually handicapped. Illustrated, 58 pages.
Hints for Parents of Preschool Visually Handicapped Children Virginia Murray	Variety Club Blind Babies Foundation 25 Taylor Street Suite 702 San Francisco, CA 94102	free	P	B L	Getting Started	Suggestions for promoting the child's development are arranged by developmental stages. 30 pages.
Where Are They Now? A follow-up study of 314 multihandicapped blind people, former pupils of Condover Hall School Stanley Oscar Myers	Royal National Institute for the Blind 224-6-8, Great Portland St. London, W1N 6AA 1975		T P	M D	Looking Ahead	After describing Condover, author reports on former students as to placement or living arrangements, employment, marital status and leisure activities. Relates characteristics of former students to their present situation. Makes recommendations for both education and welfare of handicapped adults. 249 pages.
Toybrary: A Toy Lending Library for Paents and Children Nebraska Department of Education	Nebraska Department of Education Special Education Branch Box 94987 309 Centennial Mall South Lincoln, NE 68509 1978		P T	L M	Taking Off Picking Up Thinking It Through	Catalog lists toys with information on their use to enhance development and how to make substitutes with household items. Final section on resources. For handicapped in general, not visually handicapped. Illustrated, approximately 240 pages.
Take charge! A Guide to Resources for Parents of the Visually Impaired Diane Nousanen and Lee W. Robinson	National Association for Parents of the Visually Impaired P.O. Box 18086 Austin, TX 78718 1980	$5.50	P T	B L	Talking It Over Looking Ahead	Designed to help parents become aware of resources for their visually impaired children. Organized around 16 questions commonly asked about services, care, rights and resources. Illustrated, 94 pages.
Picture Books for the Blind Philomel (a member of Putnam Publishing Group)	Philomel 200 Madison Ave., Suite 1405 New York, NY 10016		P T	B L	Thinking It Through	Books which are designed to be read by blind and sighted children, ages 4 to 8. The books are in braille and standard type and have "pictures" that can be felt as well as seen.

Publication and Author	Available From:	Cost	Most	Main	Relevant to "Reach Out and Teach" chapters:	Description
Games and Toys for Blind Children in Preschool Age Pielasch, Helmut, Ed.,	World Council for the Welfare of the Blind 58 Avenue Basquet 75007 Paris, France 1978		T P	B L	Getting Started	Published as a contribution to the International Year of the Child, it is intended to help parents enhance the development of their blind preschoolers. Photographs, 65 pages. In four languages
Get a Wiggle On Sherry Raynor and Richard Drouillard	American Alliance Publications P.O. Box 870 Lanham, MD 20706 1975	$3.75	P	B L	Getting Started	First in a two-part set; contains basic suggestions for helping the blind baby to grow and learn like other children. Simple text applicable to all visually handicapped. Cartoons, 77 pages.
Get Ready, Get Set, Go! Jeanette Schuch	International Institute for Visually Impaired 1975 Rutgers Circle E. Lansing, MI 48823 1980	$5.00	T P	B L	Getting Started	Manual with specific activities for blind children and advice for parents on helping them to master ordinary tasks and motor skills. Illustrated, 38 pages
Can't Your Child See? E. P. Scott, J. E. Jan, and R. D. Freeman	University Park Press 300 N. Charles St. Baltimore, MD 21201 1977	$9.95	P T	B L M	Getting Started Talking It Over Looking Ahead	Guidebook for parents of visually handicapped children with much emphasis on the early years of life. A chapter on multiply handicapped is included. Photographs, 201 pages.
How to Fill Your Toy Shelves Without Emptying Your Pocketbook: 70 Inexpensive Things To Do or Make Southwest Education Dev. Lab. Austin	Council for Exceptional Children 1920 Association Drive Reston, VA 22091 1976	$3.95	P T	L M	Getting Started	The manual contains suggestions for approximately 70 inexpensively constructed games, activities, and manipulative materials for use with handicapped and nonhandicapped young children.
Elizabeth Sharon Ulrich	University of Michigan Press 615 E. University Ann Arbor, MI 48106	$5.95	P	B	Getting Started Talking It Over	Biography written by mother covers period from birth to 5 years of age. Blindness was diagnosed at 2 months. Two experts provide commentaries applicable to blind children in general. Photographs, 122 pages.
A Practical Guide to the Training of Low Functioning Deaf-Blind Watson, Marcia J. Nicholas, Judith L.	Connecticut Institute for the Blind 120 Holcomb St. Hartford, CT 06112 1973	$2.00	P T	D	Taking Off Picking Up Coming Across	Guidelines for parents and teachers working with severely handicapped deaf-blind children. Deals with teamwork of parents and professionals, motor development, communication, social and daily living skills. 49 pages.
The Road to Freedom: A Parent's Guide to Prepare the Blind Child to Travel Independently Richard Webster	Katan Publications 2012 Cedar Street Jacksonville, IL 62650 1977	$7.00	P T	B	Getting Started Thinking It Through Looking Ahead	Practical suggestions for parents on how they can logically and sequentially introduce their blind child to the world so that the child will later benefit from professional mobility training. Very comprehensive from the point of view of overall development from birth on. A few diagrams, 115 pages.
Selecting A Preschool: A Guide for Parents of Handicapped Children Pamela J. Winton, Ann P. Turnbull, and Jan Blacher	University Park Press 300 North Charles Street Baltimore, MD 21201 1984		P	L M B	Getting Started Looking Ahead	Applicable to all handicaps. Provides substantive information about mainstreaming, special services, rights under PL94-142, etc. and a discussion of the social and emotional factors involved for both parent and child. Some photographs, 237 pages.

Most appropriate for:
P — Parents
T — Teachers

Main focus on:
B — Blind
L — Low vision
D — Deaf-blind
M — Multiply handicapped

Publication and Author	Available From:	Cost	Most	Main	Relevant to "Reach Out and Teach" chapters:	Description
Tune In! Virginia Yates	Virginia Yates 4 Glen Creek St. Louis, MO 63124 1980	$2.00	P	B L	Coming Across Thinking It Through	A guide for developing listening skills in young visually impaired children; activities for parents and children to enjoy together. 49 pages.
Periodicals						
Exceptional Parent	Exceptional Parent Magazine 296 Boylston St., 3rd Floor Boston, MA 02116	$15.00	P	L M	Talking It Over Looking Ahead	6 per year For parents and professionals, deals with all disabilities. Articles range from language development to estate planning and from family problems to legislation. Little on blindness but rich material on matters common to disability in general.
National Newspatch	Oregon School for the Blind 700 Church St., S.E. Salem, Oregon 97310	$4.00	T P	B L M	Taking Off Picking Up Coming Across Thinking It Through	Quarterly newsletter for educators of visually impaired preschoolers. News of meetings, programs and publications. Articles and suggestions for parents and teachers.
Newsletter of the Sibling Information Network	Sibling Information Network School of Education Departments of Educational Psychology Box U-64 The University of Connecticut Storrs, CT 06268	$5.00 Dues per year	T P	M	Talking It Over	The Network was formed to assist professionals and families concerned with the well being of siblings of handicapped children. Information on services, projects, research and literature.
VIP Newsletter	The International Institute for Visually Impaired 0-7 1975 Rutgers East Lansing, MI 48823		P T	B L M	Getting Started	Quarterly newsletter of short articles with suggestions for parents of visually impaired aged 0-7, questions and answers, news of activities, publications, toys. Parent participation.

About the Author

KAY ALICYN FERRELL is National Consultant in Early Childhood, American Foundation for the Blind, New York. Dr. Ferrell holds her Ph.D. in Special Education from the University of Pittsburgh, and has taught visually and multiply handicapped children from infants through high school, and has trained teachers to work with infants and preschoolers as well as school-age children. Dr. Ferrell is a past chair of the Infant and Preschool Division of the Association for the Education and Rehabilitation for the Blind and Visually Impaired, as well as being a member of the Council for Exceptional Children and an Associate Member of the National Association for Parents of the Visually Impaired. She has published extensively on the development and education of infant and preschool visually handicapped children; most recently, she was guest editor of a two-volume special issue on preschool of the *Education of the Visually Handicapped* journal (Summer/Fall, 1984).